Reshaping Social Work Series

Series Editors: Robert Adams, Lena Dominelli and Malcolm Payne

The **Reshaping Social Work** series aims to develop the knowledge base for critical, reflective practitioners. Each book is designed to support students on qualifying social work programmes and update practitioners on crucial issues in today's social work, strengthening research knowledge, critical analysis and skilled practice to shape social work to meet future challenges.

Published titles

Social Work and Power Roger Smith
Social Work Research for Social Justice Beth Humphries

D0071364

Forthcoming titles

Anti-Racist Practice in Social Work Kish Bhatti-Sinclair
Social Care Practice in Context Malcolm Payne
Critical Issues in Social Work with Older People Mo Ray, Judith Phillips and
    Miriam Bernard
Social Work and Spirituality Margaret Holloway and Bernard Moss

Invitation to authors

The Series Editors welcome proposals for new books within the *Reshaping Social Work* series. Please contact one of the series editors for an initial discussion:

- Robert Adams at rvadams@rvadams.karoo.co.uk
- Lena Dominelli at lena.dominelli@durham.ac.uk
- Malcolm Payne at M.Payne@stchristophers.org.uk

Reshaping Social Work
Series Editors: **Robert Adams, Lena Dominelli and Malcolm Payne**
Series Standing Order ISBN 1–4039–4878–X
(outside North America only)

You can receive future titles in this series as they are published by placing a standing order. Please contact your bookseller or, in the case of difficulty, write to us at the address below with your name and address, the title of the series and the ISBN quoted above.

Customer Services Department
Macmillan Distribution Ltd
Houndmills
Basingstoke
Hampshire
RG21 6XS
England

Social Work and Power

Roger Smith

Published by
PALGRAVE MACMILLAN
Houndmills, Basingstoke, Hampshire RG21 6XS and
175 Fifth Avenue, New York, N.Y. 10010
Companies and representatives throughout the world

PALGRAVE MACMILLAN is the global academic imprint of the Palgrave Macmillan division of St. Martin's Press, LLC and of Palgrave Macmillan Ltd. Macmillan® is a registered trademark in the United States, United Kingdom and other countries. Palgrave is a registered trademark in the European Union and other countries.

ISBN-13: 978–1–4039–9124–9
ISBN-10: 1–4039–9124–3

This book is printed on paper suitable for recycling and made from fully managed and sustained forest sources. Logging, pulping and manufacturing processes are expected to conform to the environmental regulations of the country of origin.

A catalogue record for this book is available from the British Library.

A catalog record for this book is available from the Library of Congress.

10   9   8   7   6   5   4   3   2   1
17   16   15   14   13   12   11   10   09   08

Printed in China

Contents

List of Illustrations		viii
Acknowledgements		x

1 **Why Do We Need to Think about Power?**   1
A persistent problem   1
The power to be late   3
What is the place of power in social work?   5
The contexts of power in social work   7
Key questions about power   9
The structure and aims of this book   10
Main points   13
Stop and think   13
Taking it further   14

Part 1 Ideas of Power

2 **Ideas about Power**   17
Power is a double-edged concept   17
Historical ideas of power   18
From recognition to definition?   19
Power as potential   23
Power as possession   28
Power as process   32
Power as product   35
Main points   38
Stop and think   39
Taking it further   39

3 **Modes of Power**   40
Interests and difference   40
The 'personal' aspect of power: the role of identity   42
Positional power   47

Relational power   52
Main points   56
Stop and think   57
Taking it further   57

4   Sites of Power   58
The importance of context   58
Situating power: three frameworks   59
Up close and personal: the family   65
The community as 'local authority'?   69
State institutions: speaking directly to practice   73
The global dimension   76
Main points   79
Stop and think   79
Taking it further   80

Part 2 Mechanisms of Power

5   Structural Influences on Practice   83
Making it real   83
Appearances count: the media and social work   84
Speaking directly to practice: the role of government   88
Law and legitimacy   92
Social work and the market   96
Main points   101
Stop and think   102
Taking it further   102

6   Professionals and Organizations   103
Practice and the impact of systems   103
The power of professions?   104
Social work: a transformative profession?   108
Professionalism and 'managerialism'   111
'Reprofessionalizing' social work?   112
Social work and other professions   114
Social work professionals and service users   118
Social work as a 'critical' profession   122
Main points   123
Stop and think   123
Taking it further   124

7   Service-User Strategies   125
The power of people who use services   125
Compliance   127
Non-cooperation   131

Resistance   133
Challenge   136
Collaboration   138
Control   141
Main points   144
Stop and think   144
Taking it further   145

Part 3 Taking, Making and Using Power

8 Empowering Relationships   149
Power and practice   149
Working with individuals: understanding power
    relationships   151
Exploring power relationships: relational practice   156
Reframing power relationships: language, choice and
    change   160
Towards user-led services: changing power relationships   165
Main points   169
Stop and think   170
Taking it further   170

9 Groups, Communities and Systems   171
Making links   171
Understanding power: systems thinking   172
Exploring power relationships: tuning in to the networks   176
Reframing (again): whose problem is it anyway?   180
Generating power: changing relationships in networks
    and systems   184
Main points   189
Stop and think   189
Taking it further   189

10 Power: Meeting the Challenge   191
The political nature of social work   191
Knowing our place: recognizing the impact of social work   193
Sites and sources of power: their meaning for practice   198
'Reframing' social work: solidarity and commitment   203
Proper social work?   203
Structural change is a legitimate objective for social work   207
Social workers, power and justice   211

Bibliography   213
Author Index   227
Subject Index   231

List of Illustrations

Figures

4.1   Thompson's PCS model   61
4.2   Dominelli's multidimensional model of power   63
4.3   Smith's model of 'The child in the world'   64
8.1   Power relations: one-way, decontextualized   152
8.2   Power relations: one-way, user-context recognized   154
8.3   Power relations: two-way, user-context recognized   156
8.4   Power relations: two-way, mutual-context recognized   159

Practice illustrations

1.1   Feeling disempowered as a practitioner   3
1.2   The power of lateness?   4
2.1   The Duluth Domestic Abuse Intervention Project   25
2.2   Family Group Conferences   25
2.3   Assessing children's needs   30
3.1   Hidden pressures?   41
3.2   Disempowerment and loss of 'identity'   46
4.1   Anti-social behaviour and the use of authority   61
4.2   A young unaccompanied refugee   64
5.1   The impact of rules and procedures   98
6.1   Competing professional perspectives   117
7.1   The Intensive Supervision and Surveillance
      Programme   127
8.1   A service user taking action   151
8.2   Domestic violence, ethnicity and culture   153
8.3   The distribution of power   166
9.1   Domestic violence and empowering networks   188
10.1 Taking a referral   194
10.2 Integrated assessment models   197
10.3 Working together   210

Boxes

2.1   French and Raven's five-fold typology of power   20
7.1   Service-user strategies of power   126
8.1   Language and social work   161

Acknowledgements

My thanks go to Catherine Gray, Sarah Lodge, Keith Povey and their colleagues for keeping things on track and providing consistent feedback and support. Thanks also to the series editors for the opportunity to contribute to this important new body of social work literature.

I should also like to pay tribute to those who have helped me to (made me) reflect on the subject of 'social work and power' and what it means in practice, especially the many students with whom I have worked at Leicester and De Montfort Universities, and my friends at Central England People First who have been an inspiration for many years.

This book is dedicated to a number of former friends, colleagues and comrades who are sadly no longer with us, but who all, in their different ways, resisted unfairness and injustice and worked for a more equal distribution of 'power'. I hope they wouldn't object to being mentioned here: Richard Carr, Rita Earl, Pauline Hardiker, Jimmy Kane, Brian Williams. Thank you all.

ROGER SMITH

The author and publishers are grateful to the following for permission to reproduce copyright material: Taylor & Francis for Figure 4.3 (www. informaworld.com) from Roger Smith, 'Globalization, Individualization and Childhood: The Challenge for Social Work', *New Global Development: Journal of International and Comparative Social Welfare* (2004) Twentieth Anniversary Special, XX: 2, pp. 71–8. Every effort has been made to contact all the copyright-holders, but if any have been inadvertently omitted the publishers will be pleased to make the necessary arrangement at the earliest opportunity.

chapter 1

Why Do We Need to Think about Power?

A persistent problem

Power is an awkward and slippery concept, and it has proved highly problematic for social work both in theory and in practice. Indeed, conventional definitions illustrate the fundamental nature of the challenge. The *Oxford Dictionary of English* offers eight variations, of which three at least are directly relevant:

> the ability or capacity to do something;
> the capacity or ability to act in a particular way to direct or influence the behaviour of others or the course of events; or physical strength or force exerted by someone ... (*Oxford Dictionary of English*, 2005)

These are abstract and neutral properties, however, which give rise to large and challenging questions when applied to concrete situations. How does someone gain the authority to 'direct' or 'influence' others, for instance? What if this conflicts with someone else's 'capacity' to act in a particular way? Is it ever acceptable to use 'force' against someone else? Where does the authority and legitimacy to act in these ways come from? These and other related questions are of particular concern for social workers whose work typically involves negotiating the boundaries between individual freedom and choice, on the one hand, and external constraints and collective responsibilities, on the other. This may, for example, include considering the use of one's authority to 'direct' the behaviour of others by setting limits to their 'capacity to do something', such as exercising the parental role.

As a result, social workers often seem to be uncomfortable with the ambiguity of their position and responsibilities. They are reported to feel 'powerless' (Jones, 2001), acting simply as the functionaries of rigid and unfeeling legal requirements and state bureaucracies; whilst, at the same time, those with whom they work often appear to identify them as wielding very substantial influence over crucial and life-changing decisions (see, for example, Fisher *et al.*, 1986).

Not only is the operational context problematic, but it is also difficult to identify consistent underlying precepts to guide interventions. Sometimes, it appears to be necessary to take authority, to be directive and to exercise a degree of coercion (child protection and mental health are two areas of work where this may be the case – see below); but, on other occasions, the emphasis is very much on establishing a sense of mutuality and seeking to 'empower' service users (when working with people with learning difficulties, for example). The subject of power thus raises some fundamental questions about the very nature and purposes of social work. The very diverse nature of the responsibilities and functions of social workers makes it difficult to establish a generalized set of rules about how and in what circumstances, and in whose interest, authority is exercised. Social workers are expected to be able to mediate between different interests and to resolve competing demands, so it is perhaps unsurprising that there are inherent contradictions in the very statements of principle which inform their actions (General Social Care Council, 2002).

In fact, the authority of social workers derives from a number of different sources, giving rise to conflicts and choices for practitioners. Their professional standing, recently underpinned by the establishment of a national accrediting body in the UK (the General Social Care Council), offers one form of legitimacy to their work, helping to rationalize and justify the discretionary exercise of authority in complex circumstances. At the same time, law, policy and procedural rules offer another, routinized and systematized, source of justification for the exercise of mechanisms of control in situations of dispute or conflict.

A third and rather more nebulous, although arguably more important, source of authority for social work practitioners is that which derives from their personal credibility and accountability to those who use services, based on the way in which they conduct their everyday working relationships, especially with service users, but also with colleagues and other professionals. In other words, the practitioner's capacity to influence outcomes may depend on personalized attributions such as 'he or she knows what he or she is talking about'.

Other sources of legitimacy and credibility should also not be overlooked, including personal characteristics, such as ethnicity, gender or (dis)ability. This adds a further level of complexity, because it is not just the social worker's professional 'identity' which is crucial, but also the implications of the individual's characteristics and behaviour for the legitimacy accorded to that individual by others. So, a sense of 'difference' may effectively undermine the practitioner's credibility, leading service users to conclude that 'he or she *doesn't* know what he or she is talking about'.

practice illustration 1.1

Feeling disempowered as a practitioner

I can recall being told as a newly qualified probation worker that I could not possibly have anything to offer an alcoholic because I had not experienced that condition myself. In this way, authority bestowed on me by law and by my professional status was effectively denied on the basis of personal qualities (or lack of them).

As we shall see subsequently (Chapter 7), the role of service users themselves in determining the shape of power relationships is crucial.

Power dynamics in social work depend on the complex interplay between these different aspects of the practitioner's identity, standing and imputed authority, and those with whom the practitioner is interacting, notably service users, as well as others who may have a part to play in 'influencing' interventions.

Right from the start we will have to accept that there are no simple answers to the kind of questions to be explored here. The paradoxical and multifaceted nature of social work's relationship to power, and its power relationships, clearly represent a significant challenge.

The power to be late

Social workers may feel themselves to be driven by overwhelming operational demands, compounded by excessive workloads, staff shortages, paperwork and limited support (Jones, 2001). This may underlie the occurrence of unavoidable problems, such as lateness or even missed appointments. Nevertheless, for people in positions of relative authority, such as social workers, there may be considerable latitude, in that lateness for appointments with service users attracts little by way of negative comment or official sanction, although service users themselves stress the importance of practitioner 'punctuality' (Department of Health, 2002b). On the other hand, people in relatively weaker positions, such as service users themselves, may face rather different interpretations being placed on their 'failure' to attend appointments or meetings. Indeed, such actions may be taken as signs of indifference or inadequacy, and this may have significant consequences in terms of the judgements made about them and decisions about practice interventions.

practice illustration 1.2

The power of lateness?

The centrality of power in social work was, in fact, neatly illustrated for me by a colleague when I first told him that I was
thinking of writing this book. His immediate response was to
relate the term to its concrete implications rather than abstract
ideas, and he framed the issue in terms of 'lateness', and the
ways in which this is defined, experienced and justified. It
seemed to him that power relations are expressed in the differing
ways in which 'being late' is dealt with in transactions between
agencies, practitioners and service users.

In his view, those in positions of formal authority are less
likely to be held accountable for being late, whilst service users
may find that their 'lateness' has adverse consequences for the
way they are perceived or treated.

This may be a relatively mundane example, but its very ordinari-
ness highlights the way in which power and its consequences are
deeply embedded in the routines of day-to-day practice, as well as the
more obvious points where authority is invoked or sanctions applied
directly. In addition, the example illustrates at least three things
which are of critical importance when we consider the place of power
in social work. Firstly, perceptions will vary depending on an individual's position in any given transaction. That is to say, the meaning of
one's actions will not always be conveyed to others as intended, and
may well be interpreted in the light of differing assumptions about
the relative status and authority of participants. 'Being late', for
example, may be an occupational hazard for the professional concerned, but for those who are kept waiting, implicit messages are conveyed about how (un)important they are seen to be. For the service
user, on the other hand, 'being late' may similarly be an inevitable
consequence of problematic circumstances or limited resources, yet
this may still be interpreted as a sign of irresponsibility by others
whose moral judgements may have significant implications.

Secondly, the distribution of power in personal and professional
relationships is likely to be perceived and experienced as unequal,
even if the imbalance may not always lie in the expected direction.
The relationship between a female practitioner and a male service
user may incorporate a number of potentially conflicting power
dynamics, for example. In general, however, the ability to prescribe

behaviour (or ascribe meanings and apply moral judgements) rests predominantly with the social worker rather than the service user.

And, thirdly, it is impossible to operate in a power vacuum. This is especially the case in the social work setting. It is important to acknowledge that social work is constantly challenged by the requirement to make decisions and to carry out interventions which may have a profound impact on the lives of service users and carers. These may be positive actions, based on the decision to provide a service, to exercise control over someone's actions, or to act to protect a vulnerable person; or they may be negative decisions, where organizational priorities require a service not to be offered, or to be removed. Crucially, however, these interventions will be influenced by the nature of the relationship between participants, and, again, this may be affected by overt behavioural indicators, such as the quality of timekeeping. In this instance, however, there may also be a consequence for the practitioner if he or she is perceived as unreliable, in terms of service users' willingness to 'cooperate' with professional decisions.

The nature of power and its exercise, then, lies at the heart of the relationship between social work practitioners and those who use services. It is a feature of mundane and routine interactions as much as it is apparent in the explicit and formal exercise of authority and control. It is clearly important that we develop a sound and thorough understanding of the concept in order to be able to bring some clarity to the challenge of establishing effective and productive power relationships in practice.

What is the place of power in social work?

Social work interventions are likely to have a profound effect on people's lives. These include the imposition of restrictions on their activities, the allocation (or denial) of resources, and the determination of their living arrangements. Inevitably, these actions are likely to have a fundamental impact on service users, and others concerned with them, such as family members and carers. There are a number of social work settings which epitomize these issues, such as the exercise of child protection responsibilities, or decisions over the hospitalization of people under mental health legislation. In other contexts, such as work with people with learning difficulties, the dilemmas of power may revolve not so much around if and when to impose constraints, but around the extent to which the autonomy of service users can be promoted.

In child protection, for example, this is clearly a context in which the social work professional is responsible for exercising critical decisions which may involve determining the way in which families are ordered, and the conduct of relationships between family members. In other words, the social worker is cast in a role which may involve acting intrusively and authoritatively in the personal and private sphere of the family, which may conventionally be seen as inviolate. The consequence of such intervention may involve transfer of parental responsibility to the state, in the form of the local authority, and the consequent disruption of what may be seen as 'natural' ties, with both symbolic and practical consequences. The exercise of power in the formal or legal sense may appear to be decisive; but it may also give rise to further and continuing conflict and challenge (Smith, 2005).

Likewise, mental health social workers have for some time held responsibility for making crucial judgements about 'risk' and dangerousness, where the rights of service users are balanced against those of the wider family and the community. Once again, the professional obligation to evaluate complex situations, and to reach appropriate decisions, lies with the social work practitioner. The consequences of these judgements may involve invoking compulsory measures of detention. This is a major step which requires substantial justification in terms of the protection of the public (Ball and McDonald, 2002). We should note that such responsibilities are further complicated by the necessity for practitioners to take account of social and cultural factors (Davis, 1996, p. 118). Professional judgements are likely to be exercised against a backdrop of inequality and oppression, where the dynamics of power are, once again, a central issue. The problem of institutional racism, for example, has a significant bearing on the exercise of power by individual practitioners.

Turning to a third example, for people with learning difficulties, social workers may well have a central role in making judgements of a rather different character. In this context, it is the expectation placed on practitioners to determine the 'best interests' of the service user which is particularly challenging. This, in effect, generates a requirement to resolve tensions between key social work principles, such as autonomy and empowerment, on one hand, and the protection of vulnerable people, on the other. This potential conflict is particularly acute in relation to the emerging recognition of the importance of enabling people with learning difficulties to take charge of their own lives, for example by managing their own finances, and commissioning their own services through direct payments schemes.

These examples illustrate a number of recurrent themes which epitomize the kind of judgements which must be exercised in carrying out the social work task. Major considerations include the problem of competing interests, the balance between respecting wishes and meeting needs, and the distinctions between personal autonomy and what is believed to be the common good.

Embedded in such processes are the currents of power, which are manifested through the exercise of social work responsibilities, but which are also encountered in the settings in which practice is carried out. Oppressive and abusive relationships will be encountered, for example, and will need to be challenged, but even in this context the processes involved are not likely to be straightforward. Questions of the legitimacy of the practitioner's actions will arise in parallel with complex interpersonal dynamics, and this will further compound the difficulty of exercising authority effectively. The nature of power and the manner in which it is realized will thus represent significant challenges.

The contexts of power in social work

The task of exercising authority in individual cases encompasses many of the professional challenges likely to be faced by social workers, such as the need to exercise their judgement sensitively, and make definitive decisions, with far-reaching implications for the lives of service users and those around them. Before moving on to consider the notion of professional power in more detail, however, it is important to acknowledge that the predominantly individualized nature of social work interventions sometimes obscures some of the wider considerations which must be taken into account. Relationships within a particular family, for example, will be shaped by an intersecting pattern of influences, including cultural norms, ideologies of gender, financial resources and, sometimes, physical strength. We must be ready to acknowledge that power is multifaceted and diffuse, representing a complex and diverse set of influences on interpersonal transactions.

Social work is not just concerned with direct interactions between service users, practitioners and their agencies, but it is also closely implicated in the conflicts and inequalities that characterize the contexts of interventions, including those that reflect wider forms of oppression and discrimination. As is widely acknowledged, those who use social work services are predominantly to be found amongst groups and communities who experience disadvantage, oppression or social exclusion (Dominelli, 2004). Thus, for example, discrimination on the grounds of 'race', gender, disability, sexual orientation or immigration status is a prominent feature of the lives of many of those with whom social workers practice. Inevitably, in these circumstances, the dynamics of power, control and authority are of major significance, since it is denial of their basic human rights and lack of ability to shape their own lives which is crucial to people.

Relationships can be characterized in a number of ways. For example, they may be perceived in terms of structural positions, such as the formal role of the representative of a state agency vis-à-vis the recipient of services. But such relationships may incorporate a number of other dimensions such as the expertise attributed to a professional as opposed to a lay person; or, in another sense, the differential access to finance or other resources may also be a central aspect of a particular interaction. Indeed, we need to think of interpersonal transactions as reflecting a number of different dimensions. They may be affected by political, ideological, financial, cultural, communal or collective influences. These can each be seen to represent a distinctive 'mode' of power, with its own means of expression and dynamics. However, these should also be seen as interactive, generating a potentially limitless variety of currents and forces.

As we can see, individually based actions necessarily incorporate a number of dimensions. Social work typically takes place in settings where disadvantage and discrimination are commonly experienced. The consequences for service users may well be experienced in the form of a loss of control over key aspects of their own lives. The ambiguous nature of the social worker's role is evident. At one and the same time, the practitioner may both hold power in the form of ascribed professional expertise and statutory authority, yet at the same time be expected to promote the values of empowerment and autonomy for the service user. In addition, interventions are likely to be further circumscribed by external forces over which neither party has much control, as diverse as budgetary constraints and media stereotypes.

It must be recognized, too, that features of the social work terrain, such as formal language and standardized terminology, may also have a bearing on the interaction between practitioners and service users. Although clearly an essential basis for communication, language also incorporates implicit assumptions and judgements which may have adverse consequences for those it purports to describe. The routine use of jargon and opaque professional terms are also likely to create a sense of distance, and may effectively devalue and disempower people who use services.

It is not just that social work is complicated. It is also necessary to take account of the differential impact of the diverse forms of power on the circumstances and experience of service users. Inequality and oppression are certain to play a part in shaping their lives. Social work practice is thus obliged to engage with power imbalances in this respect. The exercise of one's responsibilities becomes a much more complex task than merely efficient resource management or the accurate application of eligibility criteria.

Key questions about power

It is the unevenness in the sites and forms of power that leads to our next significant observation. It may be an attractive notion that power is held in measurable form by individuals or institutions, for example, that the rule of law, and the ability to exercise statutory authority, solely depend on the legitimacy accorded to agencies of the state. However, as we shall see, such assumptions can be challenged in a number of ways. The notion of authority being held in a particular place seems to underestimate the extent to which different and competing sources of legitimacy can be seen to apply.

Neither is it realistic to think of power simply as a fixed quantity, subject to processes of transfer or exchange, but incapable of changing in overall capacity. This view is held by writers from quite different theoretical traditions, such as Parsons (1969) and Poulantzas (1973). Both argue that power cannot be reduced to a 'zero sum' equation. It does not, according to this view, represent a fixed entity, whereby one group or individual can only gain at the expense of another, and to an equivalent extent: 'In short, power relations do not constitute a simple expressive totality, any more than structures or practices do; but they are complex and distorted relations' (Poulantzas, 1973, p. 113).

We can see, therefore, that the shape and nature of power vary and its dynamics are unpredictable. At the same time, the manner in which it is exercised and realized is a fundamental issue in social work assessment, decision-making and intervention. It seems that there are four key questions which must be addressed in order to provide an effective understanding of power as a central element in social work practice. Firstly, it is critically important to gain some insight into *the nature of power*, that is, can we conceptualize its essential characteristics and, if so, how? Secondly, we need to acquire an understanding of *the sources of power*, that is, where does it come from, and how is it represented in any given social work transaction? Thirdly, it is important to achieve a practical awareness of *who has access to power*, that is, what are the resources (in terms of influence and authority) available to participants in specific contexts? And fourthly, we need to know *how power can be realized*, that is to say how practice can draw on the dynamics of power in order to achieve effective outcomes, which also reflect principles of fairness, equality and social justice.

The structure and aims of this book

In attempting to provide a constructive approach to the questions set out above, this book will focus on three broad areas. Part 1 (Ideas of Power) will consider some of the theories which have been developed to account for power and the means by which it is realized. Chapter 2 will explore key questions about the meaning of power and what it consists of – for example by exploring the distinction between what Fitzpatrick (2001) refers to as 'power as quantitative capacity', that is, as a possession; or 'power as production', that is, as the outcome of a particular social process. The differing implications of these (and other) conceptualizations will be explored, and I will endeavour to illustrate these with reference to aspects of social work practice. Despite its structure, it is not the intention to maintain a rigid demarcation in the content of the book between theory and practice.

Chapter 3 will link theories of power itself to a more detailed discussion of the 'sites of power'. In this context, notions of authority and legitimacy are particularly important, as well as the distinction mentioned earlier, between 'formal' and 'real' power (Poulantzas, 1975). Clearly, for social work practitioners, the sources of legitimacy are of particular significance, especially for those working in statutory settings. The authority to act derives to a great extent from legislation and official policy, and it is important to recognize this. However, authority also derives from a number of other sources, including expert knowledge and professional organizations, which may sometimes come into conflict with formal statements of policy. It is also clear that informal understandings and mutual solidarity provide a basis for practical decision-making, when it appears necessary to act in a way which is not sanctioned by official policy. Here, too, the idea of 'resistance' (Dominelli and McLeod, 1989; Housley, 2003) will be considered, particularly in the light of the emerging strength of service users and the potential for them and their organizations to act as sites of power. Thus, it will become apparent that 'authority' is not the same as 'legitimacy', since the latter depends on the extent to which a range of stakeholders, including service users, accept the formal authority bestowed on practitioners by their statutory powers and professional status.

To conclude this part, we will consider some of the processes by which power is realized in practice. In order to do so, it will be important to identify the mechanisms by which legitimacy is achieved, and authority established. For example, the primacy of managerial and business-orientated approaches to service delivery (Harris, 2003) is neither inevitable, nor self-evidently justified. The impact of ideology, and its relationship to power, are of particular importance because of the way in which the possibilities and impossibilities of practice are framed. For example, what counts as knowledge depends on dominant assumptions – sometimes referred to in terms of 'hegemony' (Gramsci, 1971) or 'paradigms' (Kuhn, 1970) – and this, in turn, sets the parameters for interventions. Chapter 4 will thus illustrate the importance for practitioners of retaining an awareness of alternative sources of understanding and bringing a critical edge to their work.

Part 2 (Mechanisms of Power) will offer an account of the way in which power is embedded in the operational structures of social work. Chapter 5 will consider the role of key institutions in setting the agenda for practice. Notably, the increasingly significant influence of government in speaking directly to practitioners will be considered here. However, it will also be important to reflect on other sources of influence, such as the media, judiciary and community leaders. These influences are of especial concern when we consider the circumstances of marginalized groups of service users, such as asylum seekers (Hayes and Humphries, 2004), where social work intervention takes place in a context of social exclusion and outright hostility.

Chapter 6 will consider the professional and organizational context in more detail, reflecting on the implications of recent changes for social work practitioners. Two trends, in particular, will be explored. The first is the continuing tension between professional standing and values on the one hand and the influence of procedural requirements and managerialism on the other. At issue will be the extent to which this represents a constraint on the independence of social workers, determining not just what they do, but how they do it. Implicated in this process are the burgeoning targets and performance indicators which appear to act as a distorting influence on the exercise of judgement, expertise and creativity.

At the same time, another emerging theme is the emphasis in training and service delivery on interprofessional working. Whilst this appears to be uncontentious, reflecting, as it does, a reasonable aspiration towards better communication and more effective practice, some concerns persist, as we shall see. These relate, again, to independence, and to the impact on practice of imbalances in status, resources and influence. Notwithstanding these concerns, this chapter will discuss some positive developments in this area, in terms of the enhanced authority of social work as a distinct professional discipline.

To conclude Part 2, there will be a fuller discussion of the relationship between practitioners and service users, in order to consider the challenges of exercising authority whilst at the same time promoting the aim of empowerment. Social workers have not always appreciated the extent to which their actions are experienced as hostile and intrusive (Fisher *et al.*, 1986; Cleaver and Freeman, 1995). Chapter 7 will explore some of the challenges of incorporating this understanding into practice, and building honest, open and productive relationships. Importantly, the aim will be to incorporate the service user's perspective, offering some insight into possible strategies to renegotiate power relationships from an apparently weak position.

Part 3 (Taking, Making and Using Power) moves from earlier analyses of power structures, formal systems and organizational frameworks towards a detailed consideration of the potential for social workers to share and devolve power effectively in the interests of service users. Here, we will concentrate on the strategies and practicalities of delivering effective and empowering interventions which pursue underlying objectives of achieving outcomes which address power imbalances and promote social justice. This part will consider the implications for practice at three distinct levels: the individual; the systemic; and the structural. The aim is to demonstrate that each of these is a legitimate and, indeed, necessary focal point for social work intervention. The connectedness of power relations means, in turn, that practice must itself be integrated, seeking systems and structural solutions alongside and in concert with personal change. Chapter 8 concentrates on the importance of recognizing the negotiable nature of power relationships in practice at the individual level. This does not necessarily mean that the social worker must relinquish all claim to power or authority but, rather, involves developing appropriate and inclusive methods for evaluating and balancing 'rights' and 'risks'. It may still be necessary to exercise measures of control and coercion, but these, too, can contribute to enhancing the power and autonomy of service users themselves. This chapter also discusses the importance of approaching interventions in ways which 'factor in' the likelihood of service users' being excluded from determining just what is the problem, and what are the key questions and choices from their point of view. In short, it is about professionals being sufficiently confident in their own skills to feel able to 'let go' and adopt an inclusive approach to problem definition and resolution.

Chapter 9 takes a more systemic view of the role of social work in reshaping power relations, based on the preceding arguments that people's needs and aspirations cannot be taken out of context, and that it is often the network of relationships around them which determine their particular circumstances. A consideration of systems and ecological theories will demonstrate the potential for social work practice to use such strategies to achieve certain goals and aspirations, for example participation, advocacy and self-determination, as set out in the Codes of Practice (GSCC, 2002). Recognizing the limitations of the 'zero sum' notion of power (Fitzpatrick, 2001) will enable social workers to consider the creative possibilities of working alongside service users and their networks to enhance their sense of autonomy and control.

Finally in Chapter 10 I will seek to pursue this theme further with a consideration of the potential role for social work in using its inherent power to promote social inclusion and social justice. This may mean reframing social work and linking individual interventions to broader strategies of social change and strengthening communities. The opportunities for developing practice along these lines will be considered here, as will the importance of seeking effective alliances with service-user and community organizations, as being part of the job of social work. This chapter will conclude by summarizing some of the strategies by which social work can deliver practice which is genuinely empowering and emancipatory (Leonard, 1997).

main points

- Power is a complex and challenging concept
- Power has a crucial impact on the relationship between social workers and service users
- Power has several dimensions, with practitioners operating at the interface between the structural and the personal
- Authority, legitimacy, and professional and personal credibility are all significant factors in the exercise of power in social work
- Social workers must be willing to take a proactive approach to considering, rethinking and changing power relationships in the interests of service users.

stop and think

- Who is oppressed/disadvantaged in a given practice setting?
- Who/what is the source of oppression?
- What form does this power imbalance take (e.g. structural, personal, financial, gender, 'race')?
- What levers are available to us (practitioners and service users) to achieve positive change in this unequal relationship (e.g. professional authority, negotiation, collective action, human rights instruments)?
- How can we generalize change to achieve collective as well as individual benefits?
- With whom can we work to achieve these goals?

- Lena Dominelli's comprehensive account *Social Work* (Polity Press, 2004) not only provides a thorough overview of the history and state of social work, but it also sets this within a context of the persistent experiences of disadvantage and oppression facing those who use social work services.
- David Garland's *The Culture of Control* (Oxford University Press, 2001) includes an insightful critical account of the everyday processes by which certain groups and communities are marginalized and 'othered'.
- Tony Fitzpatrick's wide-ranging book *Welfare Theory: An Introduction* (Palgrave Macmillan, 2001) also includes a helpful framework for conceptualizing power in the context of social welfare.
- Peter Leonard's contributions to the pursuit of positive strategies for renegotiating imbalances of power and promoting social justice is a helpful antidote to the tone of pessimism which sometimes seems to infuse discussions about the inevitability of disadvantage (*Postmodern Welfare*, Sage, 1997).

part 1 Ideas of Power

2 Ideas about Power

Power is a double-edged concept

Social workers have for a long time been uncomfortable with the phenomenon of power. They are, at one and the same time, acutely aware of their own relative powerlessness in an organizational and structural sense, and yet concerned as to how to manage their own authority over service users. Indeed, it seems that they are confronted with a very real irony; whilst having limited capacity to change structural aspects of oppression, they are also expected to exercise further controls and constraints over the oppressed. Jones's (2001) survey of practising social workers found this to be a matter of great concern. One said:

> I think the ... government is into having a two-tier system and the clients we work with are not needed so we are there to keep those at the bottom in their place and out of sight, or to be blamed if things go wrong. I think most local authority social workers today, unless they are completely apolitical, would accept that most of what we do is about policing. You can still do some useful things for your clients but it is more difficult than ever. (quoted in Jones, 2001, p. 550)

For those in this position, the task of exercising statutory authority, in the public interest supposedly, and at the same time identifying and representing the interests of service users, represents a complex challenge. Power relationships must be continually renegotiated, and opportunities for constructive solutions pursued, if social workers are to make an effective contribution to securing social justice. Sometimes it may feel as if pragmatic and individualized solutions are all that can be achieved; however, I want to suggest here that wider understanding is important, in both analysing the task and devising workable options. In developing this argument, I hope to demonstrate that the gulf between theory and practice in the context of power is not unbridgeable, and that it is worth the effort to travel this journey.

Historical ideas of power

Theorizing about power has been going on for a long time, and has originated from very diverse perspectives and interests. As Westwood (2002) points out, the distribution and mechanics of power have been the subject of thinking and debate over many centuries, and probably across all cultures. She notes the subject's appearance in Hindu texts, biblical writings and the works of Greek philosophers and Arab historians. She suggests, for example, that the work of Ibn Khaldun (2005 [1377]) represented a fundamental contribution to the early development of the understanding of power and power relations (Westwood, 2002, p. 7).

Modern thinking about the subject is clearly influenced by the ideas of earlier scholars, such as Machiavelli and Hobbes. Importantly, these writers began to focus attention away from a belief in power and its relationships as 'natural' and predetermined, towards a recognition of its 'social', and thus constructed and changing, character. Hobbes, for example, writing in 1651, distinguished between natural powers, such as physical or mental attributes, and 'instrumental' power, which is acquired through gaining wealth, influence or status: 'The power of a man (sic), to take it universally, is his present means to obtain some future apparent good, and is either original or instrumental' (Hobbes, 1998 [1651], p. xxx).

In setting out this definition, he also argued that power was not a fixed entity but could be extended, and could take a number of different forms. In this sense, there are parallels with the later work of Parsons (1969), who resists the idea that power is subject to specific and quantifiable limits.

Machiavelli's (2005 [1513]) contribution was to make explicit the contingent nature of power:

> Machiavelli offers us an ethnography of power as it is constituted and re-constituted ... Power is not an absolute, nor is it vested in the Prince or sovereign. Power is simply the effectiveness of strategies for generating a wider scope of action, *vis-à-vis* other people who must then operate within these arenas. (Westwood, 2002, p. 9)

Machiavelli did not make moral or ethical judgements about the use of power, but treated it simply as a means to an end. He was concerned with the efficiency and effectiveness of the methods used, rather than their justifications. However, his insights also draw our attention to another distinct perspective on power, in that he was concerned with the *processes* by which it could be realized, rather than with the *possession* of authority. This is an important distinction, to which we shall return.

Whilst modern theorists have attributed a degree of oversimplification to early discussions of power, Westwood (2002, p. 10) points out that their achievements were substantial in opening up the concept and drawing attention to its qualities as a social production: 'their texts demonstrate the ways in which, from the earliest attempts to theorise power, power has been bound to theorisations of the social'.

From recognition to definition?

Since the early attempts to describe and quantify power, there has emerged an extensive series of debates about its nature and implications. It has been a matter of concern for scholars in successive ages, and has repeatedly been recognized as fundamental to social and political analysis. However, underlying these debates, there appears to have been a marked lack of consensus about exactly what is meant by the term itself. Indeed, a number of competing definitions can be seen to apply, both implicitly and explicitly. For some (e.g. Lukes, 1974, p. 9), it is no bad thing that power is an 'evaluative and contested' concept. For others, however, it is seen to be of crucial importance that a definition is agreed. Dahl, for instance, is concerned to define the term in the form of coercive capability: '*A* has power over *B* to the extent that he can get *B* to do something that *B* would not otherwise do' (Dahl, 1969, p. 80).

This notion of power as the capability of securing compliance is consistent with the position taken by others, too: '*Power* is simply the probability that men (sic) will act as another man wishes. This action may rest on fear, rational calculation of advantage, lack of energy to do otherwise, loyal devotion or a dozen other individual motives' (Gerth and Mills, 1954, p. 195).

However, even with these fairly straightforward definitions, there are grounds for potential differences of emphasis and disagreement. According to the former, power resides with the dominant *interest*, which is able to secure the desired outcome through its exercise. Indeed, as Lukes (1974) observes, it is the 'successful attempt' by *A* to secure *B*'s compliance which is held to provide evidence for the exercise of power.

For Gerth and Mills (1954), on the other hand, the nature of power depends at least in part on the *relationship* between individuals, since the 'motives' of participants will significantly affect their likelihood of acting in the desired manner. As they point out, there is a distinction to be made between legitimate power, in the form of 'authority', on the one hand, and coercive power, or the exercise of force, on the other (p. 195). This consideration leads, in turn, to the development of 'typologies' of power (Lukes, 1974), which may take the form of coercion, influence, force, authority or manipulation. In this way, the definition is broadened, going beyond the overt exercise of authority by one individual over another in a decision-making situation, to one in which power may be implicit in social settings; and, indeed, underlying interests and dynamics may be hidden from view (Lukes, 1974, p. 25). Alternative typologies of power have been offered by a number of writers; these are a helpful aid to understanding, but also clearly a matter of some debate. The version offered by French and Raven, for example, introduces the key element of 'legitimacy' into the equation.

Box 2.1 French and Raven's five-fold typology of power

- *Referent power*, meaning the effect arising from the identification of one individual with another individual or group
- *Expert power*, that is, the extent to which someone is attributed with authoritative knowledge and skills in a given situation
- *Reward power*, by which is meant the ability to determine how resources are distributed
- *Coercive power*, by which is meant the ability to impose force or punish others
- *Legitimate power*, 'probably the most complex' (p. 264), in their view, but essentially meaning the sources of authority bestowed by the state, religious bodies or other normative institutions.

(based on French and Raven, 1968)

One way in which the 'social' characteristics of power have been elaborated is through the work of Parsons. For him, power can be generalized as a '*specific* mechanism operating to bring about changes in the action of other units, individual or collective, in the process of social interaction' (Parsons, 1969, p. 299).

The interesting feature of this definition is its characterization of power as an independent factor in social processes. Power is a means of securing and maintaining social order, which is not necessarily vested in any individual or interest: 'Power then is generalized capacity to secure the performance of binding obligations by units in a system of collective organization when the obligations are legitimized' (Parsons, 1969, p. 308).

It is the legitimacy of power which therefore justifies the threat and/or exercise of coercive action in the case of non-compliance. The right to make and enforce decisions derives from the collective interests of the social system as a whole. Power and legitimacy originate not with individual interests, but in the pre-existing goals of the established social order. For Parsons, legitimacy infuses all aspects of the exercise of power, somewhat at odds with French and Raven (1968) who distinguish it from other forms, such as coercive power.

Whilst Parsons helpfully illustrates the social basis of power relationships, he appears to underestimate the place of conflict and inequality in the establishment of societal norms and collective goals. The justifications for the exercise of authority and coercion are taken as given.

Parsons's definition offers some analytical benefits, notably in suggesting that power can be shared, and that therefore it offers the capacity for mutual benefit and the development of common interests. This, in turn, offers analytical support for the key social work concept of 'empowerment'. However, significant flaws run through this conceptualization. For Lukes, the reduction of 'power' to a function only of legitimate authority and consensual social goals conceals

> the whole range of problems that have concerned so-called 'coercion' theorists, precisely under the rubric of 'power'. By definitional fiat, phenomena of coercion, exploitation, manipulation and so on cease to be phenomena of power – and in consequence disappear from the theoretical landscape.
> (Lukes, 1974, p. 29)

Whereas Parsons appears not to recognize the possibility of conflicting interests, Lukes argues that the exercise of power necessarily involves the assertion of one interest over another. Power cannot be reduced to an abstract process of maintaining social order, but must involve a decisive move to exert control: 'A exercises power over B when A affects B in a manner contrary to B's interests' (Lukes, 1974, p. 74).

Power, in this sense, is not merely the capacity to exert influence, but it is the process of realization of one set of interests over another. It has been noted that this definition is helpful in that it looks further than a 'behaviourist concern with outcome' (MacKenzie, 1999, p. 75), but that the notion of 'interests' is not developed, leaving an unresolved tension between the individual actor and the underlying social factors which may come into play. As MacKenzie (1999) points out, this highlights an important contrast between those who have tried to capture the essence of power in individual transactions and those who have sought to highlight the role of social systems in determining power relations. The importance of collective interests is highlighted, for example, by Poulantzas, for whom, like others, power is a 'capacity', but one which is vested in different social classes, rather than the common good, interest groups or individuals. Power is 'the capacity of a social class to realise its specific objective interests' (Poulantzas, 1973, p. 104).

This definition, too, offers some useful insights. Firstly, it underlines the social nature of power, suggesting that it is realized in the interaction between specific and divergent collective interests. In this way, it becomes clearer that individualized transactions, such as that between social worker and service user, must be understood in the wider context of the class relations of the participants. This is particularly helpful when we come to consider the 'sites of power' (Westwood, 2002) within which particular social interactions are played out.

At the same time, the problematic nature of class and agency create potential difficulties for this analysis, as Poulantzas (1975) himself acknowledged. It is impossible to reduce power to a simplistic single dimension based on class, given the range of other interests (gender, race, disability, sexuality, and so on), which can be seen to have an influence on social interactions. Indeed, for the individual who may be acting at the interface between several differing interests, the source of her/his power (or its lack) may be the product of a complex interaction between competing factors. Dominelli (2002), for example, illustrates this with reference to a series of 'dyads' representing relations of dominance and oppression (such as male–female, white–black, able-bodied–disabled) which operate both independently and in combination to compound the effects of discrimination for particular groups, such as women, ethnic minorities and the disabled.

These concerns have led, in turn, to further attempts to capture the essence of power in what is seen as an increasingly diverse and multifaceted world. For Foucault, for example, power relations are to be seen as central to, and constitutive of, all forms of social interaction. Power is 'the multiplicity of force relations immanent in the sphere in which they operate and which constitute their own organisation' (Foucault, 1981, p. 92).

The insight offered here seems to be that power is inherent in all social interactions, that it is complex, and that it therefore has a kind of self-reinforcing character, whereby its exercise tends to confirm its legitimacy. Thus, for example, certain kinds of abusive and exploitative behaviour may come to be 'normalized' if they are not confronted. The problem with Foucault's analysis, though, is that it is essentially circular, and does not allow for a full understanding of the historical sources of power or the development of a capacity to challenge or change its relationships.

In concluding this discussion of the search for a definition of power, it is worth reminding ourselves that

> There is no consensus among theorists regarding the nature of power, the way it operates in the social and political world, [or] the manner in which it relates to associated concepts (such as authority, domination, resistance and empowerment). (MacKenzie, 1999, p. 69)

Despite this, it is possible to offer a conceptualization of power which may be helpful in the present context. It can be described as *the capacity, held individually or collectively, to influence either groups or individuals (including oneself) in a given social context.* This encompasses both the individual and social dimensions of power, although it clearly makes no attempt to give an account of its dynamics, or any inequalities in its distribution.

For the present, it may be sufficient to rely on this working definition, but it is clear that it must be developed and contextualized in order to provide any kind of detailed understanding applicable in the practice setting. In order to assist with this, I shall now move on to explore in more detail a number of aspects of power which will help us to begin to think in more depth about its development and application. These are:

- Power as potential
- Power as possession
- Power as process
- Power as product.

As will be seen, each of these represents a particular way of characterizing power relations, and each in turn will be shown to have potential value in understanding the power relationships between social work practitioners and service users.

Power as potential

According to Fitzpatrick (2001), the notion of power as 'quantitative capacity' is attractive because it suggests something substantive which can be identified and measured in terms of both its exercise and its outcomes. As he points out, this does not presuppose a particular distribution of power, and, indeed, it is compatible with quite divergent analyses of the state and social order. For example, power may be fairly evenly and fairly distributed, according to a pluralist analysis; whilst others may view it as being held predominantly by elite interests, who will then use their position to extend and perpetuate control.

Parsons (1969, p. 252) provides further support for this approach when he draws parallels between 'the conceptual schemes appropriate for the analysis of the economic and political aspects of societies'. So, 'power' can be conceived as a form of currency in the political sphere, just as money functions in the economic sphere, representing the capacity to achieve certain desired ends within the social system. Parsons argues that power is not to be seen in terms of different *forms*, but simply as a means of acquiring and exercising control. In this respect, it matters little whether power is exercised through influence, or through coercion, since these issues are subordinate to the question of whether or not the means of power is accorded legitimacy within any given social grouping. Legitimation, in power systems, achieves the same end as does confidence in monetary units in the economic sphere; therefore, the legitimate exercise of power is based on a consensual commitment to social structures and norms.

Parsons's analysis also enables him to deal with the question of 'authority', which is not associated with the status or characteristics of particular individuals, but relies on the position held within the social organization. Like Weber (1957), in this respect, he depersonalizes power and associates it with the roles and statuses arising from the way in which social systems are organized. The exercise of authority is simply the means of expressing the legitimate application of power, according to this view.

Consistent with this, Parsons views power as a neutral entity which exists and can be changed outside of the specific relationship between individuals or interest groups. It can be equated with financial capital, with similar processes of 'investment' and 'accumulation': 'Our concern is with the "real" outputs of the political process – the analogue of the monetary here is output of power' (Parsons, 1969, p. 254).

In passing, it is interesting to note here the contemporary emergence of the term 'social capital', with its connotations of investment in community well-being (O'Neill, 2004). Significantly, his approach enables Parsons to address what he terms the 'zero-sum problem' (1969, p. 271), which holds that 'a gain in power by a unit *A* is in the nature of the case the cause of a corresponding loss of power by other units, *B*, *C*, *D* ...'. Power need not be seen as a fixed quantity, according to him, but it can be built on and enhanced, such that the capacity of the collectivity as a whole can be increased. Parsons (1969, p. 276) suggests that effective leadership can mobilize members of the collectivity to assume new obligations, which are then capable of being converted into additional commitments to act in the promotion of the common good. Whilst initiatives of this kind may involve a degree of risk and uncertainty, they also provide routes towards 'altogether new levels of collective effectiveness' (Parsons, 1969, p. 278).

practice illustration 2.1

The Duluth Domestic Abuse Intervention Project

This project adopted a strategy based on principles of empowerment to change the way in which the community collectively responded to incidents of male domestic violence. The project thus challenged all concerned, including key agencies and practitioners to 'hold offenders accountable and place the onus of intervention on the community, not on the individual woman being beaten' (Pence and Paymar, 1993).

This model of practice operates systemically, aiming to empower those who experience 'domestic abuse' by coordinating community responses to incidents of harm drawing on principles of community organizing and advocacy. Importantly, the programme seeks as part of its work to challenge assumptions and practices embedded in formal response systems which might compound the victimization and oppression of those who experience domestic abuse.

(See: http://www.duluth-model.org.)

Thus, a committed group of practitioners have been able to reframe conventional assumptions about victimization and responsibility and generate a collective movement to shift power relations significantly in the interests of those who have been harmed.

practice illustration 2.2

Family Group Conferences

The practice of establishing Family Group Conferences (FGCs) to consider the needs of children who may be at risk of harm is one way in which power dynamics between practitioners and service users can be transformed to seek mutually beneficial outcomes. This model, deriving from Maori traditions and pioneered in New Zealand/Aotearoa, puts family members in control of the process, giving them responsibility for deciding who attends the conference and how it is conducted, as well as the decisions that are made and the interventions agreed upon.

> The following case shows how the FGC helped the family to prove that this was a suitable placement for the children. This case came about as a result of the death of the children's mother.
>
> The children, Maya (6) and Mubeen (10), were placed with the maternal aunt, Mrs Begum, following the death of their mother.
>
> There was no social services intervention until Mrs Begum asked for assistance for school placements. Social services decided to do an assessment and concluded that Mrs Begum was not a suitable carer as she herself has 7 children and the children were placed with their maternal uncles.
>
> The maternal uncles said that they were willing to care for the children if they had no other alternative. However, I discovered that the aunts were not happy with the children being placed with them. The children were also not happy about this arrangement and expressed a wish to live with Mrs Begum.
>
> The family group conference was well attended by family and other members of the Bangladeshi community. The FGC took place in the family's language, Sylheti (a Bangladeshi dialect), with the use of an interpreter required for the social worker. As a Sylheti speaking co-ordinator I was able to promote an environment where the family had trust in me and confidence in the FGC process.
>
> The fact that the FGC was held in the family's first language was empowering for the family and a complete contrast to previous meetings, which were held in English. This enabled them to confidently discuss with the social worker their needs as a family [and] gave the family the opportunity to make sense of the nature of social services involvement which they had previously struggled to understand.
>
> Through the family group conference Mrs Begum and the wider family members were able to convince social services that she had a very large support network and would be able to manage the two children as well as her own family. Social services agreed to the family plan which proposed that all of the children be placed with Mrs Begum.

(From *Together*, summer 2004, p. 5; reprinted by permission of the Family Rights Group.)

It can be seen that this perspective on power has some potential value in relation to social work practice in the context of autonomy and the promotion of user self-determination (Biesteck, 1961). As has been observed, this helps us to think about power not simply as a matter of struggle between opposing interests or hostile forces:

> Power as an interactional negotiated force is not simply a matter of control over others, as is suggested in zero-sum conceptualizations that produce winners and losers ... It can be a force that creates positive environments for communication and action which can result in 'win–win' situations. (Dominelli, 2004, p. 41)

However useful the idea of power as currency may be, there is clearly a danger in taking the analogy between power and money too far. Parsons devotes a lot of attention to developing the notion of 'power-credit' (1969, p. 277), whereby mutual commitments can be expanded beyond what is formally agreed in the same way as financial loans operate. However, it is difficult to sustain the argument that power behaves in exactly the same way as money. Despite its symbolic character, it remains quite straightforward to trace the circulation of money, and to observe that once it is spent, its location and ownership has changed. This is not necessarily the case for power, which may still be 'spent' in the same way, through the exercise of influence, but this does not necessarily result in a transfer to another group or individual. Clegg argues that this is because power crucially depends on its organizational context:

> Consider the 'rights' that possession of each entails. For money, the right to possession means access to market transactions; for power, the right to its exercise means having a position in a hierarchy of power relations in an organization. (Clegg, 1989, p. 133)

This problem, in part, derives from the second difficulty with Parsons's formulation, which is that it operates at too high a level of abstraction. For all that his notion of power as a kind of lubricant for the maintenance of consensual norms and social order is instructive, problems arise when trying to quantify and give substance to this concept. If, as Clegg suggests, power is dependent on specific organizational arrangements, it also depends on legitimation, that is, on the acceptance of the authority of those who exercise it. In order to understand how it operates in practice, it is therefore necessary to have some understanding of the specific nature of the organizational arrangements which apply. However, once attention is turned to the precise nature of these structures, it becomes clear that consensus and shared interests are not the norm: 'Discursive participation in consensual goal formation is not a normal condition for most organization members' (Clegg, 1989, p. 135). As Clegg observes, the consequences may be somewhat familiar for many members of formally constituted bodies:

> To be invariably told, rarely asked, infrequently consulted and be expected not to participate in the formulation of collective goals is hardly a secure basis for obtaining commitment to these goals. Hence the *realpolitik* of power and resistance are the normal conditions of membership and meaning for many organization personnel. (Clegg, 1989, p. 135)

Related to these concerns, a further problem with the abstract nature of Parsons's account is his apparent disregard for the 'forms' of power. In treating it as a form of currency, he suggests that its character is irrelevant, given that it can be translated into a common unit of exchange. As we have observed, this argument has some value, in that it may help to draw attention to the possible equivalence between different forms of power, such as money and familial obligations. However, to take this to the point of suggesting that this enables us to dispense with concerns about the 'forms' of power seems ultimately to be unhelpful. It renders it difficult, for example, to consider the substance and meaning of different power relations, such as those based on gender or ethnic differences, since different interests are seen as being both equivalent and capable of being 'integrated' with those of the social system 'as a whole' (Parsons, 1969, p. 269). In a very practical sense, this provides us with little support in the essential social work task of trying to understand difference, and then deal with the diverse interests and pressures which apply in complex social settings. Parsons claims that his formulation of power as a form of currency applies as effectively to its coercive use as to its consensual aspects (p. 251), but his reliance on the 'integration' of interests to achieve this (p. 280) is too neat, and does not resolve continuing concerns about inequality and injustice. Clearly, longstanding and systemic inequalities based on ethnicity and gender cannot simply be wished away in this oversimplified equation of all forms of power relations with the common good (Dominelli, 2002).

Power as possession

In contrast to the notion of power as a kind of facilitative resource, which works to sustain and develop social relations, stands the conception of it as an attribute, held by an individual or a body, by virtue of certain characteristics. This formulation is associated closely with ideas about institutional sources of authority and discipline. Indeed, Dahl encapsulates this position quite neatly: 'The base of an actor's power consists of all the resources – opportunities, acts, objects, etc. – that he [*sic*] can exploit in order to affect the behaviour of another' (Dahl, 1969, p. 81).

His illustration of this point contrasts the standing of an ordinary citizen ordering all drivers to do as directed with that of a police officer carrying out the same function. It appears that there are particular qualities attached to the police officer which confer the authority to compel obedience. The power exercised in this way is not arbitrary, but depends on a set of rules and responsibilities which determine the nature of the relationship between the official and other members of the community. This leads us to think of power as in some way being 'held' in particular locations and capable of being exercised to affect the actions of others. Clearly this leads us, in turn, to think about structures and state power.

Underlying Hobbes's *Leviathan*, for example, was the view that a central and authoritative source of power would be essential to curtail self-interest and to promote the common good. Without a common source of authority, the fear was that society would dissolve into a 'warring mass of individuals all striving for a power that none can hold absolutely' (MacKenzie, 1999, p. 71). According to his original formulation, the common interest could be protected by the location of authority by consent with one individual, who would have absolute sovereignty (Hobbes, 1998 [1651]). Whilst there have been many criticisms of this apparent oversimplification (MacKenzie, 1999), it does provide the basis for subsequent, more sophisticated, attempts to understand the nature of state power. Weber (1957), for example, developed a typology of different 'ideal types' of state power and 'legitimate' authority, identified as traditional, charismatic and legal–rational authority. These derive their legitimacy from different sources, namely social customs, the power of the individual, and formalized rules and practices. It is the last of these, epitomized in the term 'bureaucracy', which is seen as particularly relevant to a modern understanding of state functions and purposes. Of particular interest here is the shift of emphasis from the idea of power being attributed to or held by an individual, to its location within a socially constructed body.

Others, typically writing in the Marxist tradition, have also developed this notion of power being held within the state structure. Althusser (1977), for example, developed the idea of 'state apparatuses'. According to this depiction the various institutions of the state, including schools, statutory services, agencies of law and order and the civil service form part of the network which controls and dictates the activities of the citizen. Indeed, this schematic frame-work was extended further by Althusser and others (see Donzelot, 1979, for example) to incorporate other institutions which could be identified with the dominant class interests, such as the organized church, the media and even the family. This also enabled him to draw a distinction between those bodies which could be seen as directly coercive, such as the armed forces or police ('Repressive State Apparatuses'), and those which work through a process of securing legitimation and consent, such as the church and the media ('Ideological State Apparatuses').

Donzelot (1979) extends this by reflecting on the possibility of the co-option of the family as an agent of social control. Importantly, in the present context, this discussion provides further insight into the distinction sometimes made by theorists of power between 'coercive sanctions' and 'consensus and the will to voluntary cooperation' (Parsons, 1969, p. 251). Functionalists of the left (Althusser, 1977) and right (Parsons, 1969) agree, that there is no real value in differentiating between these, since they are merely aspects of a common social order. On the other hand Lukes (1974) suggests that a more nuanced account is necessary, in order to account for the differences between coercion, influence and persuasion.

practice illustration 2.3

Assessing children's needs

The legislative framework offered by the Children Act 1989 incorporates a number of alternative routes to securing the participation of children and their parents in assessments of need, depending on how serious the situation is perceived to be and what is the level of risk.

Choices may need to be made between carrying out an investigation under Section 17 and Section 47 of the Children Act 1989, and in some cases it may be deemed necessary to pursue a court order to secure compliance. The role of social workers as 'agents of the state' may thus become increasingly explicit as concerns heighten, moving from a negotiated strategy based on influence and persuasion to one which is explicitly coercive.

(See *Framework for the Assessment of Children in Need and Their Families*, http://www.dh.gov.uk/asset/Root/04/01/44/30/04014430.pdf.)

Whilst some have concentrated on the machinery of the state and its networks in securing authority and control, others have emphasized human agency in this process to a greater extent. Mills's (1956) discussion of the 'power elite', for example, has highlighted the way in which apparently diverse interests can be seen as sharing social and personal ties, such that they tend to act in mutually supportive ways. He demonstrates the close relationship between business interests and political power-holders in America, as an illustration of this. In taking this argument further, Miliband has suggested that the ownership and control of key elements of the social terrain, such as the media, are concentrated in the hands of conservative interests, such that 'ideas "seep downwards", and provide an ideological and political framework' (Miliband, 1973, p. 205), which establishes the ground rules for what appears in the public domain and how it is presented. Power is thus said to be held and exercised predominantly by elites in their own interest, and contrary to the aspirations or interests of the population in general.

It is possible to distinguish between those who offer a rather more impersonal view of the power held by state institutions and other bodies (for example, Weber, 1957; Althusser, 1977), and those who emphasize the role of human agency in securing and exercising dominance (such as Mills, 1956; Miliband, 1973). However, for present purposes, the key point is that they share a perception of power as something vested in specific interests and exercised partially, through particular mechanisms, to further their own ends.

There are, however, significant criticisms of this approach, namely that a static and highly structured characterization does not allow easily for divergence of interests or the possibility of any change in power dynamics. It has been argued that this kind of analysis is historically specific, and whilst it may account for the distribution of resources and authority at certain points in time, it is less well suited to an era of change and increasing diversity. As Clegg puts it: 'the situation in late capitalism is far more complex than any instrumental application of a dominant ideology view may suggest' (Clegg, 1989, p. 165). Dominelli puts this rather differently, but helpfully offers a personal dimension: 'People who are oppressed in one aspect of their lives may be oppressive in other elements ... they may be simultaneously oppressed by others and oppressive of others' (Dominelli, 2002, p. 13).

This does not necessarily refute the argument that power can be seen primarily as a possession, since it could be the case that it is just held more widely and by a greater number of interests. However, the need to understand the way in which power circulates and shifts requires us to move beyond a fixed view of the phenomenon. Clegg

(1989, p. 215), for example, tries to develop a multidimensional model based on the idea of 'circuits of power', in which power should be seen as 'multifarious' and 'episodic'.

Power as process

By contrast, there has been a developing body of work which has tried to elaborate an understanding of power as contingent, and as something which is manifested only in the course of human interaction, rather than as a fixed entity. Clegg's view on this is graphic:

> In the post-modern world, power consists less in the control of the relational field of force in each circuit and more in the way in which the obligatory passage point of the market has become a 'black hole', sucking in ever more agency and spewing out an ever more diffuse power as the pursuit of all things becomes an all encompassing passion. (Clegg, 1989, p. 275)

The pervasive nature of the phenomenon is thus its most distinctive feature. This thinking derives from the work of Foucault, whose portrayal of power as something with which all action is imbued is the most clearly articulated. In his view, power is to be understood not as a fixed phenomenon, but as a set of relations which are played out in practice. Power 'must not be sought in the primary existence of a central point' (Foucault, 1981, p. 93). It 'is everywhere; not because it embraces everything, but because it comes from everywhere'. Whilst it is difficult to grasp the fluidity of the concept when presented in this form, it is nonetheless a very helpful counterpoint to those formulations which attribute permanent and quantifiable characteristics to the notion of power.

Foucault (1981, p. 94) sets out a number of key characteristics of power:

- It is not an object, but is exercised in the 'interplay of nonegalitarian and mobile relations'
- It is not external to other types of relationship, but is 'immanent' in them
- It comes from below; that is, it is given substance in the direct interactions between people in specific settings, rather than superimposed upon these
- It is 'both intentional and nonsubjective'; that is, it is exercised according to the aims and objectives of social actors, but, at the same time, these may be inspired by other networks and influences
- It is also characterized by 'resistance': it encounters sporadic and unpredictable acts of non-compliance or counteraction.

These ideas are given substance most famously in Foucault's (1979) account of the techniques of punishment and surveillance. According to this analysis, all aspects of the processing and control of offenders are imbued with power relations. Thus, prisons and other penal sanctions are not simply methods of punishing or containing those convicted of crimes, they are also to be seen as means by which behaviour is 'normalized' (Garland, 1990, p. 145). Such methods have become assimilated in wider frameworks of surveillance and behaviour modification which traverse all aspects of social life and institutions. Foucault also discusses the ways in which notions of professionalism and expertise are bound up with these processes, such that resistance becomes irrational and illegitimate by definition. Clearly, this analysis has implications for present day practices in fields such as youth justice and mental health (see Chapter 7).

Although Foucault is probably the most influential theorist of power as process, there have been other contributions along these lines. For example, as already noted, Clegg has tried to articulate a complex framework for understanding the subject, which seeks to integrate both fixed and moving elements. Difference and disagreement are the norm, he argues: 'negotiation, contestation and struggle between organizationally divided and linked agencies is a routine occurrence' (Clegg, 1989, p. 198). As a consequence, analyses of power must take account of the interaction between different 'circuits' which represent 'rules, relations and resources' (Clegg, 1989, p. 211). Different individuals and interests will have variable access to these elements and as a result, their interactions will be uneven, and perceptions of authority and control will vary, even over the course of specific interactions. In this way, the notion of 'power as process' is also able to account for the perpetuation of established inequalities.

Contemporary ideas of postmodernity have also generated new ways of thinking about power, suggesting in effect that it has become fragmented and diffuse, with no single source of authority or legitimacy: 'The postmodern habitat is a complex (non-mechanical) system ... [T]here is no 'goal setting' agency with overall managing and co-ordinating capacities or ambitions' (Bauman, 1992, p. 192). As a result, individuals and groups have a substantial degree of freedom: 'Autonomy means that agents are only partly, if at all, constrained in their pursuit of whatever they have institutionalized as their purpose' (ibid.).

Under these conditions, power is also less likely to be anchored to specific interests, becoming 'episodic' (Clegg, 1989), which means that it can be seen as resulting from a momentary combination of circumstances or interests which generate substantial momentum in a given direction, only to be swept away in the next moment. Social relations are characterized by a chronic state of *'indeterminacy'* (Bauman, 1992, p. 193), of which changing power dynamics is one dimension.

Fook (2002) is an enthusiastic advocate of the value of postmodern thinking for social work. In particular, she believes that it offers an important contribution, precisely to the extent that it acknowledges diversity and allows for 'multiple discourses' (p. 14). She explains how she, herself, has been able to make positive use of this kind of thinking: 'I participate as an active player in a much more creative process in which I use ideas to develop critical possibilities' (*ibid.*).

Fook suggests that this has significant consequences for social workers. Notably, the loss of certainty associated with rapid social transformation has implications for the idea of professional expertise. The control of professional status and the definition of what counts as specialist knowledge come into question when their very legitimacy becomes fluid and negotiable: 'Professionals therefore stand to lose quite a bit of power if alternative perspectives are accepted, so a challenge to the exclusive knowledge of professionals is a direct challenge to their power base' (Fook, 2002, p. 37). As she points out, this generates some interesting dynamics for those involved in social work practice. Whilst it is important to respect the perspective of service users, their professional status and expertise remain important to social work practitioners. As Fook says, social work appears sometimes to want to 'have it both ways'. Nevertheless, this sense of ambiguity and uncertainty may still be used creatively, to 'move things on'.

Despite the apparently liberating aspects of postmodern thinking about power, there are also some criticisms to be made of it. In particular, its strong emphasis on process and contingency does tend to decontextualize it. The loss of any sense of groundedness tends to de-emphasize those aspects of power relations which derive from structural difference and inequalities. Postmodernism may be a source of 'emancipatory' thinking, but it has not shown that it can provide a strong base for 'reconstructing welfare as an emancipatory project' (Leonard, 1997, p. 149). This may well be because it offers limited insight into the structural aspects of power discussed previously. Despite their own limitations, such perspectives draw attention to the significance of 'interests' and ideologies as providing support for particular manifestations of power.

Likewise, Foucault comes in for criticism for attending only to the 'local' nature of power relations (MacKenzie, 1999, p. 83) and understating the extent to which such localized interactions are representative of broader structural relationships. These considerations are critically important when considering specific aspects of power dynamics, such as gender inequalities, racism or the disadvantages experienced by people with disabilities. In other words, the recurrent and pressing problems of inequality and oppression (Dominelli, 2002, p. 45) are not easily explained if we focus solely on the processual nature of power.

Power as product

The final characterization of power which I wish to consider here is, in many ways, the most attractive to social work practitioners, since it offers support for the idea of empowerment and, indeed, 'emancipatory practice' (Leonard, 1997; Fook, 2002).

Giddens has offered some useful insights into the notion of power as the consequence of processes of social and structural interaction, rather than as their precursor. His starting point is an attempt to resolve the tensions between those who see power solely 'in terms of intent or the will, as the capacity to achieve desired and intended outcomes', and others who see it 'above all as a property of society or the social community' (Giddens, 1984, p. 15). It is more apt, in his view, to see power as generated at the interface of individuals and structures: 'Power within social systems which enjoy some continuity over time and space presumes regularized relations of autonomy and dependence between actors or collectivities in contexts of social interaction' (Giddens, 1984, p. 16).

Power can thus be seen not simply as the determinant of social interactions, or even simply the medium through which they take place, but also as a product of dynamic change. He agrees with Parsons (1969) that power is not a fixed quantity, but is capable of variation depending on developments in the social system. Unlike Parsons, however, this is linked, for Giddens, to the idea of 'domination' by one group or interest over another; thus, power 'is generated in and through the reproduction of structures of domination' (Giddens, 1984, p. 258). The resources which support the particular form of domination at any one time can be classified according to a number of characteristics as either 'allocative' or 'authoritative'. The former equates to the various means by which material resources are controlled, and the latter to the kind of hegemonic mechanisms according to which the social order is organized. The precise nature of power relations at any given time depends on the interaction between these elements. It is not simply a matter of who owns or controls material resources in any given context.

Giddens points us towards the role of ideology and belief systems as significant elements in the constitution and exercise of power. As an illustration, he draws attention to the role of 'storage' in constituting authoritative understanding of social relations, and in ensuring that these are

> perpetuated across time-space. Storage presumes *media* of information representation, modes of information *retrieval* or recall and, as with all power resources, modes of its dissemination. Notches on wood, written lists, books, files, films, tapes – all these are media of information storage of widely varying capacity and detail. All depend for their retrieval upon the recall capacities of the human memory but also upon the skills of interpretation that may be possessed by only a minority within any given population. (Giddens, 1984, p. 261)

In the context of social work practice, for example, the way in which information is processed and recorded in both official documents and other formats both reflects existing power relations, and provides the basis for their reproduction and/or transformation. Thus, the extent to which service users (do or do not) have access to, hold and create their own records becomes a focal point for the negotiation and reshaping of their relationship with professional practitioners. The potential to own and control the production of knowledge, especially about oneself, is thus linked to the expansion of 'life-chances' (*ibid.*), providing one potential route towards 'empowerment' (Adams, 2003).

Even where 'knowledge' is conventionally produced by 'experts' who thereby control the ways in which needs and behaviour are defined, there is scope for reshaping the distribution of power (see also Chapter 7): 'all forms of dependence offer some resources whereby those who are subordinate can influence the activities of their superiors. This is what I call the dialectic of control in social systems' (Giddens, 1984, p. 16). Arendt, too, argues that power is best seen as the product of social interaction:

> Power is never the property of an individual; it belongs to a group and remains in existence only so long as the group keeps together. When we say of somebody that he is 'in power' we actually refer to his being empowered by a certain number of people to act in their name. (Arendt, 1970, p. 44)

The concept of empowerment has been particularly helpful to thinking about social work, given that it offers a means by which apparently fixed and oppressive systems and practices can be challenged and overcome through practice. The achievement of substantive improvements in the capacity of service users to control their lives depends on social workers adopting these principles. 'Social workers need empowerment to render their practice transformational' (Adams, 2003, p. 3).

Fook believes that it is important for practitioners to recognize that this process is not simply one of improving the circumstances of one individual or group 'at the *expense* of another'. She argues that this reflects a 'commodified' view of power which has severe limitations, in that it

> assumes that there is only a finite amount of power ... so that only one group or person can be empowered. It implies that we have to make choices about who can be empowered and the priority often implied is that whoever is the most disadvantaged, oppressed or marginal should be the chosen group. (Fook, 2002, p. 48)

As she points out, this kind of assumption can lead to situations of resentment or conflict between marginalized groups, where some perceive themselves to be losing out in order to benefit others. Other problems associated with this conception of power, in her view, include the assumption that there are two groups, those who are *powerful* and those who are *powerless*. According to this view, changes in power relations depend on the concession of power and control by those in dominant positions. Those who have no power are seen as being incapable of making changes in their own right, and this leads to a self-fulfilling perception of personal weakness and 'victimhood'. As Fook also points out, this approach to the distribution of power also creates real difficulty in allowing for and promoting difference, since everything depends on the perceptions of those who hold dominant positions, and who may therefore represent partial interests. As a consequence, 'the experience of being given power may not be experienced as empowering, but in fact may have disempowering effects' (Fook, 2002, p. 51).

For empowerment to be a fully developed concept, therefore, it is important to build in an appreciation of the processes by which service users 'exercise and create their own power' (Fook, 2002, p. 104). The process needs to be seen as one of both 'deconstructing' existing power relations and 'reconstructing' new forms which reflect both service users' and practitioners' interests, and allow for the possibility of mutual gains. Power, in this sense, is about development and renewal.

Whilst the liberating aspects of this analysis do, indeed, offer real support for creative and user-centred practice, it is also important to acknowledge some potential criticisms, as with the other positions discussed. It is, for example, quite difficult to perceive the role of 'structure' in the production of power, since much of the emphasis seems to be on the outcomes of interactions between actors, with little discussion of context. Giddens is criticized for understating the influence of structures or objective interests in the elaboration of power relationships. For Clegg (1989, p. 140), 'Giddens' resolution of the [agency–structure] problem in his conception of power is one in which the agency perspective is dominant'. Relying too heavily on the motivations and actions of individual agents tends to underplay the influence and importance of structural factors and external interests. In this way, relations of domination and subordination may be reduced simply to specific relationships. This may have significant implications for our understanding of racism, for example, where it is difficult to account for its institutional dimension if we concentrate principally on its 'direct' manifestations.

This, in turn, leads to two consequences for ideas of empowerment. Firstly, individual actors may not necessarily be aware of the systems and structures which shape and constrain their attempts to acquire power. Secondly, empowerment may become somewhat idealized, whereby transformation can be viewed simply in terms of 'wishing away' deep-rooted impediments to emancipation. Whilst empowering practice has many strengths, as we shall see (Adams, 2003), it is important to remain conscious of the structural constraints which apply, and which also need to be contested.

main points

- ■ Power can be viewed as:
  - – potential
  - – possession
  - – process
  - – product.

- ■ Power has a structural dimension, being vested in state agencies and other influential social institutions

- ■ Despite its structural elements, power is also diffuse and subject to continual change

- ■ Power is negotiable, and need not be thought of simply as a fixed quantity

- ■ Collective action can lead to mutual empowerment

- ■ Core social work principles such as autonomy and self-determination help practitioners to recognize the importance of seeking to transform unequal power relationships.

taking it further

- Talcott Parsons's analysis 'On the Concept of Political Power' (in Bell *et al.*, 1969) is helpful in that it refutes the 'zero-sum' notion of power and provides the basis for the idea of mutually empowering interventions.
- Stuart Clegg's *Frameworks of Power* (Sage, 1989) is an interesting and original account which illustrates the fluidity and negotiable nature of power.
- Michel Foucault's *Discipline and Punish* (Penguin, 1979) has been hugely influential in its portrayal of the machinery of power and the way in which the state acts systematically to control unacceptable behaviours.
- Jan Fook in *Social Work: Critical Theory and Practice* (Sage, 2002) offers practitioners a series of productive insights and practical options for renegotiating power relationships in the interests of service users.

Websites

http://www.duluth-model.org
This site gives details of an innovative approach to tackling domestic violence and abuse which consciously and explicitly addresses power dynamics and oppressive ideologies within communities.

http://www.shapingourlives.org.uk
A national organization dedicated to promoting the interests and rights of service users, especially to control the organization, management and delivery of services.

http://www.frg.org.uk/fgc/FamilyGConference.pdf
This is a guide to the principles and practice of Family Group Conferences, published by the Family Rights Group.

3 Modes of Power

Interests and difference

Having attempted to clarify some of the theoretical issues surrounding the nature of power, the key question to be addressed in this chapter is: how is power exercised and experienced? This will precede a more detailed consideration of the contexts within which power relations are played out (Chapter 4). It is clearly a matter of some relevance that power and its relationships can be differentiated, notwithstanding Parsons's (1969) view that this is unnecessary. Any attempt to operationalize the concept, that is, to provide a 'definition-in-use', must consider the characteristics which determine its exercise in specific settings.

Lukes, for example, relates the exercise of power to the concept of 'interests'; in other words, power relationships will depend on the perceptions of the actors concerned with regard to how these will serve their own purposes: 'talk of interests provides a licence for the making of normative judgements of a moral and political character' (Lukes, 1974, p. 34).

Bachrach and Baratz also underline the importance of 'interests' in the exercise of power in setting out a framework for the analysis of political decision-making. For them, the exercise of power depends firstly on a conflict of interests and subsequently on the acquiescence of one party to another's wishes. According to them, interests are not only expressed directly in this way, but also by control of the decision-making context. It is possible, thus, to argue that dominant interests are reflected even in the absence of concrete outcomes:

> The other side of the coin is *non*decision-making. When the dominant values, the accepted rules of the game, the existing power relations among groups, and the instruments of force, singly or in combination, effectively prevent certain grievances from developing into full-fledged issues which call for decisions, it can be said that a nondecision-making situation exists. (Bachrach and Baratz, 1969, p. 109)

The ability to set the terms of discussion and effectively to rule out certain issues from the agenda elaborated here shares much in common with the Gramscian notion of hegemony. According to this view, social structures and processes are infused with an understanding of what is acceptable and what is not, thereby creating the appearance of consensus and denying the legitimacy of alternative perspectives (Gramsci, 1971). Certainly Lukes feels that this is an important consideration in the context of the exercise of power:

> A may exercise power over B by getting him to do what he does not want to do, but he also exercises power over him by influencing, shaping or determining his very wants. Indeed, is it not the supreme exercise of power to get another or others to have the desires you want them to have – that is, to secure their compliance by controlling their thoughts and desires? (Lukes, 1974, p. 23)

The possibility seems to be that people may not only be persuaded to act against their own interests but actually to espouse aspirations and beliefs which are also not consistent with their own well-being.

practice illustration 3.1

Hidden pressures?

Amy, an older person with dementia, wants to remain in the familiar surroundings of her own home. Her relatives, however, appear keen for her to be somewhere 'safe'.

Apparently, under some pressure, in the presence of other family members, Amy comments that she does not want to be a 'burden' to anyone. When you see her alone, however, she is obviously very worried about having to move away from familiar surroundings.

Her family continually emphasize their concern for her 'safety', but appear less interested in other aspects of her well-being.

It is quite possible that Amy has been influenced both by tacit pressure from her relatives and by her own beliefs about her own self-worth as a woman and as an older person.

Whether or not the contentious notion of 'false consciousness' is sustainable, there is no doubt that the task of identifying and articulating the 'real' interests of service users is a key issue for social work practice (Rojek *et al.*, 1988). It is clear that in many practice settings there are significant challenges in gaining a reliable view of someone's best interests, particularly where these are subject to external influences. These problems are likely to arise in the context where abusive relationships exist, for example. Feelings of powerlessness and personal inadequacy may well have an impact on an individual's perceptions of what is desirable and achievable in a situation where he or she is experiencing oppression; in turn, these feelings may be induced or reinforced by the oppressive behaviour itself.

The importance of understanding the relationship between power and interests also highlights the need to acknowledge and incorporate the idea of 'difference' into our analysis. Interests do not become problematic until they encounter opposition from other perspectives, where competing needs and wishes are evident. Underlying these conflicts, there are likely to be substantive differences between the groups or individuals involved. These may be reflected in recognized variations in their characteristics, such as race, gender, disability or sexuality. They may also be a product of different personal or professional status; and they may originate from specific features of their individual relationships.

In such circumstances, the way in which conflicts are dealt with necessarily depends on the resolution of the power relationships between those concerned. Understanding the nature of 'difference' and its implications for the exercise of power is thus an important prerequisite for practice in social work settings.

In order to make sense of the questions arising from these important aspects of the subject, it will help to develop a more detailed analysis of the various 'modes' of power which may be identified. I want to suggest that there is value in attempting to distinguish different aspects of power relationships which will help us to give substance and depth to the concept. For present purposes, these are characterized as *personal*, *positional* or *relational*. As the term indicates, the 'personal' aspect relates to the characteristics attributed to people, such as sexuality or class position; 'positional' qualities of power relations derive from the structural location of those involved in a given interaction; and 'relational' features derive from intrinsic qualities of the relationship, such as the dynamics between family members, or the influence arising from peer pressure. While these aspects of power are separated here for analytical purposes, clearly they are likely to interact in practice.

The 'personal' aspect of power: the role of identity

At the core of our social relationships lies the sense of identity. In other words, who we believe we are is fundamentally influential in determining how we relate to others. Equally, of course, how we are treated may depend on others' attribution of a particular identity or identities to us. Identity therefore involves the generation of a set of characteristics by which, on the one hand, we categorize ourselves, and, on the other, the identification of qualities and attributes which are associated with those who are 'not one of us' (Garland, 2001, p. 137).

Robinson (1998) draws attention to the importance of the creation of shared meanings in the establishment of 'positive social identities'. A common language, for example, is an important element in the creation of a sense of group membership. Physical attributes, too, such as skin colour, may provide the basis for positive affirmation of one's sense of self. However, as theorists such as Dominelli (2004) and Garland (2001) have argued, the issue of identity is also closely connected with 'othering' processes. Indeed, this seems to lie at the core of the establishment of difference and potential conflict:

> The 'self' exists because there is an 'other' to whom one can compare oneself. The self–other dichotomy or binary dyad enables the self to externalize the 'other', and facilitates the act of viewing the 'other' in an antagonistic and hierarchical relationship to itself. (Dominelli, 2004, p. 76)

As Thompson (2003a, p. 28) points out, the act of 'identifying a difference' leads to the creation of boundaries. Such boundaries are created through the assumptions, beliefs and actions of both the self and the other. It is suggested further that these very basic features of the establishment of a sense of identity themselves contribute to the creation of unequal and hierarchical relationships. Negative perceptions and routine stereotyping can thus be seen as entirely predictable. The consequences are clear, in terms of labelling (see, for example, Becker, 1963) and the development of explicit distinctions between categories such as 'deserving' and 'undeserving', or 'desirable' and 'undesirable' (Dominelli, 2004, p. 76). The process of negative attribution can be seen to achieve two linked objectives; that is, it reinforces the sense of membership and social value of the group to which the self belongs, and, at the same time, it also underlines the negative value associated with those who are seen as 'not one of us'. In this way, divisions based on assumptions about identity become increasingly impermeable, and more likely to be sustained over time, even in the light of contrary evidence.

Dominelli (2004) expresses real concern about the implications of this kind of process for social work: 'Unitary conceptualizations of identity are extremely powerful and deeply embedded in social work. All women, black people, older people, are treated as if they were like all others in their particular category' (Dominelli, 2004, p. 78). This, it is argued, leads to a number of partial assumptions which have adversely affected practice. Individual characteristics come to be identified as representing membership of a particular group, which then determines the nature of the practitioner's response. These characteristics override other aspects of the individual's identity, and, at the same time, they are seen as 'fixed and immutable'. Practitioners tend to 'think about identity as something that an individual acquires at birth and sticks with until death' (Dominelli, 2004, p. 77). Not only are people expected to behave in a certain way, in accordance with their ascribed identity, but also they may be misperceived by professionals if they do not comply with these expectations. By contrast, Dominelli argues, identity needs to be seen as a much more fluid and emergent concept, arising from social interactions and reflecting both individual and group dimensions. Identity formation is held to be 'dialogical', based on the nature and content of exchanges with others. It is also to be seen as a *conscious* process, whereby people draw on 'available discourses' to establish a sense of self, and to establish the nature of their relationships to others. This means that interactions, say between professionals and service users, will partly be influenced by those 'identity attributes' which each participant chooses to reveal (*ibid.*). Interpreting what may be seen as secretive or dishonest behaviour thus becomes a more complex task, given that it may be readily understandable for people to seek to present a socially acceptable view of themselves and their actions in dealing with representatives of officialdom (see Chapter 7).

Lukes has probed the concept of identity somewhat further in his attempt to link it to the analysis of power. He argues, for example, that it is important to relate identity to the idea of human nature and to consider the role of identity in creating people's 'natures'. In his view, this argument leads to a rather more complex understanding of identity than that which sees our distinctive human qualities arising simply as a product of 'practical reason and sociability' (Lukes, 2005, p. 118). Indeed, the notion of identity is best seen as representing the intersection of two separate dimensions: the distinction between individual and group identities, and the question of whether it is self-defined or ascribed by others: 'We speak today of individual and collective *identities* – and thereby neatly express ambivalence over whether the nature of individuals and groups is objectively given or subjectively, and inter-subjectively, constructed' (*ibid.*). As he points out, the term is used both in the sense of attempting to apply an objective measure of the defining characteristics of individuals and groups, and in the sense of achieving a sense of our own being through a process of 'self-discovery and self-invention'.

It is precisely because identity can be constructed in these different ways that the exercise of power in this context can also be seen as multifaceted. This may firstly be represented by the promotion of a particular image by a dominant group. The control of 'means of interpretation and communication' (Lukes, 2005, p. 120) ensures that clear and consistent messages about what is desirable are projected. As a result, certain properties and human characteristics become identified as the preferred norm. At the same time, and partly as a consequence, the characteristics of certain other groups may become marked down as less socially valued, even though they may have positive meaning for their members. This involves the rejection of certain forms of identity, including: 'the non-recognition or mis-recognition of ethnic or cultural or religious or geographical identities, which the members of subordinate and minority groups in a society endorse and to which they cleave' (Lukes, 2005, p. 119).

That is to say, identities which are held by some groups and the ways in which they are expressed may not be recognized as positive attributes by others, who may be in a position to define what is acceptable or desirable. This is well illustrated by the example of disabled children, whose identities are clearly shaped by their experience of receiving messages about what is desirable, in terms of body image and functioning. As Middleton points out, these messages are often conveyed in very direct and painful fashion. She describes the 'experience of physically disabled girls', which 'involved a great deal of physiotherapy', and whose purpose was to make their bodies conform with the image of the ideal woman (Middleton, 1999, p. 23). In another case, a young man with 'a deformed but functional hand' experienced three painful but unsuccessful operations to try to correct it (Middleton, 1999, p. 21). It is argued that the messages that disabled children receive are inconsistent, but generally present a negative or patronizing view of disability. For example:

> Consultants have the answers, and operations to make them [disabled children] normal should take precedence over social or educational needs. It does not matter if these operations hurt, or need to be repeated, or are totally ineffective. They will add to the sum of scientific knowledge. (Middleton, 1999, p. 24)

This is to be contrasted with the activities of disabled people and their organizations which have focused on encouraging a spirit of 'self-confidence and pride, rather than the guilt and shame associated with the individual tragedy model' (French and Swain, 2002, p. 395).

As well as a failure of recognition, Lukes argues that the ascription of identity can have significant consequences in terms of fixing people into specific roles. In this way, people come to be seen, and even to see themselves, as having a particular place within the social structure. He cites the example, from another source, of widows from a particular culture, whose identity is determined in the light of their status as 'daughters, mothers, wives and widows' (Lukes, 2005, p. 119); that is, their social position is 'invariably' represented in relation to men. Thus, the exercise of power through the ascription of identity may both devalue certain groups, and, at the same time, consign people to specific positions within the social order. The clear tendency for most child care responsibilities to be undertaken by women, both domestically and in early years settings, is one manifestation of the way in which such assumptions appear to percolate the social fabric and influence the division of labour within society.

As Lukes observes, these processes do not operate solely in terms of establishing groups and assigning people to particular categories, but they also impact on the ways in which individuals negotiate their own identities. In this respect, his argument coincides with that of Dominelli (2004), to the extent that oversimplistic assumptions based on observable characteristics may result in 'unwanted recognition'. Thus: 'individuals are, in various ways and for differing reasons, disinclined to identify with some group or category ascribed to them, but are pressured into conformity, public self-ascription ... and solidarity' (Lukes, 2005, p. 119). The different dimensions of an individual's identity may be overlooked; the importance of asserting positive but undervalued aspects of one's personality may not be recognized.

practice illustration 3.2

Disempowerment and loss of 'identity'

Black and mixed heritage children and young people in care have sometimes been found to aspire to a 'white' identity, changing aspects of their appearance to conform to this apparently desirable status.

Feminists, significantly, have focused on the role of power in constructing identity (MacKenzie, 1999). In particular, they have emphasized the way in which this extends beyond an understanding of 'interests' and how these are defined, to a consideration of the ways in which they are generated. Thus, the fact that many women *want* to take up caring roles must be explained in terms of the origins of their hopes and desires, rather than simply taken at face value. The feminist argument is that this can only be explained in the context of a historical process of systematic oppression and male domination. In this sense, compliance is secured by a process of coercion, whilst complicity is ensured through the creation of a sense that unequal gender relationships are part of the natural order of things. Such arguments can also clearly be applied to other aspects of inequality and oppression, whether based on class, ethnicity, disability, sexuality, religion or any other difference arising from the negative classification of a particular group.

The focus on the oppressive potential of power tends to a view that identities are constructed and maintained by and in the interests of dominant groups. In other words, it may be assumed that identity merely reflects the prevailing social order. However, feminists and others (e.g. Castells, 2004) have recognized the capacity of individuals to self-consciously renegotiate and transform identity, and, in so doing, to realign power relations. Whilst some perspectives have concentrated on the personal aspects of emancipation and empowerment (MacKenzie, 1999, p. 82), others have emphasized the context of a fragmented and increasingly diffuse globalized society. Castells argues that we should see identity, and the power relationships it represents, in three distinct ways: as *legitimizing identity*, *resistance identity* or *project identity*. Legitimizing identity represents the way in which interests and perceptions of self are created by, and reflect, the interests of dominant sectors of society. Resistance identity arises out of the experience of 'otherwise unbearable oppression', and represents the rejection of negative ascriptions, for example through the affirmative expression of 'gay pride'. And, project identity is identified as a transformational state, whereby actors utilize whatever 'cultural materials are available to them' to establish a new identity and thus change social relations (Castells, 2004, p. 8).

In brief, then, identity should be seen as not merely a product of power relationships, but also as a focal point for their expression and eventual redefinition. For practitioners, the key point is that identity emerges from power dynamics, but, as a result, it is also fluid, multi-faceted and capable of redefinition and change.

Positional power

As the previous section illustrates, power relationships depend in part on the identities we hold and the way in which they are constructed and change. However, power also has at least two other dimensions, which are of interest here: that which relates to the positions we occupy, and that which is experienced through the process of interaction amongst individuals and groups. These are less dependent on the characteristics of individuals and more on their relative places in the social order.

Firstly, then, we shall consider the importance of social position. Power of this kind can be seen as consistent with the idea that it is a 'possession' or attribute, as discussed in the previous chapter. Originally, this view of power was associated with the Hobbesian idea of 'sovereignty', whereby a particularly powerful individual could impose her or his will over others (Clegg, 1989, p. 35). However, the practicalities of maintaining dominance required the development of social and political structures whereby this position of authority could be maintained:

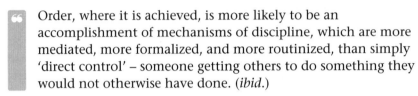

> Order, where it is achieved, is more likely to be an accomplishment of mechanisms of discipline, which are more mediated, more formalized, and more routinized, than simply 'direct control' – someone getting others to do something they would not otherwise have done. (*ibid.*)

Historically, this process can be seen in the form of the development of relatively complex mechanisms, whereby power could be exercised as an expression of state authority. However, in the process, the loci of power also appear to have become more diffuse (Poulantzas, 1975). It may be seen as deriving from any of the following, for example: organizational position, social status, religious standing or political office. In this respect, power has a kind of formal quality, which is attached to the position rather than to the individual who holds it. In this context, too, it can be seen that there is an implicit assumption that authority and control are organized in hierarchical fashion.

Weber is probably the source most closely associated with this notion of power (Gerth and Mills, 1948), as articulated through a formal, rational system of social organization and action. Weber is concerned, firstly, with the nature of 'domination' and the ways in which this comes to be legitimized (Weber, 1948, p. 78). Without legitimacy, there is no basis for the state to exercise control over the actions of its citizens. As opposed to 'traditional' and 'charismatic' forms of domination, the modern state and its functionaries gain authority for their actions by virtue of their 'legality', that is 'by virtue of the belief in the validity of legal statute and functional "competence" based on rationally created *rules*' (Weber, 1948, p. 79).

The arrangements by which these objective and impersonal rules are maintained and imposed are to be found in the development of the bureaucratic form of organization. The place of 'trained officials' within a 'fully developed bureaucracy' is to ensure the efficient and effective administration of the machinery of state in order to achieve its objectives. In this sense, the organization has no moral or political viewpoint, but is simply concerned with carrying out its assigned tasks effectively. The standing of officials themselves follows from this, in that their duties are objectively derived from these requirements; they are therefore responsible for carrying these out systematically, consistently and impartially (see also, Parsons, 1969). The status of individual functionaries, and the power relations which derive from that, arise solely from the authority ascribed to the role of competent official. As a result, personal interests and beliefs have no influence over formal interventions in the state arena:

> it was left to the complete depersonalization of administrative management by bureaucracy and the rational systematization of law to realize the separation of public and private fully and in principle. (Weber, 1948b, p. 239)

Power within the sphere of bureaucratic activity can be said to be 'positional'. Given that, according to Weber (1948b, p. 232), the modern state is characterized by increasingly bureaucratic tendencies, then the exercise of power in this context must be of central concern. However, he also acknowledges the importance of other forms of 'domination', including by economic interests (Weber, 1978). Nevertheless, for present purposes, the recognition that status and power are ascribed to people because of their position as representatives of state bureaucracies is quite important. The authority of social work professionals is closely associated with their organizational status. Clearly, too, the extent to which the idea of bureaucracy has become discredited is likely to have implications for the acceptance (or not) of the legitimacy of their interventions.

Like Weber, Simmel is also interested in the idea of domination and the mechanisms by which it is realized. He is concerned, in particular, with the ways in which coercion and compulsion are supplanted (or supplemented) by willing obedience. Why do people do as they're told, short of being forced to comply? Where does someone's authority come from, and what gives it its 'objective' character? (Simmel, 1986, p. 205).

According to Simmel, it is possible for a 'person of superior significance or strength' to lay claim to legitimacy. In other words, by drawing on this relatively greater strength, he or she is able to ensure that his or her subjective interests achieve an objective character – they become more widely acceptable or desirable. This hints at the exercise of physical, economic or other resources, not just as a means of coercion, but in order to gain institutionalized status and recognition. But Simmel is also concerned with the way in which institutions and interests are able to bestow authority and status on individuals:

> authority may be attained in the opposite direction. A super-individual power – state, church, school, family or military organizations – clothes a person with a reputation, a dignity, a power of ultimate decision, which would never flow from his [*sic*] individuality. (*ibid.*)

As a result, the individual concerned is empowered to take action and make decisions with a degree of 'certainty and automatic recognition'. Associated with this view of authority as having a natural and logical quality, he argues that compliance depends on the 'more or less voluntary faith' of the person or people who are subject to the exercise of authority. In the absence of coercion, therefore, compliance must assume a degree of freedom on the part of the person concerned, which also leaves 'room for criticism' (Simmel, 1986, p. 206).

There are, therefore, two potential complications introduced by Simmel, which impact on the idea of the exercise of power being essentially positional or dependent on status. Firstly, as he notes, the source of an individual's status may not just be the state, but it may also derive from a number of other significant social groupings, such as the family, churches or other bodies. Secondly, by seeking voluntary compliance based on claims to legitimacy, the possibility of alternative and potentially conflicting claims must also be allowed. For the social work professional, such competing status claims may become very acute in certain circumstances, such as facing the challenge of responding effectively to young women seeking to avoid arranged marriages (Smith, 2005, p. 137). In this context, clearly, claims to authority are likely to be contested, and interventions must seek to negotiate these, rather than merely relying on the presumed legitimacy of a statutory body. Here, the idea of 'status' assumes some significance: '*Status* involves the successful realization of claims to prestige; it refers to the distribution of deference in a society' (Gerth and Mills, 1954, p. 306).

Importantly, status can be seen to derive from any of a number of attributes; these may be consistent with one another, or contradictory. For example, one's professional status as a female social worker may be inconsistent with one's ascribed position within the family or one's religion. Status and social position, therefore, are likely to be multifaceted, and this may lead to conflict, both internal and external.

In a different sense, though, status may also be transferable, so that social standing in one sphere may also give one credit in another setting. The routine assumption that business skills and experience are of value in the social care field, as in the case of the Griffiths (1988) report on community care, is one example of this kind of transferability – significantly, it does not seem to flow in the other direction, though (see Harris, 2003)!

Power may thus be seen as a function of the status derived from a variety of intertwined social roles:

> all roles that are instituted, no matter in which order, involve authoritative relations – the family no less than the political, military, economic, and religious orders. The power of a person thus depends on a great variety of possible roles. (Gerth and Mills, 1954, p. 308)

In the practice setting, social workers must be concerned not just about the authority they derive from their place within formal organizational structures, and the legitimacy accorded to state agencies, but also about the power dynamics deriving from the status of others.

To take this further, it has been suggested that in order to understand the specific context in which status is used to exercise power, it is important to understand the basis of claims to authority or 'prestige' (Gerth and Mills, 1954, p. 315). The perspectives and attributes of all parties must be considered. From the point of view of the participant claiming authority, the factors to be considered are:

> (1) the status claim, (2) the way in which the claim is raised or expressed, (3) the basis on which the claim is raised. And correspondingly from the bestower's side: (4) the status bestowal or deference given, (5) the way in which these deferences are given, (6) the basis of the bestowal, which may or may not be the same as the basis on which the claim is raised. (*ibid.*)

Importantly, this formulation relates the notion of status to the perceptions of those concerned in any particular interaction. In this way, it becomes possible to factor in differing perspectives, and to allow for the fact that compliance may be conditional or temporary. Thus, for example, a service user's acceptance of a social worker's authority may be dependent on the professional securing a favourable outcome, such as a change in accommodation. In other words, the practitioner's claim to authority may be judged in terms of performance and results, rather than her or his ascribed professional standing.

Of course, these ambiguities open up a significant area of potential difficulty for the idea that power is derived straightforwardly from the position occupied by a particular individual. Indeed, it throws sharply into perspective the notion of legitimacy and the question of where consent derives from. The problem can be portrayed as one of ideology and the manner in which the rules and systems underpinning organizations and social structures can be sustained. For Clegg, the issue is that the notion of 'sovereign power' becomes highly problematic, unless it can be seen to be supported by some form of ideological justification. One mechanism for the establishment and maintenance of consent is suggested by the Gramscian notion of 'hegemony', as mentioned earlier. Hegemony is typified as a process of securing the 'active consent' (Clegg, 1989, p. 160) of all parties to the continuing domination of particular sectional interests. It is a process whereby appeals to particular sectors and demands are linked under the umbrella of a carefully defined common agenda, which maintains and enhances prevailing power relations. The agents for this process are located in a wide range of settings, including welfare organizations; and, indeed, their very diversity contributes to its objective of appealing selectively to a wide range of social groups and distinct interests. Part of the effectiveness of hegemonic power is in ensuring that its forms are appropriate to the context in which it operates.

For social work, this has been a perennial matter of concern and ambiguity. The organizational and structural location of social work practitioners places them in the role of legitimate agents of state power. Indeed, for statutory social workers this is the source of their authority to act. Dominelli (2004, p. 107) argues that this aspect of social workers' activities may lead them into a position of 'regulating' the family. They are involved in a process of 'normalization', whereby certain family forms and practices are rendered acceptable, and others subject to surveillance and coercive intervention.

Whilst this aspect of social workers' officially sanctioned role may be about defining and maintaining social norms, they are also expected to promote service user interests non-judgementally (Banks, 2001). Their value commitments to empowerment and advocacy on behalf of service users appear to place them in potential conflict with the structures within which they operate (Dominelli, 2002, p. 34). This raises significant issues of concern, not just in terms of the protection of one's own employment status, but also in terms of the ability to act effectively on behalf of less powerful and disadvantaged groups and individuals.

Relational power

The third mode of power to be discussed here differs from the previous two in that it attempts to capture a sense of power as *interactive*, in the sense that it depends not on fixed characteristics, but on the relationships between individuals, groups and interests. In this sense, the ways in which it is experienced will depend very much on situational specifics, and on the precise nature of exchanges in any given setting. Viewed in this way, it is argued, the aspects of power which derive from institutional structures and personal identity can be integrated, and thus related to the contingent aspects of relationships between social actors.

Lukes suggests that it is helpful to think of power as having a variable impact, in the sense that it may be applicable in a specific context in relation to a limited number of issues at one extreme; whilst, at the other end of the scale, power can be seen as something which 'transcends' contexts, and applies across a range of issues (Lukes, 2005, p. 79).

Some parties to the decision-making process may be said to hold 'more power' than others:

> 66 With respect to an agent's power over a given issue, or a given set of issues, we can say that another agent's power, over that issue or set of issues, is greater if it exhibits greater contextual range, brings about further significant consequences or involves less cost to the agent. (*ibid.*)

As he points out, it is possible to argue that one person's power exceeds that of another where that individual has greater influence over a larger number of issues. Clearly, the political allocation of financial resources to social work and social care is an example of this kind of imbalance, which ultimately has a direct impact on what can and cannot be done in practice.

However, as Lukes acknowledges, comparative judgements of this nature are usually more complex, because 'most commonly, we are comparing the power of different agents over different issues' (Lukes, 2005, p. 80). In addition, the differential ability to influence outcomes may assume greater or lesser significance depending on people's subjective 'interests', for example; that is, whether or not they are affected directly.

In some respects, acknowledgement of the complexity of power relations finds an echo in postmodern analyses, which suggest that processes of fragmentation and 'de-centring' social relations have significant consequences for the nature of power itself. Bauman (1992) believes that the social milieu has changed to the extent that there has been a significant growth in the extent to which people feel themselves to have the capacity to change aspects of their lives and circumstances. This is a feature of the 'postmodern habitat', that is to say, a contemporary living environment within which rules and lifestyles are constantly negotiated and renegotiated. The nature of relationships between organizations and individuals is increasingly complex, multifaceted and indeterminate. Agencies, for example, become seen as increasingly specialized, able to exercise authority and expertise over narrower and narrower domains. At points where different interests interact, therefore, there emerges a constant sense of 'indeterminacy', where competing claims for legitimacy and authority are played out (Bauman, 1992, p. 193). In terms of individual interactions, this widening sense of uncertainty and the provisional nature of outcomes combine to ensure that identities and relationships are continually renegotiated and recreated.

Clearly, if we are experiencing an increase in the capacity of individuals to assert their own subjective judgements, this must raise significant challenges for agencies and practitioners who claim objective justification for their interventions, given that they are likely to have to establish their credibility and authority with each new encounter, and repeatedly as their relationships with the users of services progress and change. The right to make decisions on others' behalf is therefore not 'given' but must be earned and sustained:

> As the pronouncements of the experts can be seldom put to the test by the recipients of their services, for most agents certainty about the soundness of their choices can be plausibly entertained only in the form of *trust* ... Trustworthiness, credibility and perceived sincerity become major criteria by which merchants of certainty – experts, politicians ... – are judged, approved or rejected. (Bauman, 1992, p. 200)

The nature of the relationship between practitioners and service users is therefore held to depend more and more on the ability to demonstrate qualities such as reliability, consistency and openness, than on ascribed position or legal status.

Giddens takes this line of reasoning further, by suggesting that it is not just formal relationships that are subject to this process of destabilization. The family, for example, is said to be subject to 'intense' debates about gender equality and the potential for structural change. The shift from 'traditional', patriarchal family forms to greater diversity has resulted, too, in a change in the nature of family relationships. Indeed, these trends have undermined the value of the very terms which have been used in the past, it is argued: '"Coupling" and "uncoupling" provide a more accurate description of the arena of personal life now than do "marriage and the family"' (Giddens, 1999, p. 59).

Personal relationships thus depend on the quality and nature of the 'emotional communication' between participants. The stability and permanence of the relationship comes to depend on the 'rewards' to be gained from this communication. In this way the successful personal relationship depends on many of the same qualities as those characterizing effective interactions between professionals and service users. Thus, it is necessary to demonstrate 'active trust' by 'opening oneself up to the other' (Giddens, 1999, p. 61).

As Fook puts it, the nature of the relationship does not depend on fixed categories (such as male–female, parent–child, black–white), but also on the immediate consequences of particular situated interactions. The origins of this position lie in the postmodern concept of identity, she argues, which is seen as a fluid notion, which only gains substance in context. This is described as 'situated subjectivity', whereby 'people's own perspectives must be interpreted in the light of changing and specific situations in which they are located' (Fook, 2002, p. 74). Not only do identities vary over time, but they can also be held in parallel, with the result that they may appear, in some respects, to be contradictory. Of course, such a level of complexity in individual identity formation and maintenance can only result in an even more highly variegated pattern of interpersonal relationships.

Structural factors such as race, class and gender may be factors in identity formation, but they are not crucial in determining specific individual personalities. However, such characteristics may act as reference points, according to how people define themselves and how others may also define them. In this way, there is a degree of coherence and continuity in the maintenance of identity, which may provide some sense of consistency even in changing situations. Identity is thus negotiable without being completely arbitrary in character. Arising from this discussion, Fook argues that two important conclusions can be drawn. Firstly, the idea that someone's identity can incorporate dynamic contradictions is helpful in accounting for inconsistencies of attitude and behaviour over time. It helps us to avoid making assumptions that these are necessarily fixed and unchangeable. And secondly, whilst we may be influenced by external, contextual factors, we still retain the capacity to develop and adapt within that framework:

> This idea that individuals are being constructed, but also engaged in constructing themselves at the same time, is important in a postmodern feminist ... and indeed in a critical and postmodern view. (Fook, 2002, p. 76)

This has supported attempts to reformulate the nature of social work practice, and in particular, to modify the use of power in the helping relationship. Thus, it is precisely the absence of 'positivist' certainties that free social work practitioners to 'do good in the flux of social care' (Folgheraiter, 2004, p. 13). However, in order to be able to do so, social workers must be able to redefine their roles and relationships with service users. It is not simply a one-sided form of transaction with the 'expert' on one side of the table and the 'client' on the other, receiving help in the prescribed manner, where the solution to the individual's problem is assumed to be a form of 'gift' from the knowledgeable and relatively more powerful professional to the dependent recipient. In this model of practice, 'diagnosis' and 'treatment' of problems are logical stages in the process, which depend on the skills of the expert, and in which the client is passive and has no input. By contrast, effective social work practice depends on a reformulation of this dyad, so that it represents a process of exchange. Social work needs to be seen as a 'creative fusion' of the practitioner's action with that of other participants (Folgheraiter, 2004, p. 99). Objective differences of status or knowledge are not wished away, and the contextual aspects of the relationship remain relevant. It is not simply a matter of being 'non-directive', for example (Folgheraiter, 2004, p. 104). Rather, it is a bringing together of perspectives and attributes, so that mutual solutions can be devised and implemented. It is only through negotiating these differences that practitioners and service users will be able to work together to generate practical and realistic solutions. The upshot of this approach may be beneficial in several respects: a greater number of options become available; a sense of mutual empowerment may be generated; and solutions may be identified which offer a greater degree of control to service users.

It is possible to offer criticisms of this argument, to the extent that it appears to underplay the structural determinants of power and expertise. The potential for pre-existing imbalances and inequalities to be brushed aside is perhaps overstated, but the notion of 'relational power' nonetheless offers something of a counterbalance to other characterizations which emphasize its fixed and enduring qualities. For social work practitioners, this is a message of hope which identifies a space for participatory and emancipatory interventions.

main points

- Power relationships are inevitably bound up with the 'interests' of those involved

- Power can be conceptualized according to different modes: the personal, positional and relational

- The relationship between social workers and service users incorporates aspects of each of these

- The capacity to negotiate positive power relationships depends on a critical and reflexive approach to pre-existing concepts of expertise and authority

- 'Relational' practice offers one means of developing a collaborative approach to empowerment.

- What are some of the advantages and disadvantages of bureaucracy as a source of legitimacy and authority in social work practice?
- How do you think the social worker's position as a qualified professional is typically viewed by service users who may be from a different class background?
- Does this create an initial sense of distance and unequal power dynamics?
- Is 'difference' necessarily divisive?

taking it further

- Stephen Lukes has been seen as a seminal author for some time, and the second edition of *Power: A Radical View* (Palgrave Macmillan, 2005) offers valuable insights into the sources and dynamics of power.
- Lena Dominelli's *Anti-Oppressive Social Work Theory and Practice* (Palgrave Macmillan, 2002) both summarizes the forms and extent of the oppressions faced by service users and provides an overview of effective practice responses.
- Franz Folgheraiter's *Relational Social Work* (Jessica Kingsley, 2004) brings an original and creative perspective to the interaction between social worker and service users, demonstrating that power dynamics need to be made explicit in order to create an effective working relationship.

Websites

http://www.relationshipsfoundation.org.uk
The Relationships Foundation is a 'think-and-do tank' which develops ideas and projects to promote positive relationship-building and seeks to demonstrate the potential of thinking 'relationally'.

http://criticalsocialwork.com
An interdisciplinary online journal dedicated to social justice which invites practitioners to question established notions of power and authority (see volume 2, 1, in particular, for significant contributions from Fook, Leonard and others).

4 Sites of Power

The importance of context

It may on occasion seem a long journey from the realm of concepts and theories to the immediate challenges of direct practice. Attempts to make these connections by discussing the ways in which power is expressed (Chapter 3) may also seem incomplete if they are not contextualized. For those concerned with the critical issues of taking professional decisions and intervening in people's lives, the value of ideas can only be realized to the extent that they are linked effectively to concrete realities. For this reason, it is important to focus on power in context, in the distinctive settings where its relationships are played out.

This is important not just because it gives greater substance to some of the ideas we have already considered, but because it will help to illustrate more clearly the relationship between different aspects of power and its effects in different settings. In a sense, this develops some of the themes of the previous chapter, in that 'relational power', for example, is likely to be associated with more personal and immediate events than is the expression of power based on status or position. Thus, alternative 'modes of power' may be more likely to be associated with different levels of the social domain.

In seeking to sketch out a kind of 'geography' of power, the aim here is not to suggest that it is manifested in particular forms only at certain points in the matrix of social relations. Indeed, the purpose is to try to provide the basis for an understanding of the possible interconnections between the various forms of power as it is experienced at different locations in the social environment. Gender relations, for example, are acted out most obviously in the personal and family spheres, but it would be unrealistic to suggest that they are not also influenced by media, cultural and political factors whose origins are structural. For practitioners, as we shall see, this might be an important consideration when reflecting on the invisible ties which seem to bind service users into damaging and unhealthy relationships.

In seeking to explore these issues further, I will first reflect on certain analytical frameworks which seem to have some potential value in understanding the links between power relations at different levels and in different 'sites'; and, subsequently, I will explore some of these specific contexts further to try to give some substance to the material aspects of power as they affect practice.

Situating power: three frameworks

For some time, efforts have been made to provide social work practitioners with effective tools for linking the immediate and pressing concerns of (usually) individualized practice with the structural context which very often sets the terms for their interventions. A particularly significant early example of attempts to reconcile these perspectives is provided by Corrigan and Leonard (1978). They have taken issue with 'the cult of individualism' (p. 109), arguing that it would be erroneous to attempt to account for personal experiences such as 'loneliness, alienation and separation from others' without considering the structural factors which give rise to them. Indeed, the risk is that, in the absence of this understanding, people might simply be blamed for the problems which befall them, whose causes largely originate elsewhere. It is vitally important, in these authors' view, that these connections are made and then utilized to underpin analysis and intervention

> because individuals are seen as directly related to their social circumstances, with their experience and personality embedded in the structure, and the structure embedded in them, we begin to see a clear connection between individual and structural factors. (Corrigan and Leonard, 1978, p. 122)

Subsequent work, particularly associated with anti-oppressive practice, has sought to develop this kind of analysis (e.g. Dalrymple and Burke, 1995; Thompson, 2001; Dominelli, 2002). The argument is made that effective outcomes depend on making links between individual circumstances and structural factors:

> Change can only be effective if the links between the subjective experiences of people and the objective social conditions are made visible. Individuals who make the connections between their personal condition and the society in which they exist begin to make changes within themselves, within their families and community and wider social structures. (Dalrymple and Burke, 1995, p. 12)

Particularly in the context of experiences of oppression, it is suggested that feelings of inadequacy, failure and powerlessness derive from three sources, which are interconnected. These are: the 'negative images' which people have of themselves arising from their experiences of oppression; the problems they encounter when engaging with 'external systems'; and, the hostile nature of these systems themselves (Dalrymple and Burke, 1995, p. 14). They argue that anti-oppressive practice can only be effective by working at all these levels and by challenging disempowering structures as well as working to build individuals' capabilities and strengths.

A number of attempts have been made to develop analytical frameworks to enable practitioners to develop these understandings and apply them in practice (Thompson, 2001; Dominelli, 2002; Smith, 2005).

Thompson (2001, p. 21), for example, has advocated an approach based on what he terms 'PCS analysis'. This, he suggests, is the product of a wider movement to take social work theory beyond fairly limited theoretical foci associated with 'traditional social work'. He argues that there is a clear need for a 'conceptual framework' which enables social workers to make the necessary connections between wider, structural factors and the problems of 'social workers and their clients'. In his view, this can best be achieved by distinguishing three levels of analysis, the 'personal', 'cultural' and 'structural', which he terms the 'PCS' model. These three elements are related in a particular way, which is illustrated schematically in Figure 4.1 in the form of concentric circles, with the P level embedded in the C level, and this, in turn, being encircled by the S level.

Personal attributes, such as thoughts, actions and emotions are 'to a certain extent unique', but also depend on the 'powerful role' of culture in shaping these individual characteristics (Thompson, 2001, p. 22). Thompson uses humour as an illustrative example of the way in which personal beliefs can be derived and sustained from cultural practices, such as the making of racist jokes. In turn, the specific cultural context can be seen to be determined by wider social forces, such as institutional racism. He argues that unless 'we are actively seeking to eliminate' racist practices from our professional dealings, then these wider collective influences will 'filter through' into our thoughts and behaviour. He suggests, further, that we should recognize that it is 'ideology' which should be seen as the 'glue' which binds the PCS levels together. By this term, he means a 'set of ideas' which legitimate the status quo and 'justifies, protects and reinforces' the prevailing social and power relationships (Thompson, 2001, p. 27).

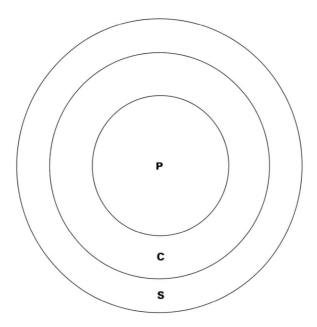

Source: Thompson (2003b).

Figure 4.1 Thompson's PCS model

Anti-social behaviour and the use of authority

A number of recent measures including Anti-Social Behaviour Orders, Parenting Orders and Acceptable Behaviour Contracts have been introduced to tackle the problem behaviour of the young.

Practitioners in social work and youth justice may feel that they are expected to resolve the 'problem' purely in terms of changing or controlling individual children and young people who give cause for concern, without being able to take proper account of relevant structural factors, such as poverty and social exclusion.

Thompson suggests that this is not just of theoretical interest:

> it is in and through human action that ideology comes into being. It is part of the complex interplay of individual and wider social forces, it is the bridge between the external objective world of social circumstances and the internal subjective world of meaning. (Thompson, 2001, p. 30)

Because of this, ideology and belief systems become crucial elements in determining actions and outcomes at the level of individual circumstances and interpersonal exchanges.

The equivalent conceptual framework offered by Dominelli (2002) does not neglect ideological influences, but tries to develop a rather more extensive schema of contexts and influences. The impact of material factors, such as resource distribution, is thus given due weight alongside the influence of ideas and beliefs. In addition, the context of interactions is said to be 'multi-layered' (p. 22), and suggests a greater level of complexity than the model offered by Thompson. Although similarly revolving around the individual, the interactive milieu includes:

- The personal level
- The institutional domain that encompasses familial relations, schools, the welfare state, social policies and legislation
- Religious or faith affiliation
- The spiritual realm
- The cultural sphere
- The local community
- The national domain
- The economy – local, national and global
- The physical environment.

(Dominelli, 2002, p. 22)

This suggests a substantial degree of complexity, in the sense that these domains inevitably interact, and there is no definite hierarchy privileging one over another. Although all social interactions are played out within this framework, specific elements will vary in the degree of influence they exert.

Dominelli has accounted for this complexity by distinguishing between the factors which impact on the individual 'client' and the forces which may impact on the specific setting. She distinguishes between levels of influence on the one hand and forms of influence on the other. The individual is located in turn within family, community, national society and the global domain, whilst the potential influences on perceptions and behaviour are enumerated as physical, economic, psychosocial and spiritual.

By drawing on our understanding of these various dimensions, both practitioner and service user can develop a sophisticated knowledge of the constraints and dynamic of their interaction. This, in Dominelli's view, promotes positive benefits to the extent that it renders power relations negotiable and capable of transformation:

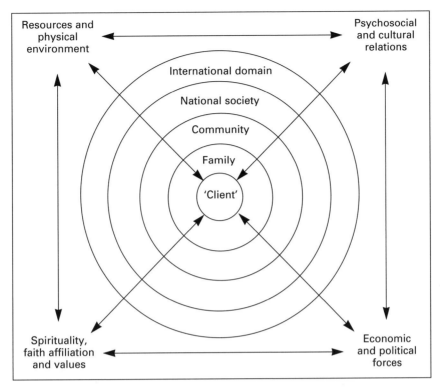

Source: Dominelli (2002).

Figure 4.2   Dominelli's multidimensional model of power

> Having a commitment to placing the individual and the practitioner in his or her social context makes the work that is done highly political, for it involves power and negotiated realities. The exercise of power involves a series of negotiations ... Thus, empowerment cannot be 'done' for or to a client ... What a professional can do ... is to ... provide an environment in which self-empowerment can flourish. (Dominelli, 2002, p. 24)

My own attempt to develop a similar framework (Smith, 2004; 2005) derives from the search for a way of understanding the dimensions of childhood.

Whilst the domains in my model are effectively the same as Dominelli's, the forces identified differ somewhat in that they are framed in terms of social, political, religious/cultural and economic influences respectively. What is more important than these relatively slight differences, however, is the common approach of relating the different 'levels' of experience and the forces which impact on them.

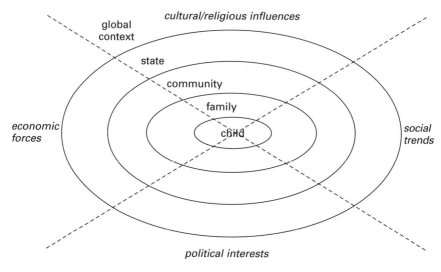

Source: Smith (2004).

Figure 4.3 Smith's model of 'The child in the world'

In the context of children's lives, it is clearly important to consider their needs in the context of family or carers, but we must also take account of their relationships to their community (peers and school, for instance), the national environment (such as media and marketing interests), and the global domain (characterized by transnational factors such as religion or forced migration).

practice illustration 4.2

Jamila – a young unaccompanied refugee

> I am very depressed because I miss my own country, I miss my family, I have lost contact with all of them. There are problems in the house [where he lives]: it's too cold and dirty and the landlord doesn't care about us, there is also the problem of not knowing how long I am going to be living here, I can't put down roots, I can't try and make a future when I don't know how long I'm going to be here and I do want to go back eventually, although I know that my own country is in a state of turmoil. (Young male refugee quoted in Marriott, 2001)

In the case of this young person, we can see that immediate personal needs for shelter and security may be shaped by a whole series of additional influences, such as the unknown circumstances of other family members, loneliness and isolation from a peer group, the need to maintain cultural and religious ties, and the continuing aspiration to be reconnected to one's country of origin. As we have seen from the three models described previously, power is manifested at different levels, which may all have an impact on the specific context of social work practice with this young person. For example, practitioners will need to take into account possibly traumatic experiences of conflict, unfamiliarity with his current social milieu and cultural norms, the possible experience of racism in his new surroundings, as well as the need to re-establish his personal relationships and take positive action to empower him to work towards longer term goals.

This example illustrates the importance of applying an analytical approach which takes account of the diversity of power relations at different levels, in order to gain a comprehensive view of the dynamics affecting people's lives. In moving on to consider a number of these 'levels' in more detail, the aim is not to detach or isolate them, but to provide a greater level of depth to assist with the process of integrating our analysis.

Up close and personal: the family

As a context for social work practice, the family can relatively easily be understood as a major area of concern. It acts as the primary setting for many aspects of social interaction, and in doing so it exercises very substantial influence on all aspects of the lives of most people. Even for those who do not live in families, family life acts as a sort of ideal benchmark against which their experience is evaluated. Inevitably, then, the question of power and its realization in and through the family takes on particular significance.

Equally, the manner in which power is exercised in this context has also been the subject of intense debate. In concentrating on just a few illustrative examples here, I will by no means do justice to the extensive range of debates to be found on this subject, but I hope to be able to outline some of the central questions to be considered. In essence, this discussion will highlight three perspectives which offer plausible accounts of the role of power within the family.

The first of these is concerned less with power differentials *within* the family, and more with the family as a *vehicle* for the exercise of authority and control from outside. This view is typified by the work of Donzelot, who sees the family as a pivotal force in organizing and transmitting social norms. In this sense, the family is seen to be subject to a number of external forces whose objectives are to utilize it as a means for sustaining compliance to social norms. The application of various forms of therapeutic interventions, which themselves are strongly normative, ensures that the family becomes a means by which dominant attitudes and expectations can be sustained: 'with its saturation by hygienic, psychological, and pedagogical norms, it becomes harder to distinguish the family from the disciplinary continuum of the social apparatuses' (Donzelot, 1979, p. 227).

In Donzelot's view, it is the pivotal nature of the family, as mediator between the state and its members, which ensures that it has come to take a central role as the means by which individuals' behaviour is regulated and controlled. His empirical observations, albeit dating back to the 1970s, suggested to him a systematic process according to which family problems were categorized and responded to by the 'social services' (p. 152). This is as much a process of establishing and maintaining a kind of moral order as it is about helping those with problems. Interventions in families are:

> characterized by a decisive tussle between the services and the recipients. In order to retrieve their children, the latter set about producing all the exterior signs of morality that are expected of them: detoxification cures, scrubbing the house ... the important thing is to show a spirit of cooperation. (Donzelot, 1979, p. 157)

The arrangement by which moral authority is reproduced through the family is, according to Donzelot, one of 'contract and tutelage' (p. 168). The autonomy of families is replaced by a system of 'supervised reproduction'. In this way, a relationship of 'dependence' is established, such that the family is used as a mechanism for imposing order:

> the working-class family is reorganized on the basis of a set of institutional constraints and stimulations that also make the child the centre of the family, to be sure, but according to procedures much more deserving of the term 'supervised freedom'. (Donzelot, 1979, p. xxi)

This rather functionalist view reflected a common strand of thought at the time in which Donzelot was writing. Since then others have taken a more nuanced view of family relations and dynamics. In this second perspective, the family is seen rather as a place where differences of interest and power imbalances are played out, so that outcomes are variable and unpredictable. Featherstone (2004), for example, notes that it is too simplistic to apply one model, or even a small number of models (working-class or middle-class, say), of the family in a context of increasing diversity, both in family forms and in lifestyles.

Whilst Donzelot was concerned with power imbalances between the state and the family, Featherstone believes that it is important to consider the unequal nature of relationships *within* families, which are both gendered and age-related. Whilst these inequalities may reflect broader social patterns, their particular implications for family life are of great significance. Featherstone traces the feminist origins of many of these contemporary discussions about the way in which power and control appear to be distributed in families, and how unequal relationships are reflected in 'family practices' (2004, p. 52). As she observes, the development of understanding in this respect has reflected a move from a simplistic conceptualization of 'patriarchy' to a more subtle and multilayered analysis. Empirical studies have found considerable variations in the way in which power is exercised and experienced within families. Indeed, different conceptual categories could be identified which capture some of this diversity. Thus, 'debilitative power' (Featherstone, 2004, p. 54) might be experienced by women as the denial of personal autonomy and selfhood, whilst 'situational power' would be a more appropriate term to define the consequences of the division of labour between women as carers and men as resource providers within families. Clearly, too, these different forces might have an interactive or cumulative effect on family relationships and behaviour.

These considerations have helped to achieve two significant outcomes. Firstly, they have clarified the way in which the lived experiences of adults and children within families are bound up with the exercise of power. It is not simply that the family reproduces external or pre-existing patterns of social organization and control. And secondly, as they have become more sophisticated, these insights have illustrated the extent to which gender is a crucial factor in the construction and experience of family relationships. The term 'parent', for example, which is commonly used to express policy goals and signify desirable characteristics, is unhelpful to the extent that it glosses over gender differences (see, e.g., Home Office, 1998).

The idea that the family is a place of ambiguity and unevenness in the exercise of power has been developed by others, too (e.g., Barrett and McIntosh, 1991). Historical understandings of the origins and development of the family provide the basis for contemporary insights into its contradictions. According to some, it is the very longevity of the family that suggests its continuing merits and vitality. Rather than acting as a means of extending state power to the level of the individual, the third of our perspectives on power and the family suggests that it is more appropriate to see the family as a constant bulwark of resistance *against* control from above. Its key features supersede historical change or political fashion:

> The family is a subversive organisation ... Only the family has continued throughout history and still continues to undermine the State. The family is the enduring permanent enemy of all hierarchies, churches and ideologies. (Mount, 1982, p. 1)

In the light of this, it is perhaps helpful to remind ourselves of Dominelli's (2002, p. 17) distinction between three aspects of power, which may all be represented within the family. Thus, individuals may exercise power *over* other members, but it is also possible to see it as a site for members to both resist oppression (*power to*), and to exercise collective strength to achieve mutual goals (*power of*).

Functions such as the provision of mutual support, the sharing of resources, cooperation, advocacy and resistance are all potential examples of the exercise of power by family members on each other's behalf (Rodger, 1996). As a result, it is argued, it is best to retain a view of the family as having both positive and negative qualities. According to Barrett and McIntosh (1991), it can clearly be understood as offering certain benefits in the context of late capitalism, such as emotional security, an institutional means of raising children, and a route to social acceptance. By contrast, these essentially affirmative characteristics need to be set against the family's acknowledged failings as a site of oppression and suffering, in the forms of gender inequality, abuse, domestic violence, hidden caring responsibilities, and the unequal distribution of rights and resources (Barrett and McIntosh, 1991; Fox Harding, 1996; Rodger, 1996).

We can conclude, perhaps, that our approach to the exercise of power within the family context must be informed by a recognition of the likelihood of encountering a variety of interests, some dependent on the exercise of control and oppression, but others representing mutuality and resistance. Different modes of power may be encountered (for instance, 'positional' vs 'relational' power), and legitimacy and authority may be contested (who determines the child's best interests?, for example), posing significant challenges for practice, to which we shall return.

The community as 'local authority'?

Whilst much attention is focused on the family as a site of intervention in social work, perhaps rather less emphasis is given to the 'community'. This may partly be to do with the amorphous nature of the concept itself, since it can be taken to incorporate a wide range of 'interlocking or overlapping networks', ranging from 'the milkman they never see to their closest relative' (Smale *et al.*, 2000, p. 90). Whilst the power in communities has often been associated with spatially bound formal structures and political processes (Lukes, 1986; Clegg, 1989), its basis clearly extends well beyond this into informal social networks and interest groups.

Whilst this is one source of potential confusion, it seems that it has proved equally problematic for social work to engage with the community, either conceptually or in practice. This clearly stems from the individualized nature of much thinking about social work. At most, social work's 'gaze' (Foucault, 1979) has typically extended beyond the individual only as far as the immediate family. Powell (2001, p. 134) suggests that this perspective has dominated at the expense of community-orientated practice, which has 'been in decline ... in recent decades'. Despite these issues, it is undoubtedly the case that communities, however defined, are highly relevant to a discussion of power and social work. Indeed, given the models of power introduced earlier, it is essential to integrate this dimension into frameworks for practice.

Communities can be seen in a number of ways: perhaps, as those people identified with a common culture, as those who share a particular interest, or as the population of a defined geographical neighbourhood. In each manifestation, however, they can be seen to have a role in shaping the power relations of both members and non-members. In particular, the notion of community has implications for the sense of 'belonging' which people might have, and consequently for the extent to which they may or may not feel a sense of 'social exclusion'. The community (or lack of it, see Jamila's case earlier) may have direct consequences for those who are at risk of being marginalized, with the resultant difficulties that this may cause.

Community may be viewed as important, too, because it is closely bound up with the notion of identity; it is viewed as the product of a 'natural union' between its members, whose ties are organic and based on a sense of mutual solidarity (Powell and Geoghegan, 2004, p. 42). This assumption of common bonds tends to have two clear consequences: it sharply defines the boundaries between those who are and are not members of a specific 'community'; and it also creates a sense of 'sameness' (Dominelli, 2002, p. 29) amongst its members. In this sense, the community plays a key role in shaping the identities and behaviour of its members:

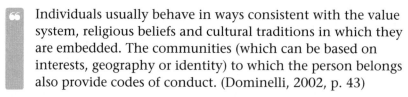

> Individuals usually behave in ways consistent with the value system, religious beliefs and cultural traditions in which they are embedded. The communities (which can be based on interests, geography or identity) to which the person belongs also provide codes of conduct. (Dominelli, 2002, p. 43)

For some, it is this very idea of homogeneity which is problematic. Garland (2001), for example, draws attention to the pressure within the criminal justice sphere to provide an increasing range of community-based interventions in response to offending behaviour. As he puts it (p. 123): 'The "community" has become the all-purpose solution to every criminal justice problem.' Associated with this shift in thinking is a process which he refers to as a strategy of 'responsibilizing', whereby the state divests itself of its crime control functions in favour of communities. This may, for example, be seen in the growth of the 'crime prevention apparatus' through the establishment of Crime Reduction Partnerships; it also appears to be typified by new measures such as Anti-Social Behaviour Orders (see Practice Illustration 4.1) which appear to bestow direct means of crime control on communities and their representatives.

However, this importation of the power to criminalize and coerce into the 'community' also helps to cement in place another process, which is also implicit in the notion of identity and belonging. This is referred to as 'othering' (Dominelli, 2002, p. 44), and has significant consequences for the exercise of power and control within communities. Garland describes some of the possible outcomes of this process in terms of the need to 'mark out' those who are identified as different and potentially dangerous (2001, p. 137), such as ex-offenders. Social work practitioners increasingly find themselves in the position of having to mediate between marginalized and often rejected individuals and 'the community'. This is especially the case where workers take on the responsibility for providing help and support to those whose behaviour or attributes mark them out as being socially unacceptable in some way, like paedophiles.

I remember as a relatively inexperienced Probation Officer in the early 1980s confronting the dilemma of how much information to share with the provider of accommodation for an ex-prisoner who had committed serious sexual offences in the past. I was acutely aware of the power relationships involved, my conflicting responsibilities, and the possible consequences of passing on this information. Whilst there have been significant changes in law, policy and procedure since then, the conflicts of interest and the task of exercising professional judgement appropriately and justifiably in this kind of situation remain.

Kemshall (2002, p. 129) illustrates this point by reference to a particular case 'vignette':

> Frank is a white, middle-aged offender currently the subject of a bail assessment in a local hostel. He has previous offences of sexual assault against children, and is awaiting a court appearance for similar offences. He is polite and cooperative in the hostel, and has assisted with clearing the garden. He is described as a 'model resident'. Despite this the task of resettlement poses some difficult questions for practitioners. For instance, Frank's interest in gardening may be exactly what it seems, or it may be connected with the fact that it creates opportunities for him to meet members of the community, including children who attend the nearby school.

Anything which demarcates him as different (even 'model behaviour') may be taken as evidence that he continues to represent a threat.

Sensitivity to signs of difference or 'otherness' may predispose us to seeing someone in a particular way, and to problematize them:

> It is what makes people and lawmakers all too ready to take up any signs that might be of service – whether it be a criminal record, a style of deportment and demeanour, or merely the colour of a person's skin. (Garland, 2001, p. 137)

Dominelli (2002, p. 44) agrees in essence with this argument. She suggests that 'othering' has direct links with processes of social exclusion, building on the notion of 'them–us', which may be rooted in the apparently benign idea of community membership. These distinctions are both substantive and normative; thus, they incorporate notions of desirability or deservingness. In this way, differences based on ' "race", gender, sexual orientation, age, disability, mental health and class' all involve valuations of superiority and inferiority. Applied to communities, this form of classification can clearly be seen to account for processes of exclusion and oppression, which means that certain individuals and groups (for example, lone mothers or asylum seekers) are both devalued and identified as a potential threat to communal norms and social order. As Dominelli observes, however, it is important not to oversimplify, since people who are excluded or oppressed on one dimension may be seen as part of the 'mainstream' on others (2002, p. 46). Nevertheless, the cumulative impact of the identification of certain groups with a range of negatively perceived characteristics has led to the emergence of the concept of the 'underclass', which is defined only in terms of its 'prescribed status as supplicant in the welfare state' (Powell, 2001, p. 93).

In terms of the challenges for social work practice, then, the idea of 'community' throws up some important issues. The community is not just a vehicle for dominant ideas and social processes, but incorporates its own dynamics of power. Working with individuals in communities requires the development of a sense of the tides and currents which are likely to influence their treatment and the way they are perceived. It also means working with service users *as* members (or potential members) of communities rather than as isolated individuals. It is important to avoid adopting an approach to intervention which reflects the exclusionary tendencies which are seen as endemic within communities:

> The individualisation of social problems involves identifying a person, typically the least powerful, as the 'problem' and so the object of concern. Meanwhile others in the network, by defining their problem as 'the person', have translated their 'problem' into the problems of that person. (Smale *et al.*, 2000, p. 91)

It is the individual's interaction with the community which is likely to be crucial in terms of countering this process and promoting social inclusion, as well as pursuing positive outcomes associated with the achievement of personal goals. It is not simply about challenging those in positions of authority or influence or competing for resources, but it is rather a matter of recognizing difference and pursuing mutual empowerment within groups and communities.

Social workers must avoid perpetuating a false dichotomy between individuals and their networks, but to engage with both. Social workers should seek to 'mobilize' both individuals and communities to achieve collective goals, according to Dominelli (2002, p. 139), whilst Mullaly (1997) lays out a set of operating principles which should underpin what he terms 'structural social work'. These are enumerated as: 'acknowledging that the personal is political; empowerment, consciousness-raising, normalisation; collectivisation, redefining and dialogical relationships' (Powell, 2001, p. 106). In short, recognition of the significance of power relationships in communities requires social workers to consider and address these directly in order to achieve effective interventions.

State institutions: speaking directly to practice

As with relationships within the family, the influence of state institutions and other national bodies is perhaps relatively easily recognized as significant for social work. Clearly, for those in statutory settings the authority, resources and means to act are provided by the state and its agencies. It is undeniable, for example, that intervention in the lives of children and families in England and Wales depends for its legitimacy on the legislative framework provided by the Children Act 1989. Where Acts of Parliament give authority to social workers to protect vulnerable people, it is argued that the 'social control function is explicit' (Smale *et al.*, 2000, p. 37). Bound up with the authority conferred by legislation are a whole series of relationships and structures which incorporate, regulate and transmit power. However, it is also the case that the law offers constructive opportunities to act on behalf of service users and to promote their interests by offering a positive framework of protections and rights, for example through the Human Rights Act 1998.

In one sense, legal structures and procedures might be seen as relatively unproblematic as a central element of social work. Nonetheless, the implications for practice are often far from straightforward, and therefore require some analysis and explanation:

> Making sense of the politics of social work is a challenging task. Very strong ideological positions have been taken up ... Much of this debate has focused on the relationship between social work and the state. (Powell, 2001, p. 1)

Social work as a discipline and its functions need to be seen as both the product and site of competing political forces, which inevitably incorporate differing and potentially antagonistic objectives. The role of social workers and their use of power are thus essentially ambiguous. This is captured from another viewpoint as a problem of multiple accountabilities:

> The dual mandate defines the role and task of social work as promoting the interests both of the state and of the service user whom they are intended to help. This dual mandate makes social work by definition a politicised activity. (Powell, 2001, p. 127)

Of itself, this does not necessarily render the use of state power in social work a problematic issue. The problem of mediating between statutory authority and the service user could be related straightforwardly to conventional ideas of 'pluralism' (Lukes, 2005, p. 5), whereby decision-making is seen in terms of the authoritative resolution of competing interests. In its purest form, the pluralist position suggests that this is a neutral process, in which all participants have an equal stake, and where the outcomes reflect a rational exercise in negotiation and debate. The state is seen purely as a mechanism for deciding arguments and delivering the outcomes of decisions made. Power is viewed in terms of the capability of achieving decisions and providing equitable solutions, and this role is ascribed to the state and its agents, including statutory-sector social workers. Pluralist notions are also based on an assumption that differing interests are able to exercise sufficient constraint on each other to avoid any one achieving sustained dominance or exercising unfettered control. The role of the state is to act as a benign arbiter and as a guarantor of the rights of all its members (Clegg, 1989, p. 104). It thus has the authority to make decisions and exercise control in the interests of every citizen:

> As a result, the argument goes, no government, acting on behalf of the state, can fail, in the not very long run, to respond to the wishes and demands of competing interests. In the end, everybody, including those at the end of the queue, get served. (Miliband, 1973, p. 4)

Applied to social work practice, this formulation would render the task relatively unproblematic. It would merely involve the application of specified skills and routine procedures to achieve consensually desirable outcomes on behalf of the community as a whole, whose interests would be ultimately indivisible. Practice would become standardized and straightforward, based on agreed professional standards and values, and dissent or disagreement would, by definition, be invalid (see, e.g., Davies, 1994).

On the other hand, it may be argued that the appearance of consensus masks a level of social conflict which is much more fundamental and arises from persistent and deep-seated inequalities. The state itself is seen as a site for the exercise of partial and vested interests, rather than as a neutral arbiter. Some observers, such as Althusser (1977) and Miliband (1973), have sought to document the ways in which the machinery of the state has been constructed and maintained as a means of legitimizing and sustaining the domination of particular class interests. Power is held and exercised partially and selfishly by these interests, and this permeates all aspects of social organization and social activity, according to this line of argument.

As Powell (2001) acknowledges, this view is associated with the tradition of radical thinking in social work, which emerged most forcefully in the 1970s (Bailey and Brake, 1975; Corrigan and Leonard,

1978). Theoretical concerns about the role of the state coincided with a developing sense of disillusionment and failure associated with the machinery of welfare provision itself. Social workers began to fear that the welfare state, and by implication their own function within it, could actually be seen as contributing to, rather than resolving, the problems of those in need. Thus, it seemed that their exercise of power on behalf of service users could not be seen as straightforwardly benevolent:

> social workers as State employees find themselves placed in a situation of considerable political confusion. In their daily lives they experience the inadequacies of State provision and the way in which the agencies of the State appear to define, categorise and dispose of clients in a manner which reinforces their problems rather than alleviates them. (Corrigan and Leonard, 1978, p. 90)

For some (e.g. Donzelot, 1979) the functionalism implicit in this kind of process extends as far as the use of the family as an informal policing mechanism, as we have seen. However, this perspective demonstrates a relatively monolithic understanding of power and its dynamics. The role of the social worker is narrowly defined in terms of acting as an agent of social control.

As Corrigan and Leonard originally pointed out, for practitioners this is a fairly uncomfortable and essentially negative view to hold of one's own function, and it seems to be contradicted by interventions which are geared to defending services on behalf of recipients and promoting service user interests. In order to account for the apparent paradox represented by the position of social work and other welfare professionals, it is argued that the state should not be seen as monolithic, but as a site of contradictory and disparate forces, which represent '*struggle* as well as the *status quo*' (Corrigan and Leonard, 1978, p. 95).

This can be linked to broader accounts of the way in which power is contested and exercised (e.g. Poulantzas, 1975). Importantly, theories of this nature enable us to appreciate the complexity of the subject and the sense in which its forms of expression are fluid and multidirectional. Poulantzas's (1975) notion of 'relative autonomy' is particularly helpful here. Whilst sharing a Marxist perspective, he develops the idea of power to illustrate the way in which institutions and interests generate their own sources of authority and legitimacy, distinguishing between 'formal power' and 'real power'. He shows that the nominal authority held by a state agency or functionary may not necessarily be reflected straightforwardly in their actions, an argument picked up by others:

> Social workers, as state employees, often enhance and negate human welfare within the same processes of their work, and it is by understanding these processes that the possibility of alternative radical practice exists. (Corrigan and Leonard, 1978, p. 106)

Whilst, for some, it may be a matter of making a deliberate decision to take a proactive approach to reshaping state power on behalf of service users, Powell (2001) argues that it is impossible to avoid making *political* choices in deciding on intervention strategies. It is not possible to adopt an entirely 'neutral' approach to the professional task, even by avoiding explicit engagement in choices about the use of one's status and authority, because power relationships are inscribed in all aspects of the interaction between practitioner and service user.

The global dimension

At first glance, it may well seem to atomized practitioners that a concern with the supranational influences which may (or may not) impact on day-to-day experience is merely a distraction from the challenge of getting on with the job. This may be because these forces, almost by definition, appear too distant to be of much immediate relevance. Or, it may be that those concerned with the delivery of welfare services feel relatively powerless in the face of fundamental shifts in the spheres of international relations, multinational economic interests, or worldwide communication technologies (Castells, 2004). There is perhaps a tendency for all of us to turn away from matters which we neither fully comprehend nor control to any real extent in order to focus on more immediate tasks which are more amenable to our interventions. Despite this, I would suggest that it is at least worth taking a moment here to consider some of the implications of globalization for social work practice and welfare provision.

It is undoubtedly the case that most analysis of the phenomenon known as 'globalization' has focused on its economic and political roots and implications. Thus, the 'reorganization of the world financial system' (Leonard, 1997) is seen as a critical feature of contemporary economic developments. The consequence has been a shift away from a concentration of business interests within national boundaries, with economic power often transcending these limits. The consequence, it is argued, is that national governments tend to become relatively weaker in relation to global capitalist enterprises. To some extent, then, individual states can be said to have lost control of key aspects of economic and social decision-making, and may be less able to protect or enhance the interests of their own citizens. The consequences associated with these changes may be felt in terms of greater social mobility resulting from transnational shifts in the labour market, internal social and political upheavals as a consequence of external economic pressures, and the cultural impacts of the emergence of global media and communication networks. Indeed, as is pointed out, there is a kind of logic at play within globalization which clearly threatens the individual welfare state:

> it becomes increasingly contradictory for firms to operate in globalized, integrated markets, while experiencing major cost differentials in social benefits, as well as distinct levels of regulation between countries. (Castells, 2004, p. 312)

Some, indeed, view the consequences of these developments and the domination of the logic of the market as potentially devastating for the contexts and practice of social work. Because globalization is driven by economic factors, and because these in turn are driven by market forces, the consequences are likely to permeate the way in which welfare interventions are organized and delivered:

> Postmodernity with its market orientation seems to be weaving a seamless web of rationality, marginalizing the human in favour of the pragmatic ... The McDonaldisation of the welfare state aims to turn the client into a consumer and welfare into a product. (Powell, 2001, p. 21)

This clearly has direct implications for the contexts of practice and the lives of those who use welfare services. Whilst this is often viewed in predominantly negative terms, as a loss of control, there are some who view these changes as neutral, or, indeed, positive in some respects (Giddens, 1999). Its effects on 'intimate and personal aspects of our lives' (p. 12) should not be overlooked, and some of these may open up new possibilities or opportunities, for example in equalizing relationships between women and men. To the extent that globalization is more than just an economic trend, it can be seen as creating the potential for transformations in human relationships which are not necessarily damaging, according to Giddens. Indeed, one of the necessary consequences of the emergence of massive transnational forces is the creation of new more localized opportunities at the level of individuals and communities which are beneath their scope. Castells argues that this leads, among other things, to observable changes in the construction of meaning and identity formation. The loss of coherence amongst societies and cultures, in the context of globalization, produces new dynamics with respect to the constitution of a sense of self: 'The search for meaning takes place then in the reconstruction of defensive identities around communal principles' (Castells, 2004, p. 11).

Norms and lifestyles become more atomized and insular, according to this analysis, based on specific personal characteristics and local and immediate social ties, rather than deriving from a wider and more open sense of community or national identity. As Fook notes, these changes, allied with some of the direct impacts of global forces, such as forced migration, can lead to new forms of social exclusion, too, such as the rejection of refugees and asylum seekers by host communities. However, as she also points out, globalization has contradictory implications, for example leading to greater fragmentation of social life at the same time as it may 'compress' differences (Fook, 2002, p. 23). As well as being potential threats, these developments represent professional challenges and opportunities.

According to some, the destabilization of old certainties and the impact of major structural change on our institutions demand a creative approach to problem-solving and capacity-building, as opposed to a spirit of anxiety or resignation:

> Many of us feel in the grip of forces over which we have no power. Can we re-impose our will upon them? I believe we can. The powerlessness we experience is not a sign of personal failings, but reflects the incapacities of our institutions. We need to reconstruct those we have, or create new ones.
> (Giddens, 1999, p. 19)

Whilst views on the implications of globalization are quite polarized, there is widespread agreement that it can be identified as a coherent phenomenon with specific and direct consequences at all levels of civil society, from the national to the personal. In terms of the implications for practice, it may be helpful here to revisit the frameworks introduced earlier in this chapter (Thompson, 2001; Dominelli, 2002; Smith, 2005), since these share the assumption that there is a connectedness between influences operating at different levels. In other words, global factors can be seen to have immediate consequences for people who use social work services. Whilst we may feel, as practitioners, that we have little influence over those economic and political forces which generate global change and social upheaval, the way in which power is generated and exercised at this level may have a critical bearing on the direct tasks of meeting personal and family needs.

In working with my own students, I sometimes draw on the example of refugees and asylum seekers (see Practice Illustration 4.2) to illustrate this point. It is not possible for practitioners to know, in a direct sense, about all the possible conflicts and divisions which prompt people to flee oppression and brutality, but there are some important common considerations which should be applied. For example, conventional social work concerns such as 'attachment' and 'identity' (Howe, 1995) may need to be understood and addressed in the context of trauma, disrupted relationships and loss originating thousands of miles away, and where current events may still be having a powerful impact on service users. There are a number of positive examples of approaches which seek to apply a 'holistic' framework of this kind: 'practitioners will not be able to engage in all the practicalities of refugees' difficult and fragmented life experiences, but at least they can show that they can hold them in mind' (Woodcock, 2002, p. 270).

The exercise of power at the global level, whether it be economic, military, religious or cultural, may be seen to have both general and specific implications for the working context and the practice demands experienced by those engaged in social work interventions.

main points

■ Power is exercised and experienced at a number of levels, from the personal to the global

■ These levels are interconnected and power flows between them

■ As holders of statutory authority, social workers may find themselves in an ambiguous and uncomfortable position, representing the state but seeking also to advance the interests of people who use their services.

■ Effective practice depends on an active understanding of the connections and contradictions of different levels of power.

stop and think

■ What do you think it means when you hear people saying: 'I'm just doing my job'?
■ What do you think this implies about their views of power and authority?
■ Why do social workers need to understand the structural dimensions of power? Can you think of an example?

- Neil Thompson's work in general is highly accessible, and *Promoting Equality* (Palgrave Macmillan, 2003) is a useful introduction to ideas about how practitioners can address the oppression and discrimination faced by service users.
- Fred Powell's *The Politics of Social Work* (Sage, 2001) offers a good analysis of the structural context within which social work operates and the politicized nature of practice, whatever form it takes.
- Bob Mullaly follows much the same line of analysis in *Structural Social Work* (2nd edn, Oxford University Press, 1997), with the inclusion of a number of suggestions about the strategies and practice available to social workers to challenge injustice.

Websites

http://www.radical.org.uk/barefoot
This is the website which claims to be the 'voice of radical social work in Britain', and which argues for structural responses to the problems encountered by practitioners.

http://www.liv.ac.uk/sspsw/Social_Work_Manifesto.html
On this site you will find a recently launched 'manifesto' for social work to renew itself in pursuit of social justice. Again, the links between meeting individual need and achieving structural change are explicit.

http://www.ciscodev.soton.ac.uk
The Centre for International Social and Community Development (CISCODEV) has been established to promote better understanding of globalization and the potential for social and community workers to build international links to share learning and improve practice.

part 2 Mechanisms of Power

5 Structural Influences on Practice

Making it real

At this point in the book, the focus will shift somewhat to bring into consideration a range of rather more concrete manifestations of power which in their different ways help to shape the context for social work intervention and affect day-to-day practice directly. I have chosen specifically to focus on three key areas: the structural forces which shape the social work agenda (see Jones, 2001); the organizational context; and the service user perspective. Each of these will be addressed over the next three chapters.

In taking this approach, I will differentiate between different levels at which power operates (see Chapter 4), but in doing so, I want to suggest that each of these can be seen as having a clear-cut impact on practice. However, it is not helpful to distinguish too sharply between them in terms of their relative significance. By its nature as a profession, social work is constantly engaged in working at the interface between structural and political influences on the one hand, and intensely personal and immediate pressures on the other. Whilst we can (helpfully) draw out distinctions between these aspects of practice analytically, the aim of this should not be to prioritize one over another.

A number of authors have sought to make this point over the years (e.g. Mullaly, 1997; Healy, 2000; Powell, 2001), stressing the interconnectedness of different aspects of the social work task. It has been suggested, for instance, that a kind of dualism has emerged over time:

> First, those who advocate a social contract vision promote the state and traditional voluntary organisations as providing an enabling relationship in which the needy are helped. Second, those who seek to promote human emancipation believe that only by changing the social structure can the political and economic basis of inequality and injustice be successfully tackled. (Powell, 2001, p. 162)

In this sense, social work appears to be faced with a choice between working to address and ameliorate individuals' problems *at the level* of the individual, or seeking to utilize alternative approaches to confront and transform those structural forces which create inequalities, fuel discriminatory attitudes, and lead to oppressive and abusive relationships between people. It has also been suggested that, historically, attempts to resolve this tension have led to practitioners opting for one approach rather than the other, and that this choice has tended to favour individualized forms of intervention:

> the problem with modern understandings is that they give too much priority to individual action as the engine of change and too little attention to the power of discourses in shaping the social realities we experience. (Healy, 2000, p. 6)

Mullaly, however, argues that it is only possible for social work to be effective and to lead to positive social change if it finds a way of making linkages between individual experience and structural factors. It is not, for him, a matter of resolving the tension between 'micro and macro practitioners' in favour of one or the other, but of developing forms of practice which integrate the two perspectives and work across and between them: 'The link between the personal and the political is made not just at the analytical or theoretical levels but at the practice level of empowerment-based structural social work' (Mullaly, 1997, p. 169).

This discussion of intervention strategies will be taken further in subsequent chapters, but for the moment it is important simply to stress that in order to adopt an integrative approach to interventions, social workers will need to have an understanding of the factors which operate to shape service users' lives at each level. Thompson (2001, p. 155) illustrates this point well with the example of the way in which the dominant discourse associated with the historical standing of the medical profession and the 'medical model' of intervention has fundamentally shaped the experiences of service users in the mental health system, acting as 'a generalised vehicle of oppression'.

This chapter will develop further our understanding of the systemic and structural factors which shape the social work environment, by focusing on four distinct engines of power: the media, government, law and policy, and the social care 'market'.

Appearances count: the media and social work

Although in this context it is easy to oversimplify and make unwarranted generalizations, it is undoubtedly the case that the media are both pervasive and highly influential. For example, as Castells (2004, p. 371) demonstrates, in the United States television is 'the most credible source of news, and its credibility has increased over time'. As he further observes, globalization has also ensured that media coverage and reach is also increasingly extensive (2004, p. 319), and that this is largely culturally specific, leading to 'cultural dominance by Western media'.

Within this context, the specific relationship between social work and the media has long been viewed as problematic (Ayre, 2001), and the primary locus of this tension has been child protection, with practitioners being exposed to attack and vilification both for intervening too much (Kitzinger, 2004) and too little (Ayre, 2001). Skewed portrayals of social work appear to have a number of unhelpful consequences, including, for example, the assumption that the central function of the profession is to police the parenting of children (see also Donzelot, 1979). Much of what social work does is effectively ignored in favour of sensational treatment of those cases where things go (or appear to go) seriously wrong, resulting in considerable harm or public outcry (Laming, 2003).

In light of this, there is a pervasive sense of social work being both misrepresented and unfairly treated by the media, but at the same time being unable to do much to redress the balance. According to some, this has had a damaging effect on the profession, which 'continues to be characterized by defeatism and cynicism … further accentuated by the low status of social work in the eyes of the general public and the poor media image that has developed' (Thompson, 2002, p. 719).

The danger here, of course, is that practice becomes defensive, and that this approach becomes embedded in the culture of social work agencies. As Ayre comments, this may result in a strategy of 'avoidance [of the media] at all costs' (2001, p. 898), which may lead to further hostility and negative coverage.

The power of the media cannot be viewed simplistically, however (Kitzinger, 2004). Whilst some have emphasized the role of the media in 'agenda-setting' or 'framing' public perceptions, others suggest that it is the nature of the audience response which is more important. According to this perspective, audiences have at least three options available to them in responding to a 'text': the dominant reading (the interpretation intended), a negotiated response, or an oppositional reaction (Kitzinger, 2004, p. 20). The idea that media portrayals translate directly into an intended audience response is open to question, not least because 'people often profess to approach the media with a high degree of cynicism' (Kitzinger, 2004, p. 184).

Despite these caveats, the media does appear to have played a substantial part in shaping popular perceptions of social work, and these are often negative. As observed, child protection often acts as the focus for intensive critical publicity about social work, with 'child abuse scandals' throughout the 1970s, 1980s and 1990s generating substantial coverage (Ayre, 2001). Kitzinger (2004) suggests that a series of connected processes can be seen to operate in respect of media representations, including the use of 'media templates' and 'story branding'. In this way, occurrences at different places and times can be linked in order to convey a consistent and compelling picture. Thus, the publicity surrounding allegations of child sexual abuse in Cleveland became the benchmark for coverage of events in Orkney four years later, when a number of children were removed from their parents as a result of similar concerns. The Orkney case became known as 'the dawn raids case' (2004, p. 84), conjuring up an image of heavy-handed removal of children from their families: ' "I just remember what was in the papers, they were took screaming from their beds" ' (research participant, quoted in Kitzinger, 2004, p. 85).

Interestingly, Kitzinger also makes the point that these portrayals are further shaped by their association with images of the respectability (or otherwise) of those who were the object of social work interventions. The representation of families in Cleveland and in Orkney as decent people casts doubt on the legitimacy of practitioners, at the same time as reinforcing other media typologies, distinguishing between respectable communities and others, where abusive behaviour might be expected. People seem to 'accept that Orkney was just not the sort of place where abuse would happen' (Kitzinger, 2004, p. 113).

Whilst Kitzinger concludes that there are strategies which enable people to resist dominant messages, the 'striking' impression is of essentially common responses consistent with the intended 'reading' of media representations (2004, p. 186). In light of this, then, it seems that there are grounds for concern at the way in which social work professionals have consistently been portrayed. Indeed, it is the very consistency of messages which gives rise to this. By contrast, it does not seem to matter that these may incorporate conflicting accounts, since they seem to reinforce the overriding impression of incompetence or insensitivity. As both Parton (1991) and Ayre (2001) report, certain characteristics are repeatedly attributed to social workers. Thus, in the context of the death of Jasmine Beckford, social workers were claimed to be naive, gullible and incompetent, whilst also being portrayed as autocratic and insensitive bureaucrats (Parton, 1991, p. 64). A similar catalogue of shortcomings is detailed by Ayre (2001, p. 890), with social workers being criticized as overzealous 'child stealers' and, at the same time, weak, overliberal and indecisive.

For present purposes, it is important to acknowledge that the substantive concerns about the way in which social workers are represented are compounded by our understanding of power, and the role that the media appears to play in 'framing' our perceptions. There are a number of significant consequences for the arena of practice. Firstly, the context is one in which 'risk' and 'danger' are recognized as endemic (Parsloe, 1999). Indeed, as Ayre points out, this perception is inevitable, given that promoting oneself as a 'child protection' service amounts to a public commitment 'to keep children safe', so it may not be too surprising that this becomes a focus for public concern and media interest:

> The inevitable but unwelcome corollary of child protection managers' emotive argument for continuing generous funding was an expectation on the part of the public, the politicians and the press that if sufficient resources were devoted to the service, children would no longer die as a result of abuse. (Ayre, 2001, p. 892)

Perceptions of social workers may thus be influenced by their inevitable failure to deliver on this commitment. Consequently, concerns about competence and training emerge (Titterton, 1999), and practice becomes increasingly proceduralized in order to address these shortcomings. As Ayre (2001, p. 893) points out, a defensive outlook is the predictable outcome, with guidance becoming increasingly tightly defined in order to create the impression of organizational competence, where each error results in guidance written 'on the spaces between the lines in the vain hope that we will eventually catch everything'.

The implications for practice of the media's influence are not just felt through increasing bureaucratization and prescription within social work organizations; there are also consequences elsewhere. The perceptions of social workers held by service users, for instance, are much more likely to be determined by what they have read or heard than by direct experience. As Kitzinger observes, beliefs about social workers' behaviour and competence are deeply embedded in the minds of the public. In discussing the Orkney case with parents of young children, she found that

> They feel that what happened to the families in Orkney could happen to them. This is not because they might be abusing their children ... but because even innocent parents are at risk. There is widespread distrust of social services and many people lack faith in social workers' training and expertise. (Kitzinger, 2004, p. 91)

It is thus likely to be the case that practitioners will encounter adverse perceptions of their competence and motivation at their first encounter with potential service users, irrespective of the reality of the situation.

The influence of the media may be felt in other ways, and it almost certainly contributes to the stereotypical views of social workers held by other professionals. Interagency stereotyping is acknowledged as a problem (Murphy, 1995), and it is suggested that this affects 'the whole child protection system' (p. 70). The consequences for social work practice may appear predictable, in that it is characterized by an overemphasis on child protection (Murphy, 1995, p. 71), and a defensive, procedure-bound orientation towards intervention (Ayre, 2001, p. 898).

At the same time, media contact is avoided in the belief that it can only lead to negative coverage (*ibid.*). On the other hand, it is suggested that a strategy of mere avoidance is not necessarily the most effective option (Ayre, 2001; Kitzinger, 2004). Social work can (and should) develop both 'better media management' and a more informed approach to understanding and changing dominant 'discourses' (Ayre, 2001, p. 899) – creating and sustaining an impression of 'competence', for example. Equally, at the level of direct practice, there is a need to demonstrate awareness of where service users are likely to be 'coming from'. For example:

> Sensitivity to everyday ways of understanding child sexual abuse, and presumptions about the intervention process, are important in working with clients and providing information and support. (Kitzinger, 2004, p. 195)

Beyond this, it is also important that social work seeks out opportunities to promote its activities in a positive light, as professional bodies such as the British Association of Social Workers and the International Federation of Social Workers seek to do.

Speaking directly to practice: the role of government

In the same way as the media has a discernible influence on practice, the actions of government may impact directly on social workers. Indeed, the relationship between politicians and the media may engender a mutually amplifying effect, in some instances. For example, the response of the then government clearly magnified the impact of the furore in Cleveland surrounding allegations of over-officious behaviour by social workers in 1987 (Parton, 1991).

Inevitably government has a formal and conventional role in determining legislation and policy (see next section), but it also seems to have a more immediate impact, in terms of ministerial initiatives and pronouncements. It is in this sense that practitioners may sometimes get the impression that they are being addressed directly, over the heads of managers and agencies. Practice may be driven by symbolic and political goals rather than through the development of law and policy based on professional knowledge and research evidence.

In some instances it is reported that government and ministers seem to be using their position consciously, engaging in a form of 'megaphone diplomacy' to get the message across:

> Nearly all the social workers I met could cite at least some of the many critical comments which Paul Boateng [as Minister of Health] had made over the years with respect to state social work's record with children in the care system. (Jones, 2001, p. 554)

Respondents saw this as part of a wider government strategy based on diverting attention away from problems of underfunding and inadequate systems and instead adopting a victim-blaming and authoritarian approach to the problems faced by practitioners. In this sense, service users and social workers appear to suffer equally as targets of ministerial concern.

Social workers believed that many of the unwelcome changes they experienced emanated directly from government, and reflected persistent distrust. The consequences are perceived to have been a tightening of mechanisms of control, imposing rigid requirements on practitioners whose competence is implicitly called into question: '"Governments believe that social workers can't do the job, therefore you turn it into a job that you do in boxes and you tick the boxes and do the job"' (social worker, quoted in Jones, 2001, p. 555).

The emergence of a new and more sophisticated machinery of control is partly attributed to this concern of government to 'micromanage' the day-to-day activities of practitioners. One illustration is the use of performance indicators and league tables to provide crude but powerful indicators of efficiency and achievement in the delivery of social services (Harris, 2003). It is suggested that the proliferation of such measures has been part of a deliberate strategy to limit discretion and determine outputs. The tools available to government are used to underpin these aims:

> The implementation of specific initiatives in relation to social work is inextricably intertwined with and evaluated by external audit, inspection and review, for example by the Best Value Inspectorate ... by performance assessment framework reviews by the Social Services Inspectorate ... by quinquennial joint reviews ... by inspections by the Commission for Care Standards and by thematic inspections by the Social Services Inspectorate. (Harris, 2003, p. 93)

This barrage of activities, in Harris's view, provides concrete evidence of a 'hands-on approach' which reflected New Labour's concern to exercise direct and close influence on interventions and outcomes. The use of regulatory mechanisms to enforce policy initiatives suggests a strong commitment to ensuring that 'governmental agendas' will be followed precisely at the level of local service delivery. The close alignment of this strategy with processes of 'managerialization' (Clarke *et al.*, 2000) is something we shall explore in more detail subsequently, but for the moment it is important to focus on its place at the heart of government thinking and action.

Closer scrutiny of the actions of service providers is indicative of a substantial level of distrust (Harris, 2003, p. 94), but, in finding evidence of omissions and failures, it inevitably reinforces this lack of trust and becomes self-fulfilling. In one sense, this provides confirmation of Beck's (1992) argument that a commitment to the perfectibility of scientific techniques paradoxically tends to result in a recognition of their own shortcomings (see also, Giddens, 1991). In short, if we search hard enough for evidence of inadequacy or failure, we will certainly find it. The consequence for practitioners, however, is that their work and procedures are increasingly adapted to meeting the demands of scrutiny and inspection, and less and less to the realities and unpredictabilities of service users' lives. As Harris puts it, this leads to a concern to achieve 'performativity', that is, to demonstrate practice that is accountable and justifiable according to standardized expectations:

> This adaptation to the process of audit on the part of auditees indicates that, in order to be regulated, organisations have to render themselves auditable. They have to produce and shape the information on which regulation relies. (Harris, 2003, p. 95)

For practitioners, the end results of this close attention originating from government is experienced as a loss of discretion and a feeling of constantly being judged, often against arbitrary criteria.

One example of this trend has been the government's introduction of targets for increased use of adoption. Not only does government appear to have a direct voice in the conduct of day-to-day practice, but it also seems to have a symbolic role in changing priorities. In the case of adoption, the dual strategy of exhortation, by way of highly publicized policy pronouncements, and coercion, through the use of performance measures and targets, illustrates this well. The starting point for this particular initiative appears to have been a brief comment included in the Home Secretary's foreword to the government's policy document on the family: 'Everybody knows that some teenage mothers may not have the necessary skills to look after their children during their childhood' (Straw, 1998, p.2).

This was not a simple statement of fact, but conveyed strong ideological beliefs held at the heart of the new government. These sentiments were quickly translated into concrete statements of intent, with heavyweight backing. The then Prime Minister, indeed, took the lead in addressing the perceived need for change in adoption policy. He was forthright in the aim of promoting adoption for more 'looked after' children:

> It is hard to overstate the importance of a stable and loving family life for children. That is why I want more children to benefit from adoption ... [W]e ... know that many children wait in care for far too long ... Too often in the past adoption has been seen as a last resort ... the Government should take a new approach to adoption, putting the child's needs at the centre of the process. (Blair, 2000, p. 3)

By putting himself at the forefront of a specific aspect of government responsibility, particularly in the sensitive area of family life, the Prime Minister had clearly signalled the importance and urgency attributed to changes in practice in this area (Smith, 2005).

It was not simply exhortation which was used in this instance to influence direct practice. Government sought also to use the kind of monitoring and inspectorial regimes described earlier to change outcomes, even in advance of specific legislative change. The Department of Health had already signalled a programme of 'modernization' of social services in general (Department of Health, 1998a) and reshaping children's services in particular (Department of Health, 1998b), and it sought to achieve these objectives in part by the aggressive use of a battery of management tools including performance indicators and targets. Amongst these, the numbers of children adopted was one of those highlighted (Department of Health, 2003). The intended direction of change was made clear:

> Good performance is generally high. There is a Public Service Agreement to increase the numbers adopted from care nationally by 40% by 2004–05, and if possible by 50% by 2005–06, from 2,700 in 1999–2000. (Department of Health, 2003, p. 58)

And, indeed, the indications were that this target-driven strategy was having effect, partway through this period. Between 1999–2000 and 2002–03, the Department of Health reported an increase in numbers adopted from care of 800 (29 per cent), 'suggesting that the target of a 40% rise ... should be reached' (*ibid.*).

This example demonstrates quite powerfully the way in which government can influence changes at the level of practice without necessarily amending the legislative framework in any way. The associated emphasis on 'stability and permanence' emanating from government (Cornwall Social Services, 2003) brings this strategy into line with existing professional concerns. For some, however, this is less a case of evidence-led reappraisal of practice than of the reassertion of traditional 'laissez-faire and familist ideologies' (Smith, 2005, p. 134). It is viewed as inappropriate for social work practice to be subject to distorting ideological influences which may impinge on the proper exercise of professional discretion:

> Put bluntly, are the most 'needy' families – emotionally and socially as well as materially – now at risk of falling through the gap between *universal family support* on the one hand, and if it fails to work, the draconian step of having their children permanently removed on the other? (Tunstill, 2003, p. 101)

The procedural requirements of processing children's cases increasingly quickly to meet government-inspired performance targets may well have the effect of encouraging practitioners to seek a 'premature answer' to difficult and demanding family circumstances (Smith, 2005, p. 134).

The conclusion to be drawn from this example is that influential figures such as those in government can be seen to have a direct impact on practice. As Jones (2001, p. 547) observed: 'New Labour under Tony Blair is very concerned to make a difference'. Importantly, we should note that such aspirations may impact on practice in two ways: firstly, to the extent that direct pressure is brought to bear through policy diktats or shifts in funding; and, secondly, in bringing about changes in the dominant 'discourse' which determines what is seen as professional orthodoxy. This, indeed, is the crux of Tunstill's (2003) concerns about a shift away from pursuing the objective of supporting families and maintaining children with their parents wherever possible, which appears to have been further downgraded through the publication of National Adoption Standards (Department of Health, 2001).

Law and legitimacy

Whilst the influence exerted by government may be understood as ideological, the authority of the law appears to offer rather more impersonal and formal guidance for practitioners. As Weber (1978, p. 213) puts it, this derives from the fact that law is created independently of personal interests and reflects some notion of the common good. He distinguishes between the law and other forms of authority, precisely to the extent that it does not depend on the qualities of individuals, but is the product of agreement or consent from those to whom it applies. Legal authority depends on the acceptance of a number of conditions:

> 1 That any given legal norm may be established by agreement or imposition ... with a claim to obedience
> 2 That every body of law consists essentially in a consistent system of abstract rules
> 3 That thus the typical person in authority ... is himself subject to an impersonal order
> 4 That the person who obeys authority does so ... only in his capacity as a member of the organization ... and what he obeys is only 'the law'
> 5 ... [T]he members of the organization, insofar as they obey a person in authority ... owe this obedience ... to an impersonal order.
> (Weber, 1978, p. 217)

To the extent that the law is seen as the product of a democratic consensus, binding all citizens equally, it effectively offers a two-sided bargain to those who practice as representatives of statutory agencies, such as local authority social workers. On the one hand, it does indeed vest in them a legitimate basis for the exercise of their functions, which may include a measure of control; whilst, on the other, it also sets out for them the constraints and rules within which they must operate. Thus, the authority vested in statutory social workers comes at a price, since it depends on their compliance with legally defined processes, and any failure to follow these in turn compromises the legitimacy of their interventions. Indeed, this sense of being both enabled and restricted by the law is likely to be one of the reasons for social workers' ambivalence towards it:

> It is important to acknowledge that the calling of social work practice to account, which is integral to many cases, can be very unsettling and uncomfortable for the social work professionals involved. (Roche, 2001, p. 12)

The law, in its specificity and rigidity, seems ill-equipped to deal with the complexities and inconsistencies of human behaviour and the need to exercise flexible professional judgements in relation to it. Nevertheless, social workers also increasingly acknowledge that the law offers a number of safeguards as well. It enables them to promote service users' rights and interests in certain circumstances, and it provides an authoritative basis for their own decisions where these involve the exercise of specific measures of control. Thus: 'the law has come to assume a significance in social work practice that would have been hard to predict in the 1980s' (Roche, 2001, p. 13).

In the context of its long history and diverse forms, the centrality of law to social work has, indeed, only been a relatively recent development. The 'statutory role of social worker' (Brayne and Carr, 2003) was defined by the Local Authority Social Services Act (LASSA) 1970. The law tries to clarify the nature and extent of social workers' responsibilities in terms which are consistent and generalizable:

> In your professional role you were created to perform – and only to perform – the jobs that parliament, through LASSA, has given you. Although there is plenty of room for good intentions, these do not define your job; the statutes do. The statutes tell you who you have responsibilities towards, and how they shall be exercised. (Brayne and Carr, 2003, p. 7)

The sense that the law *determines* social work practice is further compounded by the substantive provisions which provide the authority for much intervention, represented, for example, by the Children Acts 1989 and 2004, the NHS and Community Care Act 1990, and the Mental Health Act 1983. These are not exclusive, and they have been supplemented by many other provisions which expand on basic responsibilities in specific areas (for instance, the Children (Leaving Care) Act 2000), or at the interface with other agencies' statutory frameworks (such as the Housing Act 1996).

In addition, substantive legislation is meant to be applied in the context of over-arching procedural principles, such as those stipulated by the Human Rights Act 1998, the Disability Discrimination Act 1995, and the Race Relations Act 1976.

Supplementing primary legislation, the duties of statutory social work practitioners are further spelt out by regulations and guidance (Brayne and Carr, 2003, p. 59), which are often directly incorporated into agency policies and procedures (see, for example, Leicester, Leicestershire and Rutland Area Child Protection Committee, 2001).

Statutory social work practice is subject to highly detailed guidance (e.g. Department of Health, 2000; 2001), which is issued by government under the authority of the relevant Secretary of State. Guidance does not quite have the force of law, but there is a clear expectation that it will be followed 'unless there are justifiable reasons for not doing so' (Brayne and Carr, 2003, p. 60).

Prescription in the form of law and guidance is, therefore, likely to be experienced by social workers, in the statutory sector at least, as highly constraining, in the degree of authority vested in it, in the level of detail, in the specificity of its requirements and in the need to justify deviation in precise terms. This, combined with concerns about one's own working knowledge and credibility, translates into a 'stressful' experience for social workers practising in legal settings, such as courts, police stations or other quasi-judicial contexts. Social workers are exposed to a real sense of powerlessness and professional inadequacy (Braye and Preston-Shoot, 2005, p. 2). This unease may be compounded by the recognition that legal accountability extends not just to the agency and, ultimately, the state, but also to service users, the exercise of whose rights might also result in challenges to practitioners themselves. Social workers may 'conceptualise the law as intimidating, conflictual, and more likely to be obstructive rather than empowering' (*ibid.*).

It may seem as if the law is a central, and not entirely welcome, force in determining the nature and conduct of social work practice. As has been noted, this preoccupation has been reflected in the prominence given to law teaching in the requirements for social work qualifying programmes; without sound legal knowledge, social workers 'open up themselves and their employing agencies' to being challenged on the grounds of a failure to carry out their duties properly (Braye and Preston-Shoot, 2005, p. 3).

However, it is also acknowledged that the power of the law in the social work context is open to question. Whilst some have suggested that the job of social work in a statutory agency is effectively defined by law (Brayne and Carr, 2003), it is noted that this position has been questioned by others, who advocate that the ethical underpinnings of social work should act as 'the cornerstone of intervention' (Braye and Preston-Shoot, 2005, p. 2). Indeed, the relationship between law, values and social work practice is complex:

> The law by itself cannot and does not provide a clear guide to action in a whole host of complex circumstances. To argue that it did would be to misrepresent the importance of law. The law is open textured and contested, and when this is considered, alongside the detail of social work decision-making, it is clear that the law cannot and does not provide the answer. Instead, it provides the framework within which social work knowledge is applied. (Roche, 2001, p. 18)

Furthermore, it is misleading to represent the law and social work as essentially in conflict. Rather, law and the language of rights have much in common with core social work values. Legislation can be permissive, as well as applying constraints, for example in those cases where service users and carers are offered positive entitlements (for example, the Carers and Disabled Children Act 2000, or the Children (Leaving Care) Act 2000). Thus, the introduction of Section 11 of the Children Act 2004 imposes a positive duty on a wide range of statutory bodies to 'have regard to the need to safeguard and promote the welfare of children'.

Legislation sometimes provides a vehicle by which power imbalances may be redressed in favour of disadvantaged and oppressed individuals and groups:

> Rights talk is the language in which differently positioned people can articulate their own definitions of their needs and interests. I would thus argue that law and the language of rights is a necessary but not sufficient condition for good practice. (*ibid.*)

There is a diversity of views about the role and influence of law in social work practice. It can be portrayed simply as the authoritative basis for all statutory social work practice, providing detailed and non-negotiable instructions which must be followed in all circumstances. On the other hand, this monolithic view has been challenged by those who see the law as a rather more neutral tool, which can provide a framework for positive interventions promoting rights and equality against vested interests. This perspective perhaps underestimates the importance of factors such as differential knowledge and access to the law and its (expensive) machinery, but it does draw attention to the contested nature of even apparently fixed and irresistible sources of authority and control. As we have seen, the value of incorporating an understanding of the negotiable and changing nature of structural forces themselves should not be underestimated in our overarching analysis of the dynamics of power.

Social work and the market

In considering further the relevance of external, systemic factors on the daily challenges of practice (Healy, 2005), we should also consider one other important influence, at least, and this is the impact of resource or economic issues. Whether or not there has been a discernible process of 'marketization' of social work and social welfare (Smith *et al.*, 2002), there is no doubt that social work practitioners feel the effect of resource considerations and constraints routinely, as they seek to negotiate services and entitlements for service users. Decisions about finance allocations and distribution appear to have a powerful effect on the nature of the social work task, it is suggested:

> The issue of finance affects social work at two points: at the strategic level of resourcing services and at the tactical level where the agency and the practitioner are charging the client for services. (Adams, 2002, p. 186)

If anything, it may be that this underestimates the extent of the influence that such matters appear to exert at the level of practice. It is not simply the mechanisms by which resources are distributed that have an effect, it is also important to consider the strategic and symbolic consequences for the nature of the social work task. For those who have to make decisions based on assessments as to whether service users' needs are of sufficient priority to warrant statutory expenditure, this reaches to the essence of their identity as social work practitioners. Indeed, this is clearly an aspect of practice with which professionals feel particularly uncomfortable, for a number of reasons. Some of this discomfort has clearly been captured in research with social workers themselves:

> Because of financial constraints our clients now tend to be at the top end with very severe impairments and difficulties such as acute dementia. Due to changes in the eligibility criteria we no longer offer any services or support to those down the scale. People we had helped in the past we are now having to say that we can't do anything now. (Community care social worker, quoted in Jones, 2001, p. 557)

In his study, Jones seems to have identified a strong sense of a changing role for social workers, associated with the expectations that they act as gate-keepers for scarce resources. This may be associated with the emergence of 'eligibility criteria' as a powerful tool of rationing and managerial control in social services agencies (Harris, 2003, p. 150). Eligibility criteria, which are constructed and adjusted through apparently objective and scientifically reliable processes, become the basis by which authoritative decisions can be made as to who does and does not qualify for a service:

> [Social Services departments] ... are able to adjust their eligibility criteria, if faced with resourcing difficulties, so that fewer people qualify for a service, thus making transparent that need is defined in the context of what a Social Services department can provide. (*ibid.*)

Jones refers to practitioners' frustrations at having to carry out repeated assessments to the point where their needs finally become so great that applicants are entitled to services:

> Community care social workers spoke of clients where support could have sustained a person's independence at home for many years and yet it was not provided because they were not disabled or ill enough. In a relatively short time many of these people met the criteria because lack of support accelerated

> their deterioration, but it also involved much messing about as people came back endlessly for assessments. I was told of some people being assessed six times in 14 months. (Jones, 2001, p. 558)

practice illustration 5.1

The impact of rules and procedures

Local authorities in England typically determine adult community care entitlements according to a four-fold categorization of need (Department of Health, 2002c):

> Critical: The risk of major harm/danger to a person or major risks to independence.
> Substantial: The risk of significant impairment to health and well being of a person or significant risk to independence.
> Moderate: The risk of some impairment to the health and well being of a person or some risk to independence.
> Low: Promoting a person's quality of life or low risk to independence.
>
> (Devon Social Services Department, 2006, http://www.devon.gov.uk/assessment-and-eligibility.htm)

Social workers involved in assessing people's needs according to this template may find it frustrating when agency policies impede the provision of preventive services which may lead perversely to an escalation of need.

In Jones's view, the informality of just being able to share a 'cup of tea' with service users (Jones, 2001, p. 557) has become a thing of the past. This may romanticize the past, but it also highlights the increasing preoccupation with the social worker's role in assessment, negotiation, resource allocation and the purchasing of services. This is partly attributed to the emergence of the concept of the social care market (Wistow *et al.*, 1996) and the influence of 'consumerism' (Lymbery, 2004a).

A number of accounts have documented the substantial changes in structures and practices that followed the community care reforms, implemented in 1993, for example, which were apparently driven by principles of choice and control for service users. The aim of these reforms was to develop a framework which would allow for personalized packages of care to be provided according to detailed evaluation of the wishes and needs of potential service users. Thus, the

> approach based on assessment and care management processes and supported by devolved budgets was intended to enable packages of care to be assembled in line with individual needs and preferences. (Harris, 2003, p. 141)

As managerial and organizational responsibilities became more distinctly defined, there were consequences for the arrangement and delivery of social work functions. Statutory agencies in the shape of local authorities were expected to undertake a number of different functions, which could be broken down into the constituent parts of 'purchasing ...; providing; and monitoring' (Wistow *et al.*, 1996, p. 168). In this sense, different aspects of the social work task can be said to have been disaggregated and relocated with different units within organizational structures, or even 'outsourced' to alternative sites. Thus, it is common for commissioning, service delivery and quality control operations to be located in a variety of diverse locations, with little direct interplay between practitioners.

The consequences, in terms of shaping practice, are demonstrable. The sense in which practitioners are accorded budgetary responsibility places them in the position of having to determine who is entitled to a service:

> where resources are limited and no ongoing negotiation of extra funds is permitted, such a system, in effect, forces staff into the position of identifying their costs, rationing resources and prioritising which clients' needs should be met, rather than focusing on assessing needs and relying on funds being drawn from elsewhere to meet the identified needs. (Adams, 2002, p. 192)

Front-line workers may be constrained to the extent that they have little control over decision-making processes (Lymbery, 2004b), and professional judgements of need may be overridden by the imposition of quotas or other gate-keeping mechanisms to limit access to services.

As a consequence of these developments, the role of social workers in assessing needs and determining eligibility has the effect of creating a sense of distance between themselves and service users, who may become aware of being scrutinized and judged. The idea of 'choice' (see Department of Health, 2006) seems to be critically compromised by the fact that entitlement is so tightly circumscribed.

These tensions have been further compounded by the increasing expectation that service users should pay towards the cost of provision, in the context of adult community care. The fact that assessment for eligibility for services may be bound up with financial assessment further impacts on the relationship between service user and practitioner. As Adams (2002, p. 195) notes, the experience of being assessed for one's ability to pay for services may be 'reminiscent of means testing' for a range of social security benefits, with all that this entails. The power relationship between professional and service user may feel increasingly unequal in these circumstances, reflecting 'positional' differences rather than 'personal' connections (see Chapter 3).

It is therefore argued that the intrusion of financial considerations and market forces into social work practice has a number of direct and sometimes unhelpful consequences. Whilst the original aims of the community care reforms were to promote a personalized service, where effective assessment skills could be utilized to support the development of a 'creative and imaginative care package' (Means and Smith, 1998, p. 120; see also, Department of Health, 1990), there are a number of predictable tensions when this approach is applied in a climate which emphasizes financial stringency and tight managerial control. The pervasive impact of 'eligibility criteria' is noted (Means and Smith, 1998, p. 120), with a heavy emphasis in practice on assessment, framed around measures of 'risk and dependency'. By contrast, interventions which emphasize the creation of effective relationships, support, advocacy and empowerment are much more difficult to sustain (Jones, 2001). Despite this, a committed approach is not just possible but is an essential antidote to routinized systems based on rationing and resource control. Social workers 'are learning to live creatively with, and at times move beyond the constraints of, the social work business, rather than being subordinated by it' (Harris, 2003, p. 185).

Those who have argued for a reassertion of social work values in the face of market principles and financial constraints have emphasized the importance of utilizing the opportunities afforded by the ethos of professionalism associated with social work. For example, the manner in which work is carried out (the process) may be as important in some cases as the end product (the outcome) (Lymbery, 2004a). Social work practice is often carried out, by its nature, away from the direct control of managerial authority, which creates space for the development of 'street-level bureaucracy' (Lipsky, 1980). In this way, practitioners utilize the licence afforded by their professional independence to reinterpret and extend organizational policies and procedures to the benefit of service users. Clearly, this also requires an approach which emphasizes the importance of working 'with' service users, involving them fully in assessment and decision-making processes (Lymbery, 2004b, p. 167).

Complex circumstances, for example, require detailed attention, and in these cases assessments cannot be rushed to fit prescriptive organizational timetables. Proposed interventions should be based on professional judgements of need, rather than financial concerns or pre-established eligibility criteria. The practitioner will need to be prepared to advocate for service users' interests, sometimes against her or his own agency:

> The care manager needs to mount an argument to justify the commitment of resources, recognising that financial considerations cannot be ignored. This involves accepting that it is necessary to present good quality evidence as justification for proposed expenditure. (Lymbery, 2004b, p. 173)

For social workers to operate as effective practitioners in circumstances of financial constraint and close control of resource allocation, their adherence to core values is of great importance. People are likely to be alienated by being made to feel as if they are the objects of an impersonal and disinterested process of needs assessment, eligibility measurement and care plan implementation (Adams, 2003, p. 63). Rather, they need to feel that they are part of the process through the provision of information and the commitment of the worker to support them in protecting their rights and promoting their interests (GSCC, 2002).

main points

- External influences play a central role in shaping social work practice
- The media have been largely responsible for generating negative caricatures of social work, which may encourage 'defensive' practice
- Government has taken an increasingly active approach to 'micromanaging' social work activities
- Law provides a framework which is often experienced as constraining, but also offers safeguards and rights to service users
- Finance and the influence of the market exercise an increasing influence, often setting arbitrary and counterproductive limits to good practice
- Social workers need to retain a sense of their own professional independence, values and creativity in the face of external pressures and constraints.

- How would you prepare to deal with possible negative perceptions of 'social work' which may be held by service users?
- How can you use your role to make sure that people know their rights?
- When services are rationed, how can we ensure that 'unmet need' is identified?

taking it further

- Jenny Kitzinger's *Framing Abuse* (Pluto Press, 2004) is a thorough and illuminating analysis of the way in which media influences affect the assumptions and attitudinal context within which social workers operate, creating a sense of what is possible and what is unacceptable in terms of practice.
- John Harris's book, *The Social Work Business* (Routledge, 2003), details the way in which business thinking and behaviours have infiltrated the world of social work and social care with the active support of government and at the expense of professional autonomy.
- The most comprehensive text on social work law is provided by Hugh Brayne and Helen Carr, *Law for Social Workers* (9th edn, Oxford University Press, 2005), and it is particularly helpful to the extent that it offers insights into the ways in which social workers can use the law as a positive instrument of empowerment.

Websites

http://www.basw.org.uk

This is the site of the professional body representing social workers' interests in Britain, where the profession is able to express its own independent views and aspirations.

http://www.dcsf.gov.uk and http://www.doh.gov.uk

These are the two principal sites where government policy and consultation documents relevant to social work are likely to be found.

http://www.gscc.org.uk

This is the site of the governing body for practitioners, where the Code of Practice for Social Care Workers can be found, offering a distinctive set of professional principles to inform and shape professional practice.

6 Professionals and Organizations

Practice and the impact of systems

In the previous chapter I set out some of the structural factors which are likely to impact on social work practice, both in the sense of conferring the authority to act and in defining the terms on which intervention takes place. However, for most practitioners there is also a strong sense of being the subject of more immediate influences, which are bound up with the organizational and institutional settings within which they work. These factors may be as diverse as operational policies and procedures, team dynamics, cultural and professional norms, or management styles, but it is almost certain that some or all of these will be experienced as significant determinants of what is expected and what is possible in the performance of the social work task.

Of course, it is somewhat artificial to create distinctions between different 'levels' in this way. Management styles, for example, are likely to derive from broader ideological perspectives and structural developments (Clarke *et al.*, 2000), whilst at the same time these will probably be experienced in the work setting as immediate and personal (Jones, 2001). However, for analytical purposes, it has become almost conventional to distinguish between distinct spheres of influence in order to aid our understanding. Healy (2005, p. 140), for example, constructs a 'systems' map which identifies three levels: 'macro', 'meso' and 'micro', arguing that this assists practitioners both to understand the way in which different systems interact and to develop effective intervention strategies. For the moment, the aim will be to focus on the middle-range (or 'meso') aspect of the operation of power within social work. This approach may be helpful in the process of analysing power relationships in the organizational setting and of developing strategies for negotiating and working through these.

It should also be noted at this point that social work is peculiar in that its professional identity, based on a distinctive (but contested) repetoire of 'knowledge', 'skills' and 'values' (O'Hagan, 1996), provides an alternative source of legitimacy and authority to that conferred by the institutional standing of the agency within which the practitioner is located. The relationship between professional identity and organizational role is almost certain to lead to inconsistencies, uncertainty and conflict. Indeed, the tension between traditions of professional independence and expertise on the one hand, and the apparently increasing concern with routinization and managerial efficiency on the other, has become a matter of significant debate, not least because it is crucially bound up with questions of where power comes from and how it is exercised. It is this terrain which will become the central area for exploration of the present chapter.

I will first introduce a brief discussion of the general issues surrounding professions and power. Following this, the specific question of professionalism in the context of social welfare will be explored further. Subsequently, some of the problems of negotiating professional power relationships will be considered, firstly in relation to the challenges of interprofessional working, and then in the light of institutional norms and organizational demands.

The power of professions

 The increase in the number of professionals and the growth of professionalism has been generally accepted by social scientists as a major if not defining characteristic of industrial societies. (Johnson, 1972, p. 9)

The implication of this statement is that the emergence of the 'professional' has been a distinctive historical development, which is associated with a particular phase in the development of societies in the industrial era. Whilst the identification and recognition of distinctive disciplines within this general movement has been quite specific to particular groupings, the overall trend represents deeper and more fundamental aspects of social change.

Clearly, there have been some differences of opinion about the meaning of these developments, and the precise social function of those groups which become identified as 'professions'. Indeed, fundamental differences on this point will be seen, in due course, to have significant implications for social work practitioners themselves. According to one interpretation, professions may be seen as an essentially benevolent development, influenced by a service ethic and orientated towards enabling and supporting social integration. The emergence of professional groups is thus seen as a response to the need to provide specific resources to assist with social cohesion and to modify the potentially damaging effects of self-interested and arbitrary economic forces. According to this analysis, then, professions have come into being precisely in response to the dynamics and tensions of economic and social change. For some, 'professional organisations were a precondition of consensus in industrial societies' (Johnson, 1972, p. 12), whilst, for others, they represented an important counterbalance to the primal forces of the market. It appeared that

> 66 community interest had been subverted by the primacy of individual self-interest, and professionalism was the major force capable of subjugating rampant individualism to the needs of the community. (*ibid.*)

It has been argued that the 'professional type' provides the institutional setting for a range of integrative social functions, such as learning and scientific research (Parsons, 1964). The development of the service ethic on which professionalism is based could further be seen to be increasingly influential in determining the conduct of activities across a range of agencies and social groupings. Indeed, the norms and standards associated with professional bodies and their activities can be seen to offer a strong safeguard against a range of destabilizing forces, including economic interests and state bureaucracies (Johnson, 1972, p. 14). Professions are seen to be distinguishable by their 'rationality, functional specificity and universalism' (Parsons, 1964, p. 42), such that they provide a range of expert services which are 'disinterested' but contribute in a variety of ways to benefiting individuals and communities who draw on their services. In carrying out these functions, and in representing altruistic values, professions contribute substantially to the cohesion and integrity of 'the wider society' (*ibid.*). By coming to occupy a professional role, the individual concerned can be seen as 'possessing' power (see Chapter 2) in the form of expertise, authority and wisdom.

This broadly positive view of professions and their role in supporting social cohesion is not shared by every commentator, however. There are grounds, too, for thinking that professionals may not always be motivated by a spirit of altruism and benevolence (Parsons, 1964). Indeed, it is suggested that 'professional claims need to be regarded critically rather than simply accepted' (Wilding, 1982, p. 3). It is important to recognize that professionals, just like any other group, need to be seen in terms of their position within the class structure. The activities and influence of particular disciplines need to be understood in light of their relationship to wider social interests. This relationship is subject to influence and change. Mills, for example, pinpoints the importance of taking account of the shifting balance of occupational distributions with the emergence of a whole new class of professional employees in the course of the twentieth century:

 Occupations are ... tied to class, status and power as well as to skill and function; to understand the occupations composing any social stratum, we must consider them in terms of each of their interrelated dimensions. (Mills, 1963, p. 307)

As a result of changing patterns of social organization, according to Mills (1951), new professional groupings became increasingly significant during the early part of the twentieth century. They began to act as distinct interest groups, 'closing up their ranks' (p. 140) and establishing increasingly stringent rules of admission, reflecting a determination to protect and perpetuate their own distinctive identity. To some extent, of course, the legitimacy and authority of any professional group depends on its ability to create and sustain a belief in the integrity and value of its own set of attributes.

The idea that the skills and characteristics of a professional group are at the same time clearly identifiable and inherently beneficial is open to question (Wilding, 1982). Firstly, it is not entirely clear that professional qualities can be straightforwardly determined. For example, distinctive claims to professional status have sometimes been associated with sets of fixed and specific 'traits' (Johnson, 1972; Wilding, 1982), which are held in common by all members. Attempts to define these have identified a number of recurrent attributes, which may be generalized across professional boundaries. These include: '(1) skill based on theoretical knowledge; (2) the provision of training and education; (3) knowledge; (4) organization; (5) adherence to a professional code of conduct; and (6) altruistic service' (Johnson, 1972, p. 23).

However, such trait approaches have been criticized on a number of grounds. They assume, for example, that the 'difference' of professional work is self-evident (Wilding, 1982), although this is not necessarily true either for particular groups or for professions in general. It is noted that many of the skills attributable to specific professionals are 'non-specific' and may be 'required in many occupational areas', or, indeed, 'in everyday life' (Blackmore, 1999, p. 24). In addition, there seems to be an assumption that professional attributes are constant, objective and non-negotiable, which fails to take account of 'complex historical processes' (Morrell, 2004, p. 8). There is little offered by way of theoretical justification for the 'traits' put forward as integral to the professional identity of specific groups (Johnson, 1972, p. 24), and this leads to a further concern that many of the attributes claimed by professionals reflect their own self-interest and determination to maintain occupational boundaries and status. It is therefore suggested that the evidence of increasing professionalization (Wilensky, 1964) and the attempted institutionalization of professional status must be understood in rather different ways.

It may be helpful to think of the way in which professions are the product of specific historical developments, rather than simply as the logical outcome of improvements in technical knowledge and expertise. It is necessary 'to place professionalism in an historical context, rather than to take it as a given, independent of time' (Blackmore, 1999, p. 25).

Indeed, the burgeoning number of aspiring professions may be associated with changing class interests, as much as with the refinement of specialist skills and competences. In this sense, it is argued, the emergence of distinct cadres of professionals is tied up with changing power relationships (Morrell, 2004, p. 17). Wilding has gone further and suggested that professions are best understood in terms of their 'functionality' for society and its dominant interests. In effect, they fulfil three roles according to this view. They represent the state's 'concern' for personal and social problems which are accepted as 'public issues' (Wilding, 1982, p. 17). Their 'expertise' provides legitimacy for interventions on behalf of the state, which may serve the purpose of exerting or maintaining social control over deviant elements. And, finally, in order to fulfil these requirements:

> the welfare professions provide a rich source of desirable jobs in the public and private sectors for members of elite and middle-class groups where such groups can enjoy varying degrees of power, privilege and freedom in their work and, through their efforts, help to maintain the system which supports them. (*ibid.*)

In this sense, the professions are seen not simply as benevolent or well-intentioned experts, but as essentially self-interested and elitist. The establishment of distinctive disciplines, rules, procedures and admission requirements serves to perpetuate a sense of specialist knowledge and social distance which maintains the unique identity of each professional grouping. For some, it seems, the question is not so much one of technical skills and expert knowledge, but of the ideological nature of claims to authoritative roles and exalted status (Johnson, 1972). Claims of 'occupational and individual independence' (p. 57) are seen as a way of sustaining the position of those who meet the defined entry criteria for each profession.

In this respect, expertise appears to be performing a different (or at least, additional) function to that which may seem most obvious. It is suggested, for example, in the field of health that the 'perception of doctor as expert' (Morrell, 2004, p. 17) not only maintains the privileged status of those who hold that title, but also helps to legitimize 'dominant ... constructions of disease'. The links here with the 'medicalization' of mental health problems and disability are clear (Shaw and Woodward, 2004). Whilst the position of the 'expert' contributes to the way in which problems are defined, it also tends to have an impact on the nature of the relationship between professionals and 'consumers' (Johnson, 1972, p. 57). It is the professional who determines that there *is* a problem, in the first place; and, having done so, this also confers the authority to determine how that problem should be seen and what its 'diagnosis' actually is. The 'power to define needs and problems' (Wilding, 1982, p. 29) confirms the professional's authority and status (see Chapter 4), and, at the same time, determines the nature of the relationship with the service user, whose knowledge and indeed ownership of the problem becomes of secondary importance.

In summary, then, it is important to take account of the diverse ways of understanding professionalism and the continuing development of professions. A professional identity clearly conveys the impression of access to privileged knowledge, organizational standing and the capacity to diagnose social problems. However, as Morrell (2004) suggests, these attributes are all contingent and contested. It is important, for example, to take account of other forms of knowledge and to recognize the 'limits' of professional wisdom. Equally, professionals are situated within particular organizational settings (see below) and may have to negotiate multiple identities and 'a complex web of relations to other individuals'. Finally, the ideological role of professionals must also be considered, to the extent that they may (or may not) contribute to maintaining and legitimizing unequal social relations and perpetuating disadvantage:

> This represents a shift away from trait accounts of [the] professional, and goes beyond simple, process accounts of professionalisation. Both of these are a legacy of functionalism. This interactionist perspective redirects analysis towards the relationally constructed nature of the professional, through three lenses: knowledge, organization and power. (Morrell, 2004, p. 23)

Social work: a transformative profession?

The ambiguities surrounding professions and the power dynamics associated with their activities are particularly acute for social work practitioners, for a number of reasons. These are bound up with the questions of hierarchy, distance and control on the one hand, and those of caring, helping and empowerment on the other. These tensions frequently lie at the heart of social work practice, and they reflect competing views about what a profession is, does and should be.

Recent developments in the UK have certainly confirmed that there is a commitment to establishing social work as a distinct and legitimate profession. The establishment of the General Social Care Council in England, along with its equivalents in Northern Ireland, Scotland and Wales in 2001, represents a clear statement to this effect. The subsequent publication of Codes of Practice for social workers and their employers, the creation of a register of approved practitioners and the restriction of the use of the term 'social worker' as a job title are all consistent with the development of a distinctive professional identity. Alongside this, the development of detailed and comprehensive specifications of the requirements for social work training provide further evidence of this aspiration. For example, providers of social work training must

> Ensure that students' achievement against the required standards is regularly and accurately assessed, and confirm that all social work students have been assessed and have met all the standards. (Department of Health, 2002b, p. 3)

These stipulations are consistent with many of the 'traits' defined as essential attributes of a profession (Johnson, 1972). In combination with the development of a distinctive knowledge base and training and qualification requirements, this seems to mark out social work as a legitimate sphere of professional activity.

However, it should also be noted that this position is not uncontested, and social work has clearly struggled to attain and justify its place alongside longer-standing established professions, such as law and medicine. Johnson (1972), argues that one of the reasons for keeping the lists of professional 'traits' relatively short is that this allows greater scope to include more problematic disciplines such as social work. Thus, for example, definitions of the nature and content of professional knowledge and skill requirements may need to be kept fairly broad and unspecific. It has been argued that social work is characterized more by the particular qualities of practitioners than any 'compact, purposefully organized' body of expertise (Flexner, 2001, p. 162). Some have taken the argument further to suggest that claims to professionalism on the part of social work are actually misleading:

> Professions such as psychiatry, psychology and social work have been successful in bamboozling the public and those who fund service programs into believing that professionals offer unique services that require specialized training and experience. (Gambrill, 2001, p. 170)

According to this argument, social work's claims to professional status are largely self-serving and do not have any sound basis in evidence or 'practice-related research' (Gambrill, 2001, p. 171). The question as to whether social work can properly be viewed as a profession has, in fact, been around for a very long time, having first been voiced in 1915 (Flexner, 2001), and yet, it is suggested,

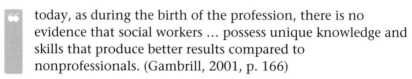

> today, as during the birth of the profession, there is no evidence that social workers ... possess unique knowledge and skills that produce better results compared to nonprofessionals. (Gambrill, 2001, p. 166)

A critical perspective on the authenticity of social work's claims to professional status also lends itself to alternative suggestions as to their true origins and motivation. It has been suggested that the search for professional respectability is self-serving, in the sense of establishing a credible *raison d'être*, whilst at the same time performing a wider function by legitimizing and reinforcing the social control of marginalized groups. Thus, the effort to create a perception of specialist knowledge and skilled interventions has also assisted in justifying forms of practice which involve intrusion into the private arena and the exercise of coercive measures. The end product is the creation of 'a self-image of neutral expertise as a legitimation of their [social workers'] personalised penetration in the lives of clients' (Jones, 1983, p. 91).

The consequences of this may be most clearly evident in formal settings, such as courts, where the considered analysis and recommendations of an expert can carry substantial weight in determining outcomes (Hugman, 1991). In this context, the professional is exercising an important function in providing a purportedly rational evidence base for the imposition of potentially contentious interventions. Thus, care orders (Wilding, 1982, p. 47) or compulsory mental health admissions acquire their justifications in the light of systematic assessments and informed recommendations, carried out by skilled practitioners.

Radical critics of state social work have long argued that the notion of professionalism provides spurious justification for the exercise of control and the perpetuation of inequality and disadvantage amongst those very groups which social work claims to help (Corrigan and Leonard, 1978; Jones, 1983; Simpkin, 1983; Mullaly, 1997). This view of the professions identifies them solely as performing a functional purpose in acting both as legitimation and vehicle for the exercise of state power over marginalized groups (see also, Althusser, 1977; Foucault, 1979). These criticisms are summarized as having four key elements, according to Mullaly (1997):

1. Professionalism is characterized by the appearance of impartiality, objectivity and technical expertise, with the result that problems are defined and dealt with in narrow practical terms, rather than within their social and political context. In the social work context, problems *for* individuals become defined as the problems *of* individuals.
2. The definition and organization of professionals into distinctive groups creates boundaries, both with other disciplines and, more importantly, with service users. This creates a sense of social and moral distance, and offers further legitimacy for social workers (and others) to intervene in people's lives and to impose control over their actions.
3. The emergence of professional structures and hierarchical forms of organization are likely to be bound up with processes that perpetuate inequalities. Processes of selection and exclusion from the ranks of professional bodies are themselves divisive. In addition, to the extent that they reflect wider inequalities, these very processes further compound such structural problems.
4. The history of other professions, 'such as law and medicine' (p. 197), suggests that their emergence is also bound up with self-interest, and the promotion of specific agendas, such as the 'medical model' of disability, which may not be helpful to people who use services.

This rather bleak view of social work as a (quasi-)profession leads to two uncomfortable conclusions. Firstly, as social work becomes bound up with the processes of gaining and maintaining its distinctive identity, it becomes less and less able to work from the perspective of service users. Secondly, the very process of achieving recognition generates structural constraints and conditions which may actually worsen the difficulties faced by oppressed and marginalized groups. Ironically, it would seem, the legitimacy of the social work profession depends to a significant extent on its willingness to demonstrate compliance with routinized procedures and control mechanisms on behalf of the state. How, for example, can a social worker reconcile her or his 'professional' role and standing with a commitment to the rights and best interests of refugee families (see Humphries, 2004)?

Professionalism and 'managerialism'

The distinctive place of social work as a 'profession' has also been questioned in recent years in light of what is identified as the growing influence of 'managerialism' (Clarke *et al.*, 2000). According to this analysis, the scope for independent thought and autonomous decision-making has been progressively limited as a result of a prevailing belief in the ability to prescribe essentially technical solutions to human problems. This is certainly held to be one of the central characteristics of New Labour thinking and the way in which government has used targets and performance indicators to prescribe the mechanisms by which services are delivered as well as the expected outcomes. This leads, in turn, to further developments such as the standardization of interventions, the emergence of routine systems and procedures which are applied universally, and the imposition of more prescriptive and authoritarian forms of compliance management (see Langan, 2000). Lymbery suggests that there is evidence of increasing 'managerial dominance over practice, as evidenced by financial controls, fragmentation of the social work process and proceduralisation' (Lymbery, 2004b, p. 163). Thus, the introduction of care management, although reputedly about ensuring greater fairness and efficiency in community care, has in fact been accompanied by a rapid expansion in documentation, leading to a form of 'checklist' practice, which is 'driven by SSDs' [social services departments] priorities not by service users' needs' (Lymbery, 2004b, p. 164).

The net effect of this changing pattern of management and control in the delivery of services has been to shift the balance of power away from the independent practitioner and towards the agency, it seems. In addition, the influence of proceduralization is also felt in a rather more impersonal fashion, to the extent that it becomes the norm, and exerts a kind of tacit inhibiting force, even when it is not expressed in the form of direct instructions or operational requirements. In this sense, perhaps, power is experienced through the very *process* (Chapter 2) of formalized assessment and resource allocation.

'Reprofessionalizing' social work

In the face of these critical observations, however, alternative arguments have been advanced. These suggest that it is not the place of social work to redefine itself to meet dominant expectations, but rather to act more proactively to challenge assumptions about definitions of professionalism itself. In this way, social work can develop a model of helping and empowering service users which is consistent with professional principles, especially those which draw on the desirable 'trait' of 'altruism' (Johnson, 1972, p. 23).

Healy and Meagher (2004), for example, argue that social workers are frequently uncomfortable with conventional notions of professionalism. They view 'status and economic rewards as unrelated to, if not opposed to, quality of service' (p. 248). This may, in their view, partly be linked to 'sexist' assumptions about the nature of caring work as essentially 'women's work'. As with other, newer 'professions' such as nursing, this draws attention to the important place of gender in constructing both 'lay-professional' and interprofessional power relationships, often along traditional, patriarchal lines (Morrell, 2004, p. 20). These considerations are important because they alert us to the importance of recognizing distinctions between professional groups; it is not enough simply to equate social work to other 'traditional professions, such as medicine, law and engineering' (Healy and Meagher, 2004, p. 248), and this has been a failing of critical functionalist analyses of practice in social services. The point which Healy and Meagher make is that a simple rejection of the mantle of 'professionalism', even if motivated by a spirit of solidarity with service users (Illich, 1977), may be counterproductive, to the extent that it abdicates the chance to reframe the professional ideal in their interests:

> Calls to abandon the project of professionalization ignore the extent to which [social] workers' knowledge claims are already marginalized through gender, class and race-based discrimination. (Healy and Meagher, 2004, p. 249).

The role of social work may, therefore, be to assist in redefining what counts as 'professional', rather than simply to reject the label altogether. Healy and Meagher (2004, p. 250) call, instead, for the 'reprofessionalization' of social work practice. Thus, for example, the diverse nature of social work practice, the provisional nature of social work knowledge, and its dependence on values rather than 'technical' expertise should all be taken as distinctive professional characteristics, rather than as evidence of failure to achieve a 'classical' professional ideal (Healy and Meagher, 2004, p. 251).

It is precisely because of social work's distinctive role in working alongside and in support of disadvantaged and oppressed groups that it should lay positive claim to a reframed notion of what it means to be a professional practitioner:

> The new professionalism finds expression in forms of professional organization that recognizes the distinctive expertise of professionals, whilst also providing opportunities for collaboration with other groups of service providers and service users. (Healy and Meagher, 2004, p. 253)

The authors here stress the value of a collaborative approach to the production of knowledge and the generation of effective interventions. Expertise is brought to bear in the sense of supporting and elaborating the expression of different forms of understanding, rather than privileging only that which is held by one discipline. This, in turn, suggests that professionalism needs to be judged by rather different criteria than those applied conventionally. For example, the application of appropriate values may be judged as of at least equal importance to the ability to utilize technical knowledge (Banks, 2004). This, too, points towards a shift in conventional assumptions about the power relationships between professionals and service users. These need not be seen as exclusively 'one-way' interactions, and they may be seen also to offer potential for 'transformational' practice (Healy, 2000, p. 24).

Social work and other professions

Whilst we have begun to consider the place of social work in redefining our understanding of professionalism, and how that can be applied in the interests of service users, it is also important to consider such possibilities within the context of interprofessional relationships and obligations. This is of particular relevance at a time when there is growing emphasis on the necessity to work across professional boundaries. For example, emerging policy initiatives for children in recent years, such as *Every Child Matters*, have consistently emphasized the importance of holistic service delivery (Chief Secretary to the Treasury, 2003). Failure to meet children's needs or to protect them adequately is attributed to 'poor coordination' and 'a failure to share information' (p. 5), and part of the necessary response is believed to be a commitment to improved multiprofessional working: 'Professionals will be encouraged to work in multi-disciplinary teams based in and around schools and Children's Centres' (p. 9). In order to achieve these aims, the UK government has put in place a workforce development strategy which aims to build on existing professional disciplines, whilst breaking down 'the professional barriers that inhibit joint working' (p. 10).

The government's vision for high quality services for adults highlights the importance of social workers being equipped to act in partnership with colleagues from other disciplines:

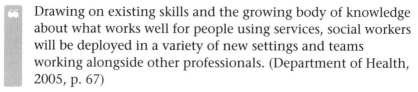

> Drawing on existing skills and the growing body of knowledge about what works well for people using services, social workers will be deployed in a variety of new settings and teams working alongside other professionals. (Department of Health, 2005, p. 67)

The stress on effective interprofessional working from government will almost certainly ensure that this is an increasingly central aspect of social work practice, in all areas of intervention. However, as the previous sections of this chapter have indicated, this, in turn, raises significant questions about the relationships between professions and the extent to which these are mediated by assumptions about power, legitimacy and authority. The implicit assumption of parity between professionals is problematic for a number of reasons. In particular, there is little evidence that professionals either see themselves, or are seen by the wider audience, as of equal standing; equally, to follow Healy and Meagher's (2004) line of argument, it may be unhelpful to think of 'professionalism' itself as representing a set of uniform characteristics. Hugman, for example, emphasizes the potential value of diversity and mutual respect in interprofessional practice:

> If interprofessional relationships are based on a mutual recognition of the skills and knowledge which each has developed then there is the possibility of an exchange of ideas and support in addressing the participation of service users, racism and sexism in the caring professions as a whole.
> (Hugman, 1991, p. 222)

Despite these aspirations, there are clearly difficulties in achieving such a degree of parity and mutuality as between disciplines. It is almost axiomatic, for example, that a hierarchy exists amongst professions, typified for Johnson (1972, p. 58) by the emergence of 'professions supplementary to medicine' whose very existence is defined by their role in relation to the position of 'physicians'. Equally, we find this kind of distinction being made between 'established' professions, such as medicine and law, 'new' professions, which include the sciences, and 'semi-professions', such as nursing and social work (Banks, 2004, p. 20).

Hugman offers a different perspective on this kind of differentiation, arguing that gender is also a fundamental factor here. Crucially, the core function of 'caring' is represented very differently as between professional orientations:

> While occupations such as medicine, law or architecture (all predominantly masculine historically) may be said to care 'about', it is occupations such as nursing, the remedial therapies and social work (all predominantly feminine historically) which care 'for' ... as well as care 'about', often acting on the pronouncements of the 'masculine' professions.
> (Hugman, 1991, p. 11)

There is thus a fairly broad consensus that there are power and status differentials in play *between* disciplines, as well as those operating at the interface between practitioners and service users.

Some differences and disagreements between professional groups appear to arise because of structural or cultural variations. Thus, for example, nurses and social workers may be found to take divergent approaches to the task of identifying and managing risk (Leiba and Weinstein, 2003, p. 70); whilst social workers and general practitioners have been seen as 'antipathetic', primarily because neither seems to prioritize the other's service needs. Social workers are unable to secure GP attendance at child protection case conferences, whilst GPs encounter unacceptable delays in obtaining assessments for community care packages (*ibid.*). Issues of status and authority in such circumstances are prominent. In child protection matters,

> the gap between doctors' views and those of social workers and health visitors suggests there is a power dynamic involved, with the former affording to be more indifferent to compliance and the latter more reliant on the procedures to induce cooperation. (Birchall and Hallett, 1995, p. 86)

In these localized but significant ways, it can be seen that professional attitudes and practices may exacerbate boundary problems through the implicit assertion of the power to decide what is important.

Empirical investigations have highlighted a number of aspects of conflict between professions. Hudson, for example, has carried out an evaluation of attitudes and perceptions operating between practitioners from different professional groups, specifically to test out assumptions that policy change automatically results in the intended outcome, that is, improved interagency working. Whilst he found cause for optimism that effective collaborative working could resolve differences in professional identity and status, this was not always the case; the evidence was equivocal, confirming 'the enduring relevance of the pessimism model' (Hudson, 2002, p. 15). In other words, conflict and power imbalances remained an issue, even where partnership working was being actively encouraged. At the same time, Hudson questions the necessity for 'enduring pessimism', arguing that the capacity to break down professional barriers in the interests of service users is often underestimated.

Nevertheless, some of the issues arising from perceived imbalances in status and authority represent significant challenges to effective interprofessional working. Koubel recounts 'the case of Naomi Angel', where the practitioner's role and expertise as a hospital social worker were called into question by other professional discourses. She suggests that hospital discharge is a point where 'two worlds inevitably collide'. This

> is an area where different values and perceptions, particularly around what terms like empowerment and client-centred practice really mean, can lead to conflicts between the professionals involved, and where the power dynamics inherent in the relationship of the medical system to the social services system are most likely to be exposed. Patients and their carers can easily be caught up in these conflicts.
> (Koubel, 1998)

practice illustration 6.1

Competing professional perspectives

Professional conflicts often arise over contested decisions about the discharge of patients from hospital. Medical judgements that someone is 'fit' to return home may coincide with resource demands and commonsense assumptions, but the necessary systems may not be readily available to ensure that the service user is safe and well supported. Social work assessments could give rise to real concerns about the individual's vulnerability and quality of life in these circumstances.

Social workers may still feel uncomfortable about challenging the authority vested in other professionals, especially when this also conflicts with financial constraints and implicit 'best interests' considerations.

The professional representing the highest level of authority (such as a medical consultant) may implicitly set an agenda leading to 'potentially oppressive decisions made for, rather than by' the patient/service user.

As Banks (2004) confirms, differences in professional orientation are of particular significance at the point of hospital discharge, with the social work value of client 'self-determination' confronting medical concerns about 'effectiveness and efficiency' and the 'general welfare (the greatest good of the greatest number)' (p. 146). We should also note at this point that similar imbalances are to be observed in most areas of social work practice where interdisciplinary working is required and, indeed, where students learn together on an interdisciplinary basis.

In child protection, for instance, it is instructive to consider the consequences of an erroneous medical diagnosis for decision-making and outcomes in the case of Victoria Climbié (Laming, 2003, p. 97). The decision to revise earlier concerns about physical harm to the child to a diagnosis of scabies 'was to have important consequences for Victoria'. Because the diagnosis had been made by a consultant paediatrician, it 'appears to have elevated Victoria's case beyond the realm for questioning by social services'.

To the extent that perceptions of a professional hierarchy derive from commonly held beliefs about the distinctiveness, credibility and authority of particular disciplines, we might infer that this will lead to unbalanced experiences of 'relational power' (see Chapter 4). Established beliefs and cultural traditions are likely to set the terms under which interprofessional interactions are played out. Equally, however, there are structural factors at work in the context of inter- and multiprofessional working. Thus, for example, the way in which Primary Care Trusts have developed appears to cement in place some of the pre-existing imbalances in professional authority and influence. Despite moves to recruit social services personnel both to strategic management and in practice settings, problems appear to persist in the 'dominance of medical culture' which presents 'major barriers' to collaborative working (Glendinning and Rummery, 2003, p. 197). It appears that the social work values of participation and self-determination may be put at risk in such structural arrangements. In relation to services for older people: 'the GPs who now dominate PCG/T [Primary Care Group/Trust] boards appear still to prefer to consult their professional colleagues, rather than older people themselves' (*ibid.*).

It must be concluded, then, that the increasing emphasis from government and elsewhere (e.g. DfES, 2004) on the need for effective interprofessional working also poses some very significant challenges given the apparently unequal nature of existing relationships. For those who aspire to effective collaborative practice, a number of important conditions must be met, including the substitution of 'professional allegiances' by 'team membership', so that power imbalances can be 'kept in check'. Thus:

> Effective *interprofessional* collaboration appears to require practitioners to learn, negotiate and apply understanding of what is *common* to the professions involved; their *distinctive contributions*; what is *complementary* between them; what may be *in conflict*; and *how to work together*. (Whittington, 2003, p. 58)

Social work professionals and service users

As we have observed, social work may be seen as being in a relatively weak position in relation to some other professional constituencies. At the same time, however, there is no doubt that service users' experience social workers as having very considerable authority over aspects of their lives, which is sometimes exercised oppressively (see, for example, Cleaver and Freeman, 1995).

The authority which social workers exercise, often in fraught and dangerous circumstances, remains a source of unease and uncertainty for them. As is repeatedly acknowledged, social work is a 'contested activity', characterized by 'continually changing identities' (Powell *et al.*, 2004, p. 1). As a result, its sense of professionalism also tends to be problematic, reflecting competing expectations (GSCC, 2002), and a lack of confidence in its own evidence base, and, indeed, the validity of 'evidence-based' approaches to practice in general (Butler and Pugh, 2004).

Living with uncertainty and ambiguity generates its own pressures, and this may be one of the reasons that practitioners are keen sometimes to assert claims to professional authority, even if this may, at the same time, exclude or misrepresent service users' interests. Detailed accounts of child protection investigations have illustrated the meaning and consequences of professional interventions for service users. Parents' accounts of the experience of being investigated suggest a number of problematic issues arising from the exercise of professional authority. Thus: 'several areas of professional practice and behaviour ... were fertile grounds for further enabling or disabling potential for working in partnership with parents' (Sharland *et al.*, 1996, p. 81).

For instance, non-abusing parents felt excluded or blamed for the harm to their children when professionals judged that they should not be informed about the investigation taking place. Equally, professionals were found in some cases to be 'misinterpreting' what they observed in interaction with parents. They did not appear to recognize the impact of their own involvement. The attempt to achieve an appropriate level of objectivity could be seen to lead to unintended consequences:

> because some social workers remained aloof and unsupportive, as if to see what responses a parent could produce unaided, some parents were denied the warmth and support for themselves that might have made them function better for their children. (Sharland *et al.*, 1996, p. 84)

A theme which emerged from this research, and is replicated in many areas of social work, was the desire of service users to be given appropriate information and a sense of choice and control over what was happening.

Whilst it is accepted that there is sometimes a need for quick, decisive and authoritative action on the part of professionals in order to protect children from harm, questions remain about the manner of intervention. A gloss of certainty may be applied to often very messy and changeable situations. This may, in part, be a consequence of a perceived need to base actions on recognized 'professional' standards:

> " discrepancies in perceptions often arise because in circumstances where clearly so much is relative, social workers are compelled to apply absolute criteria ...
>
> In this context, parents who accept help almost always perceive it as control. (Cleaver and Freeman, 1995, p. 137)

In this setting, perhaps understandably, the relationship between professionals and service users is not experienced as equal. Professionals are able to lay claim to the right to make objective, expert judgements about behaviour and outcomes which may still be the subject of ambiguity and disagreement, on the part of those affected.

The potential consequences of this mismatch between professional judgement and service users' experience is graphically captured in the accounts of those parents who become the subject of unsubstantiated child abuse allegations (Amphlett, 2000). The definitive nature of professional decisions, and the legitimacy which this confers, leave no room for doubt or the revision of fixed assumptions. Personal experience of being on the receiving end of the investigative process seems to suggest that ownership and the power to define what counts as valid knowledge can quickly be annexed by those with authoritative status in situations which give cause for concern. Despite being able to account for a series of injuries to her daughter, Sue Amphlett's family became the subject of a child protection investigation, and her children were placed on the local Child Protection Register. As a result, the family was reduced to a state of 'constant fear' and subjected to a series of enquiries in which they 'felt powerless, isolated and marginalised' (Amphlett, 2000, p. 176). Although, as she puts it, they felt relatively well-equipped to deal with the consequences of this kind of experience, it was impossible to establish credibility with the agencies involved, and the results, for the family, were 'overwhelming. We seemed unable to control our own distress, loss of self-esteem and feelings of inadequacy, even though we knew it was affecting our children badly' (Amphlett, 2000, p. 177).

She goes on to characterize this experience as one of 'system abuse', whereby the processes of investigation and intervention in child protection cases are, of themselves, abusive and likely to have long-term consequences. The '"social violence" perpetrated by ... the child protection system' (Amphlett, 2000, p. 184) may lead to persistent feelings of anger, fear and distress. It does not matter whether this 'misuse' of professional authority is intentional, the results are still highly damaging, and they may lead to a complete breakdown of trust between those affected and the 'helping agencies', including social work.

The consequences of people's experiences of unequal power relationships with professionals are thus shown to be of particular significance. Researchers have identified that a breakdown in mutual trust and understanding is commonplace between practitioners and parents in child protection cases. For example, 45 per cent of parents interviewed in one study were reported to 'actively' dislike and distrust the social worker concerned following their experience of being investigated (Farmer and Owen, 1995, p. 190). Further, parents' responses were interpreted by professionals as further evidence of their 'intransigence'. Indeed, there is some suggestion that it may be a relatively common occurrence that professionals interpret parents' responses to the investigation itself as confirmation of their shortcomings:

> For example, one mother was described as 'resigned', when in fact she was numb; a second was described to us as 'over the top' when in fact she was struggling with painful feelings from her own past which no-one had asked about. (Sharland *et al.*, 1996, p. 83)

It seems that on at least some occasions the ability of the professionals involved to impose a definition on a particular situation is likely to have a direct impact in and of itself, irrespective of the prior reasons for their involvement. The sense of 'violation' represented by an allegation of abuse, or of failure to protect a child, is always a potential consequence of social work intervention in this context (Cleaver and Freeman, 1995, p. 126). This is described by researchers in the form of a 'shocking loss of control over their own affairs' on the part of parents, whose basic competence to care for their children is placed in question.

We should also acknowledge that similar consequences are likely to be experienced by service users in a number of other service areas, such as mental health (Wilson and Beresford, 2000) and learning difficulties (Stalker *et al.*, 1999). In terms of social workers, service users and power, the central concern here is with the processes by which 'clienthood' is constructed (Hall *et al.*, 2003). The means by which service users come to be understood and classified as the subjects of social work intervention are of considerable importance, because this both demonstrates the nature of the power relations at play, and frames the way in which services are delivered (and received). Indeed, the very starting point for intervention may involve certain assumptions imbued with power and control:

> social work always ... involves managing and categorizing people in order to control a range of deviations ... Thus, categorization is often negative and based on the definition of shortcomings and problems. This places the social worker hierarchically above the client. (Juhila *et al.*, 2003, p. 13)

The problem implied here is compounded by the continuing search for certainty and definitive answers in the classification and treatment of social work problems. There appears to be a distinct contrast between the 'accumulation of evidence about the efficacy of various interventions' (White, 2003, p. 177) and the problematic and provisional nature of much professional reasoning. Indeed, according to White, much of what passes for considered judgement is actually inextricably tied up with more pejorative assessments of 'blameworthiness and creditworthiness' (p. 181). In the context of this researcher's work, these concepts were found to operate as a kind of conventional device, offering practitioners a range of standard ways of making sense of parent–child interactions. The argument derived from these observations is that professional evaluations carry substantial weight in determining the nature of the 'problem' and assigning responsibility and blame, but, at the same time, these judgements are conditioned by conventions and cultural norms. The conclusion is that

> professional common-sense must be defamiliarized ... Preferred models of causation and assumptions about the trustworthiness or otherwise of parents' or children's accounts need to be made explicit, available and reportable so that practitioners can debate them properly. (White, 2003, p. 192)

Thus, it is argued, aspirations to develop effective 'evidence-based practice' may be problematic, to the extent that they underestimate the contested nature of professional knowledge, skills and values, themselves.

Social work as a 'critical' profession

A number of critical accounts (e.g. Healy, 2000; Lorenz, 2004; Lyons and Taylor, 2004) have suggested that it is important to retain a clear view of the progressive meaning to be attached to 'professionalism' in the social work context. We might, for example, take a gendered view which suggests that the 'women's professions' such as social work (Lyons and Taylor, 2004) should emphasize their distinctive approach to what counts as knowledge and the positive value of welfare practice. These disciplines should not be judged to be of lesser value or their practitioners of lesser competence simply because they take a reflective and developmental approach to processes of assessment and intervention.

Equally, Lorenz refers to the challenge for social work of operating 'between system and lifeworld', and not simply becoming 'incorporated into public systems of social policy and national agendas of social and cultural integration' (Lorenz, 2004, p. 147). The pressures on social work practitioners to define and classify people and their problems in order to justify their decisions and interventions may be understandable given the '"colonisation" of the lifeworld by the system'. That is to say, 'arguments embodying instrumental rationality and conducted with reference to money and power have come to dominate the welfare state project, at the expense of communicative processes' (*ibid.*). However, the role of social work remains to mediate between these two poles, and to ensure that the mechanisms of organization and control represented by 'the system' are not simply replicated in practice, but moderated by principles of valuing diversity and promoting 'empowerment'.

main points

- Professional status confers authority on social work practitioners
- Social work's claims to professionalism are sometimes questioned, and often given less weight than those of others, such as medics
- The professional role can sometimes create a sense of distance and difference between practitioners and service users.
- New models of professionalism can provide support for social work's distinctive knowledge, values and skills and encourage progressive user-centred practice.

stop and think

- What are the barriers to effective interprofessional working?
- Is it helpful to distinguish between 'positional' factors, such as status and credibility, and 'personal' factors, such as gender and ethnicity?
- Is 'professionalism' incompatible with 'user-led' practice? How do you balance different sources of 'expertise'?

- The 2004 *British Journal of Social Work* article by Karen Healy and Gabrielle Meagher makes a strong case for reframing our understanding of what it is to demonstrate 'professional' qualities, arguing, in effect, that social work should redefine professionalism, rather than the reverse ('The Reprofessionalization of Social Work: Collaborative Approaches for Achieving Professional Recognition', *British Journal of Social Work*, 34, pp. 243–60).
- Sarah Banks has consistently challenged us to think carefully and constructively about the place of professional values in social work practice, for example in *Ethics and Values in Social Work* (3rd edn, Palgrave Macmillan, 2006).
- As the relationship between social work and allied professions becomes an issue of increasing prominence, books such as *Collaboration in Social Work Practice*, edited by Jenny Weinstein, Colin Whittington and Tony Leiba (Jessica Kingsley, 2003), offer a helpful introduction to this subject.

Websites

http://www.caipe.org.uk

On the theme of interprofessional learning and practice, the site provided by the Centre for the Advancement of InterProfessional Education (CAIPE) is useful.

http://www.scie.org.uk

The Social Care Institute for Excellence offers a resource intended to promote the development of 'best practice' in professional social work.

http://iassw-aiets.org

On the international stage, the International Association of Schools of Social Work seeks to promote professional standards and learning exchange between social workers and social work educators globally.

7 Service-User Strategies

The power of people who use services

Although this book is written by a social work academic and is addressed to those involved in social work practice and learning, it would clearly be an omission to ignore the perspective of service users. It is of crucial importance, both to our understanding and to the achievement of good practice, that recognition is given to the capacity of service users themselves to influence power dynamics. We should not diminish the overarching impact of structural factors, inequality or oppression, but it would be erroneous to believe that power operates only in unilinear fashion, from the top down. The context is undoubtedly crucial, and we have already noted the significance of ideology, the state and other institutions in creating the frameworks within which social work and other interpersonal transactions are carried out. Jones (1983; 2001), for example, has argued repeatedly that state social work is constructed and managed in a way to ensure that control is maintained over disadvantaged and marginalized groups in society:

> State social work, unlike many other aspects of state social policy provision such as health and education, is very class specific and always has been so. It is an activity imposed on the most vulnerable, impoverished and damaged in society. (Jones, 2001, p. 549)

As we have seen in previous chapters, this has major implications for the way in which 'professional' values and practices are shaped.

The prevalence of this kind of perspective in social work is confirmed by other sources (Beresford, 2001, p. 343), which suggest that this is consistent with a wider sense of alienation amongst public service professionals. Structural forces, represented by 'state and market', are experienced as being 'opposed' to the 'rights and interests' of practitioners and service users alike. However, it is important to recognize that interpersonal transactions, such as those represented by social work interventions, are interactive, even in the most structured and prescriptive settings. It is unhelpful to conceive of power as flowing purely in one direction. As already observed, 'power' is situated in a number of locations (Chapter 4), and it can be expressed in a number of different forms (Chapter 2).

Whilst power relationships may set the terms for, enable, or constrain, interactions, they cannot predetermine every detail. We can expect a degree of mutual influence:

> This is not to suggest that there is equality or parity of influence, authority or power, but to acknowledge that all parties to an interaction are just that, and they each have some control and power over different aspects of the relationship, decisions, indecisions and judgements that influence subsequent outcomes. (Smale *et al.*, 2000, p. 28)

Thus, just as there is an element of professional discretion implicit in social workers' actions, so too there is an element of choice exercised by others, including users of services and their carers, about how to respond. Importantly, choices will be influenced by the perceptions and resources available to participants, so that, for example, they will be 'limited by their repertoire of behaviours' (*ibid.*). Nevertheless, this repertoire, and the judgements people make, offer them a degree of freedom and even control over practice outcomes. As Beresford (2001) points out, the agendas and experiences of service users are (and should be) of crucial importance in contributing to mutual exchange and the development of agreed interventions.

In order to provide a basis for understanding the part that service users play in negotiating power relationships, it may be helpful to offer a possible framework (see Box 7.1) for considering the strategies available to them, and how these might be applied in concrete terms.

Box 7.1 Service-user strategies of power

1. Compliance
2. Non-cooperation
3. Resistance
4. Challenge
5. Collaboration
6. Control.

There is a continuum of possible service-user responses to social work intervention, from relatively passive forms of engagement to those which involve taking the lead in shaping services and determining outcomes.

In setting out this framework for understanding the ways in which service users negotiate power, it is important to stress that the intention is neither to be formulaic, nor pejorative. Thus, it is likely that certain contexts are more likely to be associated with one form of response rather than another, but this does not mean that service users will only respond in that way. For example, negotiating an agreed series of short-term care placements may be undertaken as a collaborative exercise, but decisions may still be open to challenge if what is offered proves to be unacceptable.

Equally, the fact that someone resists a certain outcome, or does not cooperate with a particular requirement, should not for present purposes carry any connotation of blame or failure. Not attending an office appointment, for instance, may be attributable to a number of reasons, and should not imply any particular degree of culpability (see Chapter 1). We are simply concerned for the moment with understanding these as the means by which service users attempt to influence outcomes in their own interests.

Compliance

Compliance is in one sense the predicted service-user response for those who see power relations in social work as simply reproducing routinized systems of control over disadvantaged groups and individuals (Althusser, 1977). It is understandable that some contexts are more likely to be characterized by expectations of compliance, notably where statutory authority is exercised, and where practitioners act as the agents of this authority ('power as possession'; see Chapter 2). Youth justice, for example, operates largely under the ambit of the criminal law (notably the Crime and Disorder Act 1998), and expectations of those who become subject to the justice process are tightly prescribed.

practice illustration 7.1

The Intensive Supervision and Surveillance Programme

The Intensive Supervision and Surveillance Programme (ISSP) which operates ostensibly as an alternative to custody stipulates in great detail what is expected of young offenders. The explicit use of control and surveillance is not intended just as a means of preventing offending, however, but also as a means of meeting social work objectives:

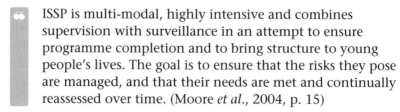

> ISSP is multi-modal, highly intensive and combines supervision with surveillance in an attempt to ensure programme completion and to bring structure to young people's lives. The goal is to ensure that the risks they pose are managed, and that their needs are met and continually reassessed over time. (Moore *et al.*, 2004, p. 15)

For social workers, the challenge is to find empowering ways of understanding and addressing welfare needs within a setting which prioritizes control and compliance.

Evaluation of the ISSP initiative seems to indicate that it is targeted at young people with disordered lives, for whom compliance with structured interventions is intended to achieve positive outcomes in terms of self-discipline and motivation. Thus, poor school attendance (59 per cent), regular absence from home (38 per cent), boredom at school (81 per cent) and non-constructive use of time (84 per cent) were commonly observed characteristics of those participating. Given these attributes, ISSP has incorporated a substantial degree of control in order to ensure 'engagement with the supervision elements of the process' (Moore *et al.*, 2004, p. 349). For example, an expectation of 25 hours' attendance per week was expected during the initial 'intensive' phase of the programme.

Whilst the initial programme evaluation demonstrated relatively moderately successful completion rates (47 per cent), it was argued that the outcomes reflected a number of positive gains, notably in relation to addressing young people's 'underlying problems' (Youth Justice Board, 2000, p.1; Moore *et al.*, 2004, p. 359). Young people themselves reported improvements in the level of family support, interpersonal skills and educational achievement (Moore *et al.*, 2004, p. 250). Both practitioners and young people are noted to have endorsed the value of an explicit and substantial attendance requirement:

> The great thing about 25 hours is that we have the time to really work and bond with the kids ... you know proper quality time with young people to get through to them, build relationships and be part of something. (Programme coordinator, quoted in Moore *et al.*, 2004, p. 252)

The disciplined framework was also appreciated by participants: 'All the activities are helpful. The 25 hours is all helpful. It is all to get you back on track' (male participant, quoted in Moore *et al.*, 2004, p. 246).

The argument put forward here is that discipline and control is sometimes an important component of social work intervention, and that programme compliance is a necessary element of the developmental process by which service users make improvements in their lives and their relationships. However, for practitioners, the problem is that externally imposed requirements can sometimes achieve formal compliance from those made subject to them, but only at the expense of an effective working relationship based on a spirit of mutuality and voluntarism.

Expectations of compliance are likely to be prominent in other areas of social work intervention, too, where compulsion or legislative authority feature significantly, such as mental health, drug treatment and child protection. In all these areas, compulsion and compliance are tied up with concerns about risk of harm, either to the service user her or himself, or to others. It is therefore often argued that enforced intervention is in the service user's own best interests, even though he or she may not recognize this at the outset. However, the fact that the service user may not accept this will have significant implications for both the level of compliance and the level of commitment it represents. Problems arise from the confusion of care and coercion:

> the dichotomy of role expectations and functions, in certain circumstances and situations, often produces unforeseen and undesirable results for clients in treatment. The vary nature of social control tactics (for example, monitoring and punishing 'deviant' behaviours and lack of compliance in treatment) can compromise the working relationship so essential to behavioural and attitude change. (Burman, 2004, p. 199)

The problem identified here is that compliance, in itself, does not indicate commitment, and may, indeed, be indicative of a distorted relationship between practitioner and service user. Whilst it may suggest a degree of commitment to the purported goals of the intervention, it may simply be brought about for fear of the consequences of non-cooperation, or it may be motivated by an instrumental approach to possible rewards. In addition, of course, cooperation may be more apparent than real. For example, in order to avoid unpleasant alternatives or the threat of compulsion, assurances may be offered by the service user about keeping to medication programmes, whereas in fact he or she has chosen not to comply (Goodwin, 1997). The experience and expectations of service users do not always encourage an open relationship with professionals. As the mental health organization Mind puts it, for example:

> Traditionally professionals have tended to recommend one plan for treatment. If users reject it they are likely to find that nothing else is forthcoming. Worse, their 'non compliance' with the treatment may be seen as a sign that they lack insight – and steps may be taken to persuade or coerce them into taking a treatment that they do not want. (Mind, 2005)

It is thus important to have a clear view of compliance as a specific strategy which is *chosen* by service users. It is not sufficient to take a monolithic view of power as something which is transmitted 'down the line' in order to ensure the intended outcome. This is to overlook the mediating factors of the service user's experience, knowledge, perceptions and motivation. Equally important may be the impact of specific individual characteristics, such as gender, ethnicity, culture and religion, which may all play a part in shaping the service user's views about whether or not 'compulsion' is necessary, appropriate or acceptable. Any social work intervention, even of the most directive kind, must be informed by an appreciation of the strategic nature of service users' responses:

> People's behaviour is not only determined by influences and 'causes', including the interventions of workers and others. It is also guided by the decisions and indecisions people make, based on their judgements of the situation. (Smale *et al.*, 2000, p. 28)

It may be helpful here to reflect on insights offered by the discipline of psychology, which has introduced the concept of 'learned helplessness' (Peterson *et al.*, 1993) to demonstrate the way in which individuals may feel that their control over events is so limited that they have no alternative but to comply with externally imposed requirements. However, such perceptions clearly differ from one individual to another, depending on both their own personalities and external influences. Thus, Rotter's (1966) notion of the 'locus of control' provides a means of understanding the way in which individuals may feel more or less able to influence events, depending on whether this is seen as 'internal' or 'external' to them.

Individual choices about 'compliance' concern an evolving and variable process of reframing and renegotiating power dynamics, depending on external forces, personal circumstances and, crucially, the perceptions held of these.

Non-cooperation

More straightforwardly non-cooperation represents a distinct statement of position by the service user. Even in the examples we have just considered, where there are significant negative consequences, there is substantial evidence that service users do not always cooperate. For example, the National Audit Office (2004, p. 23) reports a figure of 44 per cent for terminations of Drug Treatment and Testing Orders on grounds of failure to comply. The likely consequence is a custodial sentence (p. 24).

Non-cooperation can be expressed in explicit fashion such as failure to abide by a court order, but it can also be demonstrated in more mundane forms, as well. It is, for example, a relatively common experience for social work practitioners and other welfare professionals to find that service users have not kept appointments. However, it is important to distinguish between differing explanations for 'not turning up' depending on the circumstances. It may be, for instance, that parents are unable to make suitable child care arrangements to attend meetings. In some cases, it may be that the importance of the appointment is not appreciated by the service user, or has not been communicated effectively by the practitioner.

For example, parents with learning difficulties involved in child protection proceedings have stated that they are not properly informed or involved in the processes going on around them. Parents' supposed lack of cooperation may flow from 'professionals' ineffectiveness in engaging' with them (Booth and Booth, 2004, p. 180), or from lack of support to enable them to make sense of formal procedures. In this in-depth study of the experiences of parents with learning difficulties:

> For most parents, communication remained a one-way street and most felt they were not listened to ...
>   Most parents struggled to understand what was happening in meetings. (Booth and Booth, 2004, p. 179)

Non-cooperation in these circumstances may be due to being excluded and unprepared. The authors conclude that it is the 'failure to address' the issues arising from parents' disabilities which sets up barriers and discourages their participation.

In other aspects of child protection, too, there appear to be perverse incentives not to cooperate. This applies, for instance, amongst mothers who are drug users, where openness about their patterns of use may be associated in their own minds with a risk of losing their children. Non-cooperation may be based on a reasonable assumption that engaging with services may increase the likelihood of intrusive interventions.

In other areas of social work practice, non-cooperation may derive from similar feelings of loss of control. For example, it is pointed out that some aspects of the formal processes of supervision and risk management may be experienced by those on the receiving end as confirmatory of their fears. Thus:

> 66 it is common for patients with schizophrenia to have paranoid anxiety about authority figures checking up on them or threatening their interests. The extent to which such irrational fears are reinforced by ... patterns of monitoring and review, can only be imagined, but it does juxtapose two complex aspects of psychosocial reality – the imagined and the actual – in which patients are quite right to feel that they are being watched by a powerful force. (Davies and Woolgrove, 1998, p. 29)

In this context, non-cooperation may feel like a way of reasserting control over the process in the only way possible. However, the consequences are likely to lead to an increasing spiral of more intensive interventions in order to reimpose the authority of the statutory agencies involved. In some cases, social workers may feel that they have to resort to a 'policing role' (Davies and Woolgrove, 1998, p. 31).

On the other side of the line from compliance, we must therefore see non-cooperation as another potential strategy available to service users for responding to external forces which are believed to have (and often do have) the capacity to determine outcomes in key aspects of their lives. It is the failure to recognize the considered and strategic nature of non-cooperation which leads to problems, as service users' actions are often interpreted negatively. The lack of willingness to comply with externally imposed expectations is liable to be interpreted as a sign of irresponsibility, or perhaps even as confirming professional concerns. Such patterns of non-compliance and avoidance can be observed across a range of service areas, including work with parents with learning difficulties (Booth and Booth, 2004), young offenders with mental health issues (Hagel, 2002); nursing homes (Kirkevold and Engedal, 2004); and health care for looked-after children (Hill and Watkins, 2003). Implicit in many of these contexts is the assumption that service users are erroneously resisting treatment which is 'for their own good'. Thus, it appears 'non-compliance' provides the justification for the covert administration of medication in nursing homes in Norway (Kirkevold and Engedal, 2004). And, for 'looked-after children', it is suggested that it is merely a matter of exercising appropriate 'parental' concern to override non-compliance:

> Children in public care often sense little control in their lives and may reject health advice to exercise autonomy. However, an effective parent will encourage and support a child to take up health advice where it is in their best interests, even if the child does not enthusiastically concur. (Hill and Watkins, 2003, p. 10)

In such circumstances, service users have a relatively limited repertoire of responses available, with which to indicate their unhappiness with what is being required of them. Far from being irrational signs of personal inadequacies (such as dementia; Kirkevold and Engedal, 2004), non-cooperation may be the only feasible means of self-expression available.

Thus, on the one hand, service users' actions may be interpreted as evidence of rejection of legitimate authority, disinterest in their own well-being or simply capricious self-indulgence; whilst, on the other hand, the same behaviour may be seen as a considered expression of their concerns and wishes, albeit expressed negatively. It may be, for example, that their sense of 'learned helplessness' (Peterson *et al.*, 1996) effectively limits their range of options to that of passive resistance.

In this respect, it is important to 'reframe' non-cooperation as a reasoned choice, and as indicative of a breakdown in the practitioner–service user relationship, rather than as further evidence of problematic behaviour which might justify coercive interventions. Again, the nature of the power relationship and the means by which it is negotiated, are crucial factors in contributing to our understanding of the context of interactions, and the nature and content of participants' actions. These actions cannot be dismissed or devalued as arbitrary or irrational.

Resistance

Moving on from service-user strategies of power which concern choices which revolve essentially about whether or not to comply with externally imposed authority or constraints, we will now begin to consider those forms of response which are more purposeful and involve a degree of agenda-setting on the part of service users themselves. The first of these, I have termed 'resistance'.

Resistance is distinguished from non-cooperation, in that it represents a more considered and intentional response on the part of the service user than simply refusing to comply with instructions. On the other hand, resistance, as the term is applied here, does not amount to the fully fledged rejection of the practitioner's right to exercise authority encapsulated by the idea of challenge. In brief, we will consider service-user resistance as a form of action designed explicitly to express reluctance or refusal to comply with expectations or requirements, and to ensure that an alternative form of agreement can be reached with the professional(s) concerned.

Juhila (2003) illustrates this quite well through her discussion of the negotiation of 'client' identity. She argues that the starting point for much social work intervention is the assumption that there are 'two basic categories available' to participants, those of 'social worker' and 'client' (p. 83). This formulation establishes certain rules of behaviour, and gives licence, for example, to the professional to act in an authoritative manner, 'mapping the client's troubles' and identifying solutions. However, people assigned roles do not

> automatically follow the rules and take the roles like marionettes. On the contrary … [t]he categories are flexible tools which the participants employ in such a manner that makes sense and is relevant in a specific institutional context. (*ibid.*)

This point is illustrated in one example, where there was 'no alignment' between the expectations of the practitioners concerned and the service user, who thereby became seen as a 'Bad Client'. The service user attended a crisis centre which had an open access policy. In his initial meeting with two social workers, he said he was 'at breaking point' (p. 86), which prompted one of the social workers to attempt to categorize him with a particular client identity, by suggesting that he may be suffering from something 'resembling depression'. He declined to accept this attribution, which 'suggests a passive resistance towards the client role offered to him'.

Further efforts were made by the two social workers to redefine the problem in a form acceptable to him, but he would not accept the client identity because of its association with negative experiences of treatment at a psychiatric hospital. The service user persisted in seeking help on his own terms and without having to accept the 'client identity'. This interchange illustrates, even in a non-hierarchical, open-access service setting, that there are certain implicit rules in operation:

> Visitors are expected to have some reason for their popping in, some problems for which they are motivated to get help and advice from the social workers with special expertise. In that sense the roles of the interactants should be asymmetrical: one party is supposed to seek and accept help whereas the other party is entitled to give it. (Juhila, 2003, p. 93)

In such circumstances, resistance on the part of the service user is seen in terms of the use of his capacity 'to disrupt the consensus.' He may want to make use of the service offered, but on his own terms, and not at the expense of accepting a medicalized client identity. At the same time, such interactions also incorporate attempts to find a mutually agreed basis for continuing to work together. Resistance in this case does not amount to rejection of what is on offer, but it is part of a process of negotiating appropriate power relationships.

Beyond the distinctions *between* categories which we have noted, it is also possible to identify differences of emphasis *within* the category represented by the term 'resistance'. Ferguson (2004), for example, draws attention to the distinction between 'passive' and 'active' resistance on the part of those affected by child protection procedures. Passive resistance may be represented by superficial agreement to participate in assessment and service provision, which is accompanied by a continuing catalogue of missed appointments and evasion (perhaps more akin to 'non-cooperation'). Active resistance, on the other hand, involves a more determined rejection of what is offered, or at least the terms on which it is offered. In one such case, a history of failure to deliver on the part of agencies, and concerns about the standards of care provided to children, is reported as leading to a virtual breakdown of working relationships:

> Mr and Mrs Jones had literally run social workers from the house. Her view of how she felt she was seen by professionals was: 'Probably that I'm a bitch! But then again I was told ... to get assertive and be more open, so! They didn't like me when I was quiet, they certainly don't like it if I don't agree with everything.' (Ferguson, 2004, p. 169)

As Ferguson implies, resistance is not always heroic or constructive, but it does need to be seen as part of a process which stems from identifiable origins and which represents understandable viewpoints. In this case, he attributes 'Mrs Jones' resistance' to a combination of factors, incorporating her own background and experience and the problematic nature of the services on offer. In other words, the effective breakdown in the relationship between providers and service user cannot be attributed to one party alone, but must be seen as part of an ongoing process of negotiation and renegotiation of difficult and changing relationships:

> The mother, father and, periodically, the children refuse to be active subjects of child protection ... There is much evidence of knowledgeability about how they are governed but this 'cleverness' is put to use in a way which mostly sabotages a better outcome for the family. (Ferguson, 2004, p. 173)

Thus, we are reminded to be wary of idealizing or romanticizing resistance on the part of service users, since it may not always lead to desirable outcomes. It is important to recognize it, however, as a strategy which is intelligible in the sense that service users may seek to negate and redefine prior assumptions about their needs, status or behaviour. As such, this poses particular questions for the social work professional, in terms of her or his own approach to renegotiating the 'rules of engagement'.

Challenge

Whereas resistance can be seen in terms of service users seeking to renegotiate or modify existing relationships with professionals, 'challenge' is to be seen as a more explicit form of rejection of their perceived authority. Indeed, the very legitimacy of their role may be called into question. This strategy may be seen as more confrontational and more explicitly rights-based. This may extend as far as rejection of the term 'service user' in favour of a position emphasizing equal citizenship and universal entitlements.

In an international context which has seen a recent expansion of formal instruments of rights, it is perhaps to be expected and applauded that service users will seek to make use of these in defining their relationship with practitioners. The ratification of the UN Convention on the Rights of the Child (1991), the Disability Discrimination Act (1995) and the Human Rights Act (1998) are just some examples of this proliferation of measures intended to provide guarantees of fair and equitable treatment (see also Chapter 5 on the positive use of legal instruments). Williams argues that the Human Rights Act has a fundamental role to play in redefining the relationship between statutory services and those who use them. Its provisions, such as the right to 'a private and family life' (Article 8),

> will be enforceable by law through the courts and tribunals of this country [the UK]. For social work, the implications are significant. Policies, practices and procedures, old and new, central and local must comply ... Provided people are made aware of their ... rights and, when appropriate, given help to enforce them, they will be empowered in a way that was impossible before incorporation [of the European Convention on Human Rights] ... No longer are they dependent on the rhetoric of good intentions. (Williams, 2001, p. 843)

At the level of direct practice, these developments have been paralleled by the prescription of formal consultation and complaints procedures. Thus, from 1991, social work agencies in the statutory sector were required to put 'accessible' complaints procedures in place (Simons, 1995). Early findings suggested that this had prompted a substantial number of recorded complaints about social services, 'upwards of 30,000' a year. Research focusing on the experiences of people with learning difficulties found that there were a number of consistent themes emerging from their complaints, such as lack of choice, rationing of services, poor relationships with professionals, lack of family support, disputed assessments and communication problems (Simons, 1995, p. 3). In addition, the complaints processes themselves were often experienced as unhelpful and alienating.

Nevertheless, the existence of formal processes had an impact on professionals' understandings of service users' rights and their mutual relationships. Some 'reacted negatively to criticism', whilst others viewed the process more positively, seeing it as a way of promoting 'justice' or forcing their own agencies to address difficult issues (Simons, 1995, p. 4).

Other studies have also identified a growing recognition of the centrality of 'rights' to relationships between agencies, professionals and service users (Audit Commission, 2003), usually focusing on representations and complaints (Aiers, 1998; Bridge, 1999; Bridge and Street, 2001), and sometimes extending beyond the statutory sector to incorporate voluntary organizations (Bradshaw *et al.*, 1998; NCH, 2003). There has been concrete evidence of changes in practice and outcomes, particularly at the individual level (Local Government Ombudsman, 2005). In cases where people have managed to access complaints mechanisms and pursue their concerns, service changes have resulted. For one service user with autism, changes in agency behaviour were required when it was found that

> social services staff did not take the time to build up a relationship with [the service user] and he kept refusing services offered because he finds new people and social situations frightening. (Local Government Ombudsman, 2005)

However, whilst there is some evidence that this emerging emphasis on rights has had some beneficial impact in some cases, there remain serious shortcomings in the ability of service users to challenge providers, whether agencies or practitioners (Audit Commission, 2003; Carr, 2004). In terms of cementing support for the underlying aims of the Human Rights Act 1998, progress is reported to be limited and 'the impact of the Act is in danger of stalling' (Audit Commission, 2003, p. 3). What is referred to as an 'initial flurry' of activity has fallen away, and particular groups (the elderly, children and people with disabilities) are identified as 'less likely to complain even where they had suffered unfair and/or degrading treatment at the hands of a service provider' (Audit Commission, 2003, p. 5).

Issues of power and control remain deeply embedded in the operation of those very systems and processes which are meant to promote and guarantee people's rights. Thus, lack of information excludes some from making representations, while others are deterred for fear of the consequences (Carr, 2004, p. 12). Analysis of the experience of user participation suggests that there are significant limitations to consumerist approaches based on 'market principles' (Harris, 1999; Bridge and Street, 2001). Whilst the impetus for change might originate with a focus on choice and control for individual 'welfare consumers', problems of isolation and exclusion leave individuals in a vulnerable position:

> Power issues underlie the majority of identified difficulties with effective user-led change. User participation initiatives require continual awareness of the context of power relations in which they are being conducted ... It appears that power sharing can be difficult within established mainstream structures, formal consultation mechanisms and traditional ideologies. (Carr, 2004, p. vii)

By contrast, it appears that there is much greater potential for effective challenge and change when service users organize and articulate their views collectively outside the established legal framework, as the example of the Wiltshire and Swindon User Network illustrates (Carr, 2004, p. 25). Thus, it is claimed that the potential for progressive developments lies in the broader 'service user movement', acting collectively. Fears of isolation and victimization as a result of articulating legitimate expectations are much less acute when these are expressed jointly by service users. Indeed, it is through the active influence of user groups that the value of participation has been recognized: 'Challenges to traditional professional modes of thinking and operating are emerging as a result of participation' (Carr, 2004, p. 28). Not least amongst these is the importance of recognizing 'challenge' as a legitimate strategy for service users to adopt in dealing with provider agencies and professionals. The result should be a readiness to consider 'power sharing' and acceptance of the principles of partnership, self-determination and independence.

Collaboration

Service users are not always in conflict with practitioners, of course. As we have noted (Chapter 2), some theorists have argued that the distribution of power need not be based on a 'zero sum' equation; it is possible for each party to a transaction to gain from the pooling of energy and resources. Partnerships between professionals and service users are both possible and productive.

Thus, service users may be ready to adopt a strategy of active engagement and participation in change processes, even where they have not chosen to become involved with social work professionals (Lupton, 1998). It has been noted, for example, that inclusive approaches to family support have been successful in creating a sense of cooperation and mutuality. Morris and Shepherd (2000) suggest that Family Group Conferences (FGCs) typify a spirit of collaboration. This form of intervention was introduced into the UK in the early 1990s, drawing on earlier successful schemes in New Zealand. In particular, the FGC model has been applied to family support, child protection and youth offending in order to place family members at the centre of planning and decision-making in relation to identified problems. Different approaches have been identified (Jackson, 1998; 1999), but they share the objective of promoting the active involvement of service users. Family Group Conferences are held to

> reverse conventional decision-making practice. Rather than the professionals ... making decisions about young people in trouble, families (including wider kinship networks) take responsibility for the action to be taken. (Jackson, 1999, p. 128)

Thus, 'positional' preconceptions are replaced by 'relational' strategies of power (see Chapter 3). Conferences are typically organized in the form of a meeting or series of meetings to deal with concerns about the well-being or behaviour of children. Whilst these concerns may originate from the professional sphere (health, education, social services or criminal justice, for example), the aim is to organize the response around the needs and wishes of the family concerned. The family therefore takes the lead in planning the agenda and attendance at the 'conference'. The event itself is organized around information-sharing where concerns are raised and intervention options discussed, 'family time' where the family members alone come up with a plan of action, and an agreement phase where family plans can only be turned down by agencies where a child is believed to be at risk of 'significant harm' (Barnardo's, 2002, p. 5). Evidence from the implementation of the FGC practice model suggests that there are a number of significant benefits (Crow and Marsh, 1998; Morris and Shepherd, 2000). Notably, conferences appear to be effective in providing the opportunity for families and professionals to agree workable arrangements to protect children. In one local authority, two thirds of conferences studied were initiated because of child protection concerns, with 83 per cent of children 'registered' at the time of the conference, yet

> Social workers thought that the great majority of the children had been better protected, or as well protected, by the family's plans as they would otherwise have been ...
> There were few subsequent child protection concerns and in only two cases were these due to the family plans. Family involvement in the planning was generally thought to have safeguarded children rather than put them at risk. (Crow and Marsh, 1998, p. 2)

Not only were outcomes believed to be 'better', but family satisfaction with the process was also identified as 'high' in this study.

The introduction of the FGC model is clearly an attempt to incorporate empowerment and partnership into formal procedures, particularly but not exclusively (Jackson, 1999) those concerning the well-being of children. Outcomes can be very positive in this respect, with families regaining 'a measure of decision-making power in relation to their children and young people' (Jackson and Morris, 1999, p. 628). Families are accorded some latitude to bring their own 'culture, style and history' to bear on the decision-making process, and thus to devise original and independent solutions (Jackson and Morris, 1999, p. 623). It is significant that the link between FGCs and Maori traditions of informal problem solving have been acknowledged.

Despite the gains achieved by the use of conferencing, issues of power and control do not evaporate in cases where the model is applied. In addition, 'professional anxiety' about giving up the ability to determine outcomes tends to limit its use to relatively unproblematic cases (Jackson and Morris, 1999, p. 627).

Just as in the example of FGCs, there is a much broader pattern of developing interest in partnership and service-user involvement as operating principles in the delivery of services (e.g. Carpenter and Sbaraini, 1997; Sinclair, 1998; Marsh and Fisher, 2000). It is, of course, open to question whether the impetus for this emerges from growing expectations and the strengthening voice of service users themselves, or the political pressures experienced by agencies in light of a 'consumerist' agenda (Harris, 1999). Whichever is the case, there is no doubt that space has been opened up for a more active role for people who use services in shaping provision:

> She [the social work practitioner] told me what she was going to do and I told her what I wanted ... as for the others in the past I mean they've always wanted it their own way ... She wrote down the things we were saying to her that we needed help with, and she did give me a copy of what was going to be done and it was done, everything we put down ... I mean as for the past that's never happened. (Service user, quoted in Marsh and Fisher, 2000)

Positive developments have been noted in areas of practice such as mental health, where service users have responded positively to opportunities to take a more active part in determining plans for care and treatment (Carpenter and Sbaraini, 1997).

An emerging emphasis on the value of partnership in service provision has coincided with a desire on the part of recipients to have a more active part in deciding what is provided and how it is delivered:

> Undoubtedly, the involvement of young people in planning their care has increased. So too have our expectations about what involvement or participation might mean. It is as though every enhancement in standards simply serves to show how much there is still to achieve. (Sinclair, 1998, p. 141)

Progress has been made, but there is still much to do to deliver full and effective participation.

Control

For some service users, there is no doubt that the preferred 'strategy of power' is to seek to exercise complete control over the way in which needs are defined, rights are exercised and interventions are determined. In the manner of Arnstein's (1969) famous 'ladder of participation', the aim is to go beyond mere 'involvement' to enable the independent 'citizen' to design, organize and deliver services around her or his own definition of needs and entitlements.

This perspective has been articulated through the 'new social movements' (Oliver, 1990) which both incorporate and transcend 'service user' interests. A primary focus of these emerging forces has been disability and the way in which this is defined. It has been seen as vitally important, for example, for disabled people to change the way in which their organizations are run: 'Crucial to this consideration is the distinction between organisations *for* the disabled and organisations *of* disabled people' (Oliver, 1990, p. 113, my italics)

Oliver cites the example of Centres for Integrated Living (CILs) as an illustration of the shift in emphasis towards self-management. As he observes, CILs are 'more or less unique to the disability movement' (p. 120), but they represent an international trend towards a form of self-organization directed at finding solutions to externally created problems. The experience of many disabled people was that their problems were largely created by 'hostile physical and social environments', and services available to them were 'restricting rather than enabling' (*ibid.*). A new strategy was necessary in order to break through the 'institutionalised social oppression' encountered by disabled people, and in the British context, CILs became concerned with finding ways of 'controlling services' (p. 121). Despite relatively slow growth in numbers, there were reported to be around 85 organizations in the UK 'officially' run by disabled people and providing 'a range of support services' by 2001/02 (Barnes, 2005).

The Derbyshire Centre for Integrated Living was one of the early pioneers in England, and was instrumental in achieving recognition that it is legitimate for disabled people and their organizations to take responsibility for deciding 'who is employed to provide their personal assistance' (Priestley, 1999, p. 99). This, in turn, presents both challenges and benefits, particularly in achieving the capacity to exercise a greater degree of flexibility in the tasks performed. In one such instance, 'everyone was able to make some use of personal assistants for social support (such as shopping, eating out, going to the pub, pursuing a hobby or attending meetings)' (Priestley, 1999, p. 103).

This is particularly important because it enables disabled people to break down an arbitrary distinction between 'care' services and those forms of assistance which enable them to play an active and full part in their chosen community (Priestley, 1999, p. 104). In this way, the extension of user control over service provision can be seen not just as a way of reallocating resources, but as the basis for redefining essential aspects of disabled people's personal and social lives, according to their own wishes and aspirations. This also helps to break down the language of dependency which often surrounds people with disabilities, since it shifts the focus from 'care' towards an emphasis on 'self-management' and autonomy, which are key values in social work (GSCC, 2002).

More recently, the move towards user control has seen the emergence of direct payments schemes (see, for example, the Community Care (Direct Payments) Act 1996). Legislation has been put in place to enable local authorities to make payments to eligible individuals to commission their own services rather than relying on those provided by or on behalf of the statutory body. The aim of this policy initiative has been to respond to service users' wishes to have control over the key decisions about who is commissioned to provide assistance, and on what terms.

In a very practical sense, direct payments schemes represent the ceding of control from state agencies to the users of services. Whilst local authorities are nonetheless generally supportive of this (Hasler *et al.*, 2000), the political and ideological shifts involved inevitably pose challenges:

> The introduction of direct payments is complex. Within a social services department it requires practical operational changes, a shift in approach to the concepts of risk and control, and a challenge to the culture of direct service provision. (Dawson, 2000, p. 1)

In light of this, it is perhaps unsurprising that developments have been uneven (Newbigging, 2005). Resistance to change from state agencies may be both practical and ideological, with a reluctance to accord responsibility to people whose very 'diagnosis' suggests that they are unable to make sound rational choices. In the field of mental health services, for example, by the end of 2003 (six years after implementation) 'only five local authorities had ten or more mental health service users on direct payments and 57% of councils had no mental health service users' receiving direct payments (Newbigging, 2005, p. 1). Elsewhere, the present author has observed at first hand the very real difficulties encountered by an organization of people with learning difficulties in gaining the support of their local authority to establish their own direct payments scheme.

Whilst there are some potential limitations to direct payments initiatives, such as the tendency to individualize collective issues, they represent an important strategic and symbolic step:

> Direct payments legislation is an important policy development for the disabled people's movement. It challenges disabling discourses of 'care' and undermines cultural associations between disability and dependence. However, there also dangers. (Priestley, 1999, p. 204)

To the extent that they challenge established paternalistic and exclusionary ideologies, it is to be expected that direct payments schemes will encounter resistance. It has been observed, for example, that there is a definite hierarchy in terms of access to direct payments, based on judgements not so much as to who is 'deserving' and who is 'undeserving'; but rather based on distinctions between who is seen as 'competent' and who is 'incompetent'. This distinction militates against the interests of certain groups, such as mental health service users (Newbigging, 2005). Nevertheless, direct payments have much to offer in terms of transforming established and unequal relationships between service providers and those who use services:

> As a result of being on direct payments I have more confidence, I have had no hospital admissions and I have a better quality of life. I now have people back for a meal and cook and bake. I have the motivation and support I need to take part in my own care. (Direct payments user, quoted in Newbigging, 2005, p. ix)

main points

- Service users play a key part in determining the shape of power relationships affecting social work interventions
- Different 'strategies of power' may be adopted at different times and in different contexts
- Power relationships and problem definitions must be negotiated with service users.
- Social workers have a responsibility to provide service users with the 'tools for the job' (information, engagement, time, resources) to enable them to engage in processes of negotiation and decision-making on their own terms.

stop and think

- Should we be concerned if service users do not seem interested in taking control of decision-making processes?
- Is there a risk that we might promise more 'control' than we are able to offer in practice?
- How should we deal with 'resistance' which is legitimately expressed but hinders completion of the social work task?

- Sarah Carr's study is a useful resource, addressing the key question: *Has Service User Participation Made a Difference to Social Care Services?* (Social Care Institute for Excellence, 2004).
- The idea of 'learned helplessness' is a useful way of approaching the question of how to respond to the apparent passivity and negativity of responses sometimes encountered by practitioners. For this, see *Learned Helplessness: A Theory for the Age of Personal Control* by Christopher Peterson *et al.* (Oxford University Press, 1993).
- The emergence of 'service user movements' was inspired largely by the experiences of disabled people. *The Politics of Disablement* by Mike Oliver is of considerable interest and value in this respect (Macmillan, 1990).

Websites

http://partnerships.org.uk
This includes a 'Guide to Participation' with some useful ideas about how to engage individuals and communities in controlling and changing services.

http://www.direct.gov.uk/DisabledPeople/FinancialSupport/fs/en
This is the official website which provides information for service users on how to access and organize direct payments.

http://www.childreninwales.org.uk/UNConvention
This includes the text of the UN Convention on the Rights of the Child and additional information about its application in Wales, following its formal adoption by the Welsh Assembly Government on 14 January 2004.

part 3 Taking, Making and Using Power

chapter 8 Empowering Relationships

Power and practice

In the final part of this book, I want to move on to consider some of the ways in which social workers can develop interventions which utilize and reframe power relationships to the benefit of service users and those around them. The aim will be to consider a number of different routes by which these outcomes can be achieved. In particular, whilst working with individuals remains at the heart of the social work enterprise, I want to incorporate a perspective which addresses the links between different practice levels, in much the same way as Thompson suggests with the PCS model.

Links must be made, according to Thompson (2001, p. 21), between the personal, cultural and structural levels of experience, in order for practitioners to be able to relate appropriately to all aspects of service users' lives. Using the example of racism, he suggests that institutional and structural oppression will find its parallel in the 'racist beliefs and practices' which are integral to our personalities; thus, interactions between individuals are shaped, if not determined, by our social and economic structures and cultural influences. The fact that people from ethnic minorities are more likely to live in poorer housing for economic reasons may nonetheless influence our views of their personal characteristics and their cultural norms. Thus: 'the tide of discrimination (the C and S levels) is so strong that, unless we actively swim against it, it is more or less inevitable that we will be carried along with it' (Thompson, 2001, p. 25).

The implication is that empowering practice must work not just at the level of individual concerns and needs, but also in the context of wider (cultural and social) forces which incorporate inbuilt oppressive tendencies. It is not simply a matter of understanding the interplay between different levels of social organization, but also of how we determine the focus of our interventions. Only to work at the individual level is likely to reproduce implicit assumptions about inadequacy, personal responsibility and blame which compound inequalities and injustice: 'In short, social workers must simultaneously operate at structural and individual levels' (Davis and Garrett, 2004, p. 31).

Adams argues that social workers need to be prepared to intervene in a variety of contexts, depending on the nature of the task. In particular, he focuses on the challenge of empowering 'individuals', 'groups' and 'communities and organisations'. He argues that there has, in the past, been a tendency to overlook the importance of working with individuals to renegotiate unequal and oppressive social relationships:

> Much of the literature takes for granted that individual people will not have to overcome difficulties in becoming involved in self-empowerment, empowering groups, networks and community organisations. In fact, traditional social work ignores either deliberately or by default the disempowerment implicit in people's everyday circumstances. (Adams, 2003, p. 59)

The aim of this chapter is to focus explicitly at the individual level in order to provide the basis for social workers to develop intervention strategies which enable people to address and renegotiate power relationships arising from their personal circumstances. At the risk of creating arbitrary distinctions, I will then go on to consider the challenges for social work in adopting a similar approach at the levels of community and society. Importantly, however, this should form the basis for integrated practice, rather than an overemphasis on one or other 'level' of intervention (Davis and Garrett, 2004).

In order to illustrate some of the commonalities between different practice contexts, I will apply a common analytical framework throughout:

- Understanding power relationships
- Exploring power relationships
- Reframing power relationships
- Changing power relationships.

The suggestion here is that effective intervention will depend on social workers being able to engage in a process with service users which leads from an initial appreciation of the implications of power dynamics in the specific practice context towards the agreement and implementation of a strategy which seeks to transform these in the interests of service users, both individually and collectively.

Working with individuals: understanding power relationships

> Before groups can work effectively to empower people, individuals in them need to feel empowered ... The worker needs to develop ways of working with individuals which empower them. (Adams, 2003, p. 60)

Not only is work with individuals at the heart of social work practice because of the way it is structured, but also, according to Adams, building personal strengths is a prerequisite of work to reshape power relationships overall.

practice illustration 8.1

A service user taking action

> I have tried to get a job but always it seems that there are obstacles in the way ... My social worker asked me if I was interested in assisting at some meetings as a service user and a HIV positive person. Saying yes to her was the way I became involved in 'Shaping Our Lives' [a national organization of people who use services which promotes user control].
>
> I found this project so interesting that I thought there might be an opportunity for me to become involved, working alongside social work students, helping them to get a greater appreciation of what [it] is like to live with a disability and the services we need.

(Shaping Our Lives National User Group member, quoted in *National User Network Newsletter*, issue 8, December 2005.)

Although working with individuals is almost inevitably the starting point for interventions, some have, nonetheless, questioned the tendency of social work practice to atomize and to decontextualize practice (Smale *et al.*, 2000). There appear to be real dangers in taking an unduly narrow focus on the problems that people experience. The use of terms which set people apart, such as 'client', 'carer' or 'patient', tend to create an implicit and unequal relationship between the individuals concerned and those whose job it is to provide for them in that assigned role. The individual becomes detached from her or his particular social milieu, and only one aspect of her or his

Social worker   Service user

Figure 8.1   Power relations: one-way, decontextualized

identity is construed as significant (Figure 8.1). Other people and, indeed, whole networks are implicitly excluded from consideration. This, in turn, may have implications for the way in which we think of our relationships, as practitioners, with those who use our services:

> The individualisation of social problems encourages, although does not justify, seeing the identified individual or family as less able than those who 'do not have the problem'. (Smale *et al.*, 2000, p. 88)

It is unhelpful merely to respond to such concerns by a mechanistic shifting of the focus from 'problem' individuals to 'problem' families, neighbourhoods or communities. The challenge is not to redefine the object of concern, but to identify a more rounded and holistic approach to understanding the power dynamics which surround the individual distinctively and uniquely. Dominelli (1998, p. 6) reminds us that it is the very complexity of individual identity and social being which lies at the heart of the social work project. Even those approaches which seek to generalize from aspects of identity in order to challenge oppression run the risk of failing to do justice to the full diversity of personal experiences. Anti-oppressive practice therefore needs to be 'rooted in people's lived-in reality' (Dominelli, 1998, p. 7).

Returning to the themes identified earlier in the book, it may therefore be helpful to consider individuals and their experiences as being influenced by a variety of patterns of power (Chapter 4).

As Dominelli stresses, it is vitally important to avoid prescribing responses on behalf of service users. It is not enough simply to 'subsume' all those within a given category as being the same, she observes (2002, p. 77). Likewise, interventions cannot be formulaic. Practitioners need to be 'experiential' in their approach, so that

> anti-oppressive practice responds to the issues and questions which are identified by oppressed groups themselves. This approach is important if anti-oppressive practice is *not* to be imposed on reluctant service users. Moreover, this concern with validating the significance of everyday experience as a legitimate source of information in designing services endorses experiential knowledge as an important source of data. (Dominelli, 1998, p. 7)

practice illustration 8.2

Domestic violence, ethnicity and culture

The position of South Asian women in the UK who experience domestic violence is a strong example of the complex dynamics which impact on the lives of those who may use social work services.

Gender solidarity can be undermined by cultural and religious ties (Chana, 2005). Support from the wider family and particularly other women may not be available for this reason, intensifying the challenge of protecting those at risk, and ensuring that they (and any children affected) are empowered to find positive solutions.

For social work practitioners, the task of intervening to protect vulnerable people must be prioritized, but the risks of making ethnocentric assumptions or appearing hostile to minority communities must be taken into account.

To rephrase this point, power relations are not simply expressed in the form of a series of external impacts on the fixed and preformed individual, but they represent an interactive process, whereby structures, influences and expectations exert a combined impact on the subject's character and identity. As such, it is important to recognize the significance of power as an aspect of subjective being. Foucault (1980) argues that practices of power are effective because they impose regimes of self-regulation and self-discipline on the individual: 'Subjects thus collaborate in the policing of their own lives' (Pease, 2002, p. 140). Whilst I would not accept that this is an entirely one-way process (see Chapter 7), what it illustrates well is that the dynamics of power do have an impact on the way we see ourselves, and they are therefore central to the establishment of individual identities and behavioural patterns. Out of this also comes an internally produced map of what is possible, justifiable, desirable or acceptable, in terms of the choices we make about our own lives. The exercise of authority and control is effective largely to the extent to which it coincides with people's beliefs about themselves:

> In this case, governance is not only something done to us by those in power; it is something we do to ourselves. We thus act upon our own subjectivity to govern ourselves. Such subjection can be more profound because it seems to originate from within ourselves and appears to us as a reflection of our own freedom. (*ibid.*)

Social worker   Service user

Figure 8.2 Power relations: one-way, user-context recognized

Whilst this overdeterministic portrayal suggests that there is little room for change in one's sense of self over time, it does make the key point that, at the individual level, the sense of what is legitimate and what is possible depends on our sense of personal identity, as well as how we see ourselves in relation to others:

> These two aspects of self, the 'internal' and the 'external', and the idea that they interact or have the capacity to act back upon and influence each other, is crucial to the idea of identity. (Fook, 2002, p. 71)

Thus, in the example introduced above, it is essential for practitioners to consider the influences of culture, religion and gender on South Asian women experiencing domestic violence, not just as external constraints, but also to the extent that they represent challenges to the individual's sense of self (Figure 8.2). That is to say, solutions to the problems encountered cannot simply be conceived in terms of supporting changes in living arrangements or protective measures to deal with the perpetrator. It is also a question of having to consider the implications for someone's sense of identity, if they have to reject conventional roles and customs in order to confront the problem.

Although this recognition may, in one sense, serve to compound the challenges faced by practitioners and service users in achieving change, it also helps to illustrate and affirm that change is indeed possible: 'This interactive idea of identity formation of course means that there is a sense of the identity being in constant state of change' (*ibid.*).

It is thus important to view relations of power as having an internal as well as external dimension, since this is crucial to the capacity of people to define and redefine themselves (see also Rotter, 1966, on the importance of taking account of the individual's 'locus of control').

For social work practitioners, this aspect of their interactions with service users is crucial precisely because it does draw attention to the way in which power is experienced and acted upon at the individual level. It is important to avoid defining the relationship purely in terms of the identity externally ascribed to the person concerned, even if the worker's intentions are sympathetic, since

> these ascriptions may take on a stigmatised aspect for those people defined as belonging to marginal or oppressed populations ... Service users might therefore take on a disempowered, marginalised 'victim' identity. (Fook, 2002, p. 72)

Two further points are important here. First, the social worker her or himself must take account of her or his own impact on the perceptions and behaviour of the service user. The tenure of a distinctive professional identity has certain consequences, notably in terms of claims to expertise and, in some cases, the capacity to exercise a degree of coercive pressure. Equally, as well as the *role* held by the worker, her or his *behaviour* is also a relevant factor, in terms of the extent to which the service user feels (or does not feel) valued as an individual and engaged in the social work process. Holland illustrates this point well with an example from her research into child and family assessments. Whilst assessments were, in the main, carried out with due regard to 'issues of fairness', this was not always observed to be the case, and

> social workers could be seen to maintain power in a number of ways that were at times intentional and at others probably unintentional. Social workers laid out the conditions for the assessment, including the timetable, who should attend, what questions should be asked and where the assessment should take place. On occasion parents were refused permission to bring a companion with them, to be interviewed together rather than singly or to see questions in advance. (Holland, 2004, p. 123)

These practices should, of course, be seen in the context of an area of practice where social workers hold a considerable degree of formal authority. Thus, both structural and relational aspects of power are significant.

The second point is that the nature of the power relations between social worker and service user has to be incorporated into the process of building a working relationship. Both participants will bring perceptions and beliefs about the status of the other. This will include prior assumptions on the part of the social worker about the 'category' or 'categories' to which the service user belongs, and, equally, the view of the practitioner held by the service user. It should be recognized that the specific nature of the interaction will be a factor in determining the behaviour of participants on both sides. Service users' perception of the social worker's power and intentions will have an impact on the way they conduct themselves, and will need to be taken into account in any evaluation of their attitudes and behaviour, whichever 'strategy' (Chapter 7) they adopt.

Exploring power relationships: relational practice

As we have observed, the attempt to understand power dynamics offers some insights into the relationship between service users and practitioners. However, it is also helpful to consider several further phases in the realization of practice, which are reflected in a process of active engagement. Firstly, it is important to share and clarify understandings of the service-user/social-worker relationship by way of mutual exploration, that is by acknowledging shared and differing perceptions and considering possibilities.

Much recent theorizing in social work has attempted to develop an appropriate framework for the process of engagement and establishing an effective basis for exchange between service user and practitioner. In particular, there has been considerable interest in approaches identified as 'relationship-based' or 'relational' (Howe, 1997; Trevithick, 2003; Folgheraiter, 2004; Ruch, 2005). Although they may differ in certain respects, theorists from these perspectives share a concern to incorporate the *relationship* itself into the intervention process. That is to say, social workers must take a 'reflexive' view of their actions, acknowledging the impact of their status, role and behaviour, on the very shape of their interactions with service users (see Figure 8.3). Equally, of course, we must incorporate in this understanding a recognition of the variable ways in which service users themselves are affected by interventions, and in which they make sense of what is happening and then determine how to respond.

Social worker   Service user

Figure 8.3 Power relations: two-way, user-context recognized

The importance of recognizing relationships as central to social work practice is a consequence of the acceptance of the 'social' nature of personal development and individual characteristics:

> If the developmental sciences are right to understand the self as something that forms *within* relationships and that human beings *are* social beings, then psychologies and practices that deny the social-ness of self not only fail to understand the

> psychological nature of social and personal problems, they
> also commit an injustice by reacting to and dealing with
> people entirely and always as independent, rational agents.
> (Howe, 1997, p. 168)

It clearly becomes important to consider the nature and quality of the relationship between the practitioner and the service user as a central element in the social work process. For Trevithick (2003, p. 165), the change that occurs in and through an intervention must be seen as a 'two-way process', which depends on an effective engagement with service users, rather than simply the application of 'detached and mechanistic' techniques. She observes that there has been a considerable research tradition in social work which has emphasized the extent to which service users value social workers who are committed to openness and understanding (e.g. Mayer and Timms, 1970). However, the relationship that is built up must not be seen simply as an end in itself. There is a specific sense in which the social work relationship has to be viewed as driven legitimately by ulterior purposes, that is, the achievement of improved outcomes for those who use services. It is thus a 'working relationship' (Trevithick, 2003, p. 167).

Ruch, too, argues that a relationship-based approach has real advantages. This is, in part, because it represents a strategy which seeks to make links between all aspects of people's experience: 'social work practice by its very nature has to acknowledge the inner and outer worlds of the individual and the structural components of experience' (Ruch, 2005, p. 114). According to Trevithick, this can be illustrated by reference to common concerns encountered by practitioners, notably where external factors can be seen to have a profound effect on the psychological state of the service user:

> practitioners who are in touch with the emotional impact that
> results from discrimination and social exclusion, and the
> suffering caused by poverty, are in a position to accurately
> reflect those feelings when advocating and mediating on
> another's behalf. In these situations, and in times of transition
> or crisis, practitioners need to have an understanding of the
> importance of holding and containing anxiety ... Containing
> anxiety involves being open and receptive to the thoughts
> and feelings of others. (Trevithick, 2003, p. 170)

Braye and Preston-Shoot (1995, p. 139) also refer to the need for workers to act to 'contain' feelings of hurt, conflict and uncertainty. They describe this as an 'important skill' which opens up the process of 'understanding and discussion' and leads to a greater sense of manageability and control.

This provides support for the argument that social work necessarily involves establishing a sense of mutuality with service users, as a prerequisite of exploring problems with them. This leads, in turn, to a more realistic appraisal of the service user's setting and the needs which arise. In both Ruch's and Trevithick's view, the result is a more complete understanding of the complexities of people's lives. For example, the ability to appreciate the diverse dynamics impacting on children and families, through establishing mutual understanding, has important consequences:

> Whilst challenging, the risks inherent in engaging in relationship-based practice appear to be worth taking if it leads to the well-being of children and their families being more sensitively and accurately understood and effectively responded to. (Ruch, 2005, p. 115).

The importance of mutuality is also underlined to the extent that it enables practitioners to explore with the individual wider influences and expectations of them, and thus to appreciate that the solution to people's difficulties does not lie with them alone (Trevithick, 2003, p. 171).

Ruch's approach links the concept of 'relationship-based practice' with that of 'holistic reflective practice'. A critical perspective is introduced which addresses potential concerns about the nature and consequences of the relationship established between practitioner and service user (see Figure 8.3). Inbuilt assumptions are challenged, and implicit aspects of the interaction are acknowledged. In particular, it is noted that reflective practice takes full cognizance of the 'processes operating in practice as well as ... its content' (Ruch, 2005, p. 117). Thus, the relationship-building exercise can incorporate conflicting perceptions:

> We get some families here who are sent, they are not customers, they are visitors, so to really listen to why they have been sent and to try and make sense with them about that ... to see if you can form an alliance you can work with ... So it's like taking a step back and talking to the family about what they understand about what it is a person has referred them for, where you can find an agreement somewhere along the line. (quoted in *ibid.*)

The reflective approach, then, enables both the relationship and its context to be open to debate. Critical reflection enables both social workers and their clients to explore the influences and constraints which both constitute and circumscribe their interactions (Figure 8.4). This helps to maintain a realistic view of the very specific nature of the relationship, which is, at one and the same time, about 'helping'

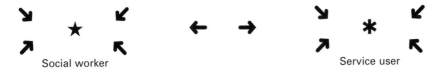

Social worker   Service user

Figure 8.4 Power relations: two-way, mutual-context recognized

people and about 'making sense' of 'organizational and professional' expectations in the specific practice setting (Ruch, 2005, p. 120). To some extent, too, this may help practitioners to overcome the feeling of being trapped within rigid and unfeeling agency structures.

For Trevithick, the formation of effective relationships between practitioners and users may provide the basis for 'capacity building', that is, to develop a greater mutual sense of power (see Parsons, 1969; also Chapter 2). The mutuality of the social work relationship potentially offers the scope for interventions to enhance the personal strengths and capabilities of those involved. This is a particularly important point, given that there is much in the nature of the social work task which can generate a sense of mutual incapacity, with limited options available to the practitioner and a disempowered service user. As Ruch (2005, p. 120) puts it, an 'increasingly task-oriented, pressurized decision-making environment exacerbates' these fears of a restrictive and prescriptive working environment. Defeatism on the part of the professional may find its equivalent in 'learned helplessness' for the service user (Peterson *et al.*, 1993; Adams, 2003), leading to apathy, depression and a belief that 'nothing works'.

In the face of this, the practitioner has a responsibility for initiating a process of determining the potential for change and development in the context of her or his relationship with the service user. This might, for example, be achieved through a process of renegotiation of prior understandings, as suggested by Folgheraiter (2004, p. 152). Thus, the 'structural distortion' brought about by the formalized nature of the practice setting can be 'attenuated to some extent'. It is possible to conduct interventions in a way which at least modifies prior understandings:

> What the practitioner can do ... is control his/her helping attitudes and utterances so that, although they occur in an institutional setting which necessarily issues latent messages to the contrary, they accept and therefore reinforce the user's capacity for action. (*ibid.*)

In order to illustrate this, he draws on the example of a mother who is convinced that her daughter is out of control, demonstrating the need to reformulate what is said in terms of the parent's own responses and capabilities. The practitioner does not 'convey a desire or decision to take action by himself', but seeks to enhance the service user's sense of control and 'self-efficacy' (Folgheraiter, 2004, p. 153). The importance of this strategy is that it both creates a sense of capacity for the service user, and, by inviting involvement in the process, provides the opportunity for concrete demonstration and reinforcement of this capacity at the same time. As he observes, however, the process of empowerment demonstrated here depends on the creation and maintenance of an effective mutual relationship, given the social worker's role in questioning and reformulating prior circumstances and existing relationships. It is neither realistic nor sufficient for the professional simply to absolve her or himself of responsibility, since this is to ignore the structural aspects of the relationship. Nevertheless:

> The surprise of a user when s/he feels accepted and respected as an actor – at the same time as his/her case is taken on because of his/her evident inability to be such – usually leads to the building and strengthening of a trust relationship, and therefore to *involvement* in the helping relationship.
> (Folgheraiter, 2004, p. 154)

Reframing power relationships: language, choice and change

It is clear from the above that an active and effective relationship between practitioner and service user is an essential prerequisite for work to examine and, if necessary, change those factors which shape and give meaning to people's lives. Building on the idea of 'reformulation' set out previously, we will move on now to consider in more depth some of the strategies available which might help with this task.

Notable among these is 'reframing', which serves an important function in introducing the potential for change in situations which appear fixed and unquestionable. Reframing is 'an opportunity to describe a situation or behaviour from a different, more hopeful and optimistic perspective' (Trevithick, 2005, p. 208). The purpose of this is to attempt to reconsider previous ideas, experiences and decisions in order to question underlying assumptions, especially where these appear to have been imposed from a position of external influence or authority (experienced as an external 'locus of control') (Rotter, 1966). The labels which people are given are often very disempowering in themselves, and the task of changing oppressive relationships may start with a questioning of accepted versions of events. 'Reframing involves taking the same "facts" but placing them in a different context or "frame"' (Trevithick, 2005, p. 208). Trevithick rejects the suggestion that reframing can be construed as 'making excuses', arguing rather that it enables negative behaviour to be seen in a new light. Indeed, it may promote a sense of personal responsibility rather than offering absolution. As importantly, the service user may also be able to challenge some of the damaging effects of being labelled or stigmatized.

Box 8.1   Language and social work

The use of language is a central factor in shaping assumptions and giving substance to underlying power relations. It provides the capacity to *define* the individuals, families and communities who are the objects of intervention; and it is sometimes used to *exclude* people or their views from discussion because it denies them access.

For example, what assumptions do the following terms encourage?

- Victim
- Offender
- Dependent
- Disadvantaged
- Inadequate
- Old
- Service user
- Carer.

And these?

- Citizen
- Partner
- Provider
- Survivor
- Self-sufficient
- Resourceful.

Fook (2002) has addressed the key relationship between language, power and social work practice in her argument supporting a strategy of 'narrative reconstruction'. As she observes, it is a crucial feature of language that it leaves 'gaps' between what is stated and the meanings applied (p. 64). However neutral sounding, words will carry additional meanings:

> Language labels may carry particular connotations or emotive implications, or may be based on certain assumptions, which may often remain unquestioned (or unidentified or not spoken about). Language labels often imply different categories, which in turn carry implicit hierarchies. (Fook, 2002, p. 65)

Language is not neutral, but represents an attempt to impose meaning, and it therefore reflects power dynamics in its use and currency. As a consequence, dominant ways of seeing and talking about particular groups or forms of behaviour can be seen to reflect the interests and perceptions of those who are able to control discourses:

> This accounts for why dominant meaning systems often go unquestioned, and even subordinate groups act against their own self-interest, because they unwittingly comply with the dominant discourse. (Fook, 2002, p. 66)

This presents some real challenges for social work practice, given its explicit commitment to principles of autonomy and self-determination. It is important to see the process of 'deconstructing' and 'reconstructing' assumptions and understandings between practitioners and service users as central to the task. Discourse analysis is not just an abstract sociological or philosophical exercise, but leads us into some important areas of practice. Fook (2002, p. 91) describes the 'critical reconstructive process' as constituting four phases:

- Critical deconstruction
- Resistance
- Challenge
- Critical reconstruction.

This means breaking down prior assumptions and reconstituting mutual understandings in a way which provides a greater degree of autonomy and control to the service user, as well as her or his carers. For example, we may find it important to question implicit gendered assumptions about what is appropriate or acceptable to expect of carers. Just because a wife/female partner has always provided for someone does not mean that it is reasonable to expect her to continue to do so, as the level and nature of need changes.

'Deconstruction' leads to the next phase, 'resistance', where the exposure of implicit assumptions leads us to question the status quo and the prevailing power relations. This, in turn, leads to 'challenge', utilizing techniques of 'naming' the different perspectives and interests represented in a particular practice context. This may be uncomfortable, since it involves questioning those who hold dominant positions, whether in agencies or in their family and other relationships.

Practitioners must be aware of the importance of supporting service users throughout, since they may also be at risk in this context.

Finally, the process is completed by the stage of reconstruction, which involves the creation of new discourses which open up alternative possibilities for the distribution of power and the way in which services are provided and received. 'Reconstruction' might involve both reframing the way in which service users and their needs are understood, and the way in which they are involved in the processes of assessment, planning and intervention:

> From a critical point of view, discourses need to be reconstructed in ways which change dominant power relations, and in ways which allow marginal and silenced perspectives to be heard. (Fook, 2002, p. 97)

Further possibilities are thus offered by 'narrative reconstruction', which enables people to change the 'stories' which define their lives and create their identities. There are a number of ways in which the discourses between practitioners and service users can be changed to transform the sense of self and promote a sense of personal control. For example, language can shift:

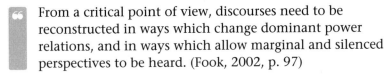

> - From 'cause' to 'effect': rather than 'how did I cause this?' to 'what effect did this have on me?'.
> - From 'blame' to 'responsibility': rather than 'who can I blame for this in the past?' to 'what responsibility can I take now?'.
> - From 'guilt' to 'care'.
> - From 'passive' to 'active'.
> - From 'failure' to success'.
> - From 'negative' to 'positive'.
> - From 'weakness' to 'strength'. (Fook, 2002, p. 140)

Thus, the importance of framing our work in a particular way from the start becomes clear. For example, the tension between the terms 'service user' and 'citizen' needs to be addressed in direct practice. Morris illustrates well the impact of this dichotomy in one particular instance, where the agency and practitioners appear to have been unable to apply a rights perspective. The individual concerned

> needs practical assistance in her home – which as a disabled person she is entitled to under the 1970 Chronically Sick and Disabled Persons Act. Her child has been providing this assistance, yet when she approached social services about an assessment of her own needs for help, they referred her to the children and families section to deal with the situation because they identified her child as a 'young carer' and therefore as a 'child in need'. (Morris, 1997, p. 55)

An approach based on notions of citizenship and rights would probably have led to a different and more empowering outcome. The focus
on 'need' and 'dependency' shifted the concern away from the independent rights of the person concerned, and concentrated attention
on her disability at the expense of her identity as a parent (Morris,
1997, p. 56).

Whilst it is undoubtedly in the fields of disability and mental
health that the strongest impetus has emerged for such challenges to
the dependent identity ascribed to service users, there is no doubt
that similar arguments are being articulated in other areas of practice.
Social work with the homeless, for example, has struggled to move
beyond the pathologizing and controlling aspects of work with a
group whose marginalized status implicitly devalues them. Living on
the streets should not override the importance of individual stories
and aspirations, nor should it undermine service users' part in determining the nature of interventions:

> A more empowering assumption would be that service users
> are 'experts' on their own lives ... Critically reflecting on the
> role of social work in the 'story-telling process' assists the
> practitioner to develop more collaborative and 'client-focused'
> approaches to service provision shifting the focus from social
> control to social justice. (Zufferey and Kerr, 2004, p. 351)

We are reminded of one of the critical functions of reconstruction or
reframing, which is to allow service users to play their part in defining the way in which their concerns are to be viewed and addressed.
It has been observed that 'being heard and having one's story understood are crucial to achieving any positive benefit for the service user
in most kinds of therapeutic relationship' (Gregory and Holloway,
2005, p. 39).

Indeed, it is the reification of terms, and the 'taken-for-granted'
nature of the language used, which must be a central focus of the
social work task. Even the term 'service user', having superseded the
terminology of 'client' and 'patient', may ultimately prove to be
unhelpful. Certainly, as I have progressed in writing this book, I have
become increasingly aware of its limitations, and I know that many
people who use services do not like its connotations of dependency
and a 'partial' identity. The term certainly does not capture the holistic nature of people's lives and aspirations, and it is felt by community organizations which represent people who use services to be an
inaccurate representation of their status and objectves. It may be the
best term available for the moment, but it is incumbent on practitioners to enter into working relationships determined not to see
people *only* as service users, but to focus on their rights and identities

as citizens, including their self-ascribed identities, meanings, hopes and fears.

Towards user-led services: changing power relationships

To what extent, then, do the kind of strategies set out previously lead us to a position where power relations can be renegotiated or transformed in favour of people who use social work services? For practitioners the key question is to decide on the most suitable approach to take in order to influence power relations in favour of their service users. Whilst we may share a general commitment to shifting the balance, the specific form of intervention clearly varies depending on the context. As Adams (2003, p. 60) acknowledges, 'not all interactions between the worker and the service user are likely to have an equal potential for empowering the person'. Despite this, we may be able to articulate some common operating principles which should be seen as crucial. These include:

- Being alert to multiple forms of oppression
- Recognizing and taking account of diversity
- Being ready to take risks to challenge oppression
- Recognizing our own authority and status in the practice setting
- Being willing to negotiate power relationships
- Acknowledging diverse forms of expertise
- Sharing knowledge and expertise
- Creating space for 'the excluded' to have their say
- Recognizing the validity of different perspectives
- Being prepared to share or devolve decision-making capacity
- Promoting assertiveness and self-determination
- Encouraging questioning and challenge (even of ourselves)
- Being willing to advocate on behalf of participants who are 'unheard'
- Looking for sources of solidarity between disenfranchised interests.

In order to be consistent, and consistently effective, in reshaping relationships of power and control, these principles must be applied across all aspects of practice, from the point of initial contact, through assessment and decision-making phases, and on to intervention and service delivery.

Thus, both the structuring and the content of assessment need to be orientated towards the concerns and issues of the service user (and carers), rather than being driven by organizational imperatives. For the practitioner, this may mean having to make hard choices between meeting the operational demands of a bureaucratic organization and active listening (Lymbery, 2001), which is focused on the

practice illustration 8.3

The distribution of power

It is sometimes helpful when undertaking an assessment of need to consider the question: 'who is in the weakest position here?'.

For example, in considering the needs of an older person, it may be important to consider the expectations placed on her or his carer, and whether or not these are legitimate or sustainable.

Bear in mind that many relationships are based on power imbalances, and that both partners may have independent needs which are not always compatible. Carers are entitled to separate assessments, for example, should they so wish.

Intervention should focus on the need to enable each individual concerned to participate and to influence the outcome in their own right.

identified priorities of the person who is being assessed and those around her or him.

This kind of distinction is supported by Smale *et al.* (2000), who have devised and developed a framework for understanding differing models of assessment. They distinguish between 'procedural', 'questioning' and 'exchange' models, which are each premised on a different understanding of the relationship between practitioner and service user. As might be imagined, the procedural model is highly prescriptive and organizationally driven, with needs measured and assessed in standardized fashion against a predetermined set of eligibility criteria. The questioning model also locates authority for judgement and decision-making with the professional as expert, although it takes a more open-ended approach to information gathering. Smale *et al.* prefer the exchange model, precisely because it provides much greater potential for power-sharing and dialogue between social workers and service users. They suggest that the worker's expertise in this context can best be demonstrated 'in the way all [the] other sources of expertise and people are brought into conjunction and successful negotiation with each other' (Smale *et al.*, 2000, p. 151). Their model of assessment depends very much on the worker's role in bringing together knowledge, experience and resources to enable participants to make informed and shared decisions, as far as possible. This is seen as a collaborative exercise, whereby the 'definition of the problem and the options for resolution or management are arrived at as much through the initiative' (Smale *et al.*, 2000, p.

136) of the potential service user, as through organizational demands or the judgement of the social worker.

The attempt to correct imbalances of power represented by this model can also be furthered by measures such as enabling service users to determine where and when meetings will take place, who will attend and how the agenda is to be constructed (Charles, 2004, p. 191).

As we move from the assessment phase to the point at which decisions are made, it may become more problematic to think in terms of genuinely collaborative approaches. It is, after all, in the hands of agencies to determine what resources will be allocated, and the authority does rest with statutory bodies to use legal means to impose interventions where this is deemed necessary. In other words, power dynamics become much more explicit at the point where choices are made about how and with whom to intervene. It may be the case that a more open approach at the initial assessment stage may encourage a greater sense of participation in decision-making, but this may equally be experienced as contradictory by service users who feel that initial promises of consultation and participation have not been met, and that 'the rug has been pulled from underneath them'. Indeed, there is considerable evidence to suggest that both lack of resources and lack of involvement may compromise ostensible commitments to the involvement of service users:

> For children and young people and people with learning difficulties, **the ability to make choices was often limited by a lack of information ... together with a lack of support or creative communication in decision-making ... Disabled people have found that assessment of eligibility for services can pose difficulties for exercising choice and control** ... the imposition of strict ... criteria for access to support services seriously undermines the notion of meaningful participation and choice. (Carr, 2004, p. 11)

These problems are compounded by professionals' assumptions about the 'decision-making competence' (or lack of it) of service users. This, in turn, suggests that the capacity for power-sharing rests at least in part with practitioners, whose own attitudes and behaviour remain important, even where other factors such as limited resources come into play (Lymbery, 2004b). Both structural and process changes may be needed to ensure that service users feel more engaged in this aspect of the intervention. For example, provision of *as much as possible* of the pertinent information will be an important prerequisite. It is also necessary to ensure that support and time (Carr, 2004, p. 20) are made available, sometimes in the face of organizational pressures. It is important to resist 'tidy' solutions in messy situations, where the demand for certainty and permanence may run counter to the service user's need to negotiate change over time. When working with complex interpersonal issues:

> A reflective practitioner will explore the dynamics of the relationship, developing the ability to use growing knowledge about this in the ensuing practice ... Practice based on technical rationality would search for the 'correct' solution ... practice grounded in reflection-in-action will seek an outcome grounded in the uniqueness of [service users'] experience.
> (Lymbery, 2004b, p. 175)

The culmination of the intervention process is represented by the service provided, or the process initiated following the assessment and decision-making stages. Here, too, the question of power and control is central. Indeed, in order to give meaning to participatory strategies, service users must be able to feel that they continue to hold some influence over the way in which interventions are delivered throughout. Despite some limitations, there are a number of models of service provision which offer indications as to how this might be achieved, including, for instance, family group conferences (Jackson and Morris, 1999; Brown, 2003) and direct payments (Stainton and Boyce, 2004; Askheim, 2005). Common to both these initiatives is a sense in which service users feel that they control key aspects of the planning and delivery process. For example, in 'conferences' involving young people, the choice lay with them as to who should attend and what information should be shared (Jackson and Morris, 1999, p. 624). For those using direct payments, control over daily routines and life choices appears to be more easily achievable:

> The advantages are that you can start to relive your life in the way that you want to. You can, say, pick your own clothes, where when you have got an agency you can't do that.
> (Direct payments user, quoted in Stainton and Boyce, 2004, p. 450)

These are specific practice innovations, both of which have experienced difficulties in becoming widely accepted, so it is important to avoid generalizing too readily from them. Nevertheless, they do highlight key points which need to be considered in addressing questions of power and control in service delivery. It seems clear, for example, that devolving control over resource allocation to service users can be a significant step (Stainton and Boyce, 2004). Equally, however, placing service users at the centre of the intervention process provides them with the authority to apply their own definitions of 'the problem', and, thus, their own strategies for addressing external concerns. This approach, though, seems to have met with some reluctance on the part of state agencies and professionals to cede control. Where 'abuse or serious offending has taken place', professionals may be more reluctant to give up 'their decision making power to families, especially when they often blame the family for the current problems' (Jackson and Morris, 1999, p. 627).

Despite such concerns, there are common strands likely to be found in approaches which seek to equalize imbalances of power in the interest of service users. Practitioners undertake their initial assessment openly, and in an exploratory fashion; they share information and options as fully as possible with service users; they seek to identify and engage with service users' own definitions of matters of concern; and they look for ways of agreeing a shared agenda, rather than imposing external expectations, either of a procedural or substantive nature. Access to resources is negotiated, and outcomes are sought which are defined in service users' rather than agency terms – narrowly prescriptive solutions are to be avoided, since they are unlikely to accord with the diversity and complexity of peoples' changing lives. Subsequent processes of evaluation and review should also seek to be participative and developmental, rather than determined by operational demands, such as performance targets which have only limited bearing on the lived experience of service users themselves.

main points

- Social workers need to take an active approach to empowering service users

- This means adopting a spirit of challenge at all levels of interaction, including the language used to define problems and needs

- Mundane procedures and behaviours incorporate implicit assumptions about power and authority, so practitioners must take a reflective approach to their own actions

- Strategies such as 'reframing' and 'reconstruction' provide practical tools for transforming power relationships with service users

- Effective empowerment, however, cannot be achieved by focusing solely at the individual level.

taking it further

- *Social Work Ideals and Practice Realities*, edited by Mark Lymbery and Sandra Butler (Palgrave Macmillan, 2004), does what the title claims in providing a series of insights into the concrete and everyday challenges faced by social workers in applying their values effectively in context.
- Pam Trevithick's comprehensive book *Social Work Skills* is a highly effective source of guidance, making clear and understandable connections between underlying principles and the reality of effective practice (2nd edn, Open University Press, 2005).
- Gerald Smale and colleagues' book *Social Work and Social Problems* (Palgrave Macmillan, 2000) is very helpful in offering ways of linking social work processes, such as assessment, to their contextual setting.

Websites

http://www.swap.ac.uk
This is a valuable resource offering a wide range of learning material relevant to the development of social work skills.

http://sieswe.org
This is the site of the Scottish Institute for Excellence in Social Work Education, which offers some valuable resources, including a detailed review of different models of assessment.

9 Groups, Communities and Systems

Making links

It has been a central theme of this book that social work practice must take account of and renegotiate power relationships in order to stand any chance of achieving effective outcomes. However, it has also become clear that these relationships cannot be viewed simplistically, for example, purely as structural forces which operate consistently and impose uniform outcomes. As we have seen previously, the dynamics of power depend on a variety of factors which operate at a number of distinct levels.

Whilst the primary focus of social work practice is usually characterized in individual terms, each service user and her or his circumstances will be crucially affected by the ebbs and flows of these patterns of power, albeit each will be affected differently.

It is because of this that social workers *must* be able to situate their work with individuals within a wider contextual framework. This involves both a willingness to analyse power relationships in terms of the interaction between individual circumstances and the social context, and a practice orientation which recognizes the need to intervene in systems and structures.

It has been argued at times that social work has no real business to go beyond the task of ministering to individual needs. For some, the central purpose of the profession should be to provide caring services to those in urgent need of help or protection, but that it should accept that such important, but relatively modest, goals should be the limits of the profession's aspirations (Davies, 1981). According to proponents of this view, characterized as 'the maintenance school' (Dominelli, 2004, p. 71), it is important to be realistic and to concentrate one's energies where they are likely to have most impact, even if this itself is limited:

 The goals of practice are determined primarily by agency policy and the social worker's contribution is to work towards the achievement of those goals ...

> [People are] not so malleable nor [their] circumstances so amenable to change as to be radically reformed by the mere intervention of a social worker ... it would be better if such changes as the social worker can prompt were to be considered rather as maintenance. (Davies, 1981, p. 116)

Social workers, it has been argued, have two main functions in this respect: working 'at the interface of the individual and society', they should be expected to 'curb some of the excesses of deviant behaviour' in the context of child protection, youth justice or compulsory mental health treatment; and, they should try to improve the circumstances of those who 'are finding it difficult to cope', by promoting personal growth and capacity for 'self-help' (Davies, 1981, p. 138). The focus of intervention should almost exclusively be on the individual and her or his difficulties. There is no sense here of an interactive process between individual service users and the social milieu, rather the social worker is 'maintaining members *in* society' (p. 139).

Criticisms of this position have tended to focus on its denial of a 'political' role for social workers, for example in terms of promoting anti-oppressive values and practice (Dominelli, 1998, p. 12). However, it is not just a matter of ideological differences; there are other limitations to an exclusively individualized approach to practice. By locating 'problems' solely with the individual, this perspective denies the validity of the service user's own perspective, and necessary connections are not made between individual needs and external factors. This also implicitly lays the blame for their problems with people themselves ('victim-blaming'), and it excludes service users from playing a part in developing their own solutions. Furthermore, it precludes any question of pursuing change in the systems and structures within which problems arise. The individualization of problems prevents us from seeing them as products of complex dynamics, which *necessarily* involve interactions between social systems, communities and individuals (Smale *et al.*, 2000). The example of youth crime illustrates this point, since culpability is often placed exclusively with young people who offend; yet, becoming a young offender can be seen to depend both on a range of influences which affect young people's circumstances and behaviour, and also on the power of the state and its agencies to define what counts as a 'crime' (Smale *et al.*, 2000, p. 89).

Understanding power: systems thinking

In the social work arena, the problem of the interaction between individuals and their social contexts has been a matter of continuing concern. This is partly, as Payne (2005) observes, because the precise nature of the social work task has also been a matter of continuing debate; our view of the appropriate intervention strategy in any particular context depends to a large extent on our theoretical and ideological orientation. Thus, social work is contested both in theory and in the 'real world' of practice. What is not in dispute is that social work involves a process of intervention with people experiencing difficulties in some aspect of their personal and social functioning. Thus, in analysing these issues and devising intervention strategies, the importance of the interaction between people and their environment cannot be overlooked by practitioners. One approach which has offered useful insights in this respect has been systems theory:

> " The focus of social work practice is on the interactions between people and systems in the social environment. People are dependent on systems for help in obtaining the material, emotional, or spiritual resources and the services and opportunities they need to realize their aspirations and to help them cope with their life tasks. (Pincus and Minahan, 1973, p. 3)

The notion of systems has proved to be very helpful to social work, because it provides a sense of the distinctive nature of people's family and community relationships, at the same time as relating these to the structures and mechanisms available to intervene. Pincus and Minahan identify three categories of 'support systems' which are available to people, and which may, or may not, be providing the resources they need. These are: i) informal or natural resource systems; ii) formal resource systems; and iii) societal resource systems. Informal systems consist of family, friends, colleagues and other members of one's natural or organic social network. Formal systems are those organizations which are constituted around common interests to provide mutual support or share activities. These might, in some instances, be carrying out social work functions such as befriending, counselling or advocacy. Societal systems include government agencies and resources which are available to provide for both day-to-day and emergency social needs. The purpose of social work is to resolve problematic issues which arise at the point of interaction between people and their social setting, that is, when one or other of their 'resource systems' is not working effectively. Intervention therefore goes beyond the rather limited goals specified by the 'maintenance' model, since it may involve changing systems as well as individual service users. This account offers positive benefits, such as moving away from a 'victim-blaming' approach and providing for the service user to engage in the problem-solving process.

Pincus and Minahan have offered a framework for intervention, which elaborates further their notion of 'systems' as the basis for practice:

> 1 *Change agent system*: The change agent and the people who are part of his [sic] agency or employing organization.
> 2 *Client system*: People who sanction or ask for the change agent's services, who are the expected beneficiaries of service, and who have a working agreement or contract with the change agent.
> 3 *Target system*: People who need to be changed to accomplish the goals of the change agent.
> 4 *Action system*: The change agent and the people he works with and through to accomplish his goals and influence the target system.
> (Pincus and Minahan, 1973, p. 63)

The social worker is the 'change agent' according to this classification, and her or his system includes the agency she or he represents and the resources available to it (Pincus and Minahan, 1973, p. 54). Service users are represented by the 'client system', and, of course, this very terminology shifts the spotlight away from the individual to the network of relationships within which she or he is located, and which may be closely implicated in the specific problem identified. The target and action systems represent those who need to be changed to achieve the aims of the intervention, and the means of achieving this. Again, the concern is shifted from the individual in isolation to the network of resources and relationships which may need to be challenged and changed.

Systems approaches are of value because they begin to develop a holistic view of the problems encountered by service users. Included in the scope of the social work task are the 'social networks' and 'power relationships' which impact on the particular practice setting (Payne, 2005, p. 146). Systems theory may be very helpful in bringing into focus aspects of service users' lives which might otherwise have gone unconsidered. The drug or alcohol problems of parents, for example, may be viewed in a rather different light in the context of oppressive family relationships, or alternatively where there are no 'informal' systems of support available. In this way, power dynamics and their implications may become more clearly understood.

Indeed, a number of advantages to the applications of systems approaches are identified. They are noted as 'interactive, concentrating on the effects of one person on another' (Payne, 2005, p. 157). They do not prioritize any particular target or level of intervention, and thus avoid the risk of stigmatizing individuals identified in the role of 'service user'. At the same time, unequal distributions of resources and oppressive relationships may well become more apparent.

However, systems theories are problematic in some respects. For example, they help to illustrate the dynamic nature of social relationships and the multifaceted nature of social work problems, but they do not offer any clues as to the substantive reasons for these. The underlying causes of disadvantage and social exclusion are not explored, and this, in turn, limits the scope of guidance as to how to intervene. There may also be an implicit assumption that the purpose of social work interventions is to make systems work better, rather than to initiate structural change (Payne, 2005, p. 158). This could be highly problematic if it leads to a perception that it is better to try to sustain or rebuild damaging relationships rather than bring them to an end – a questionable strategy in the context of domestic violence, for instance.

Despite these concerns, systems theory provides an important starting point for our consideration of the impact of power dynamics between individuals, groups and communities, and the implications of these for social work ideas and practice. Thus, ecological theories have sought to go beyond the rather mechanistic language suggested by 'systems' in order to consider the importance of relationships and social networks in constituting the context within which problems arise (Jack, 1997; Payne, 2005). Such work suggests that people's capacities, personal resources and resilience are significantly affected by the quality of the social environment in which they are living. It is noted that the quality of life can be affected by the community resources available. Thus, in 'the socially impoverished neighbourhood', levels of informal mutual aid are diminished, and lack of 'emotional support from social networks' has been observed to have a negative impact on lone mothers' interactions with their children (Jack, 1997, p. 111). Related to this kind of approach are models which emphasize the importance of the 'fit' between people and their social environments. The quality of this fit clearly depends on the interaction between the two, and this, in turn, is influenced by a number of factors, including the individual's 'social position' and the power relationships impacting on the individual (Payne, 2005, p. 151). In both these examples, the distribution of power in networks and communities is seen as an important factor, having a direct impact on the quality of life of those who are likely to use social work services.

For Smale et al., similarly, the community is a critical factor in setting the stage for social work practice. They criticize a rather romanticized view of communities as simply offering a repository of 'untapped resources', suggesting that they must also be considered as a source and incubator of problems. They cite the example of wide-spread racial harassment, suggesting that the community and the way in which it is experienced are shaped by such behaviour:

> Many people are in communities which ignore, neglect, reject, persecute or in some other way cause them stress, or leave them alone with their pain. Most people are in communities and networks where resources are unevenly distributed, and some feel powerless relative to others. Often people known to workers are in networks that label them as 'clients'. The worker will deliberately, or unwittingly, but nevertheless inevitably be part of these processes. (Smale *et al.*, 2000, p. 90)

Thinking about communities in terms of systems or networks enables us to identify the overlapping and interactive nature of people's relationships. Whilst social work practitioners are part of formal, organizational systems, which may be perceived as having certain characteristics (such as authority and control of resources), service users will inevitably also be members of 'different interlocking or overlapping networks' (*ibid.*). The interplay of these networks may be of crucial importance in determining their current experience and the difficulties they face. For social work practitioners, it is important to bring this view of 'the problem' to bear, in order to avoid reinforcing dominant perceptions. This is an important step in resisting the tendency to 'individualize' problems, imposing definitions on those who are least able to resist them. It also represents a challenge for practitioners who may find that tackling prevailing assumptions and behaviour becomes an integral part of the task, if solutions are to be found which genuinely empower and create new opportunities for service users.

Exploring power relationships: tuning in to the networks

Having set out the reasons for seeing people's systems, communities, networks and relationships as important in social work, we must now consider approaches which will enable us to explore these, particularly the patterns of power which might be observed.

A colleague who has worked with disabled children comments that she found a 'systems' approach particularly helpful in evaluating children's circumstances and determining the appropriate focus for intervention (Fitchett, 2005). As she points out, children with disabilities and their families often find themselves caught up in a complex array of statutory services, with health, social work and education all having distinct but related responsibilities. In addition to the sometimes confusing and intrusive part played by these various formal 'systems', other networks are also likely to be important, such as the wider family, community resources and organizations representing service user interests. However, the sheer number of different perspectives may have the effect of shining the spotlight ever more intensely on the child, in the manner of Foucault's (1979) 'army of experts'.

The consequence of this may be that the focus of concern is limited to negatively perceived aspects of the child's behaviour or personal characteristics at the expense of both positive personal qualities and the role of other influences which have an impact on her or his life. The potential for problematizing or 'scapegoating' the individual is clear.

By contrast, an approach which *begins* with an attempt to locate the child within a network of power relationships may provide a much more complete picture. A number of benefits may flow from this. Firstly, it will be possible to de-emphasize those aspects of the child's behaviour or experience which seem particularly problematic. These will be addressed only *within* and in relation to the wider context. In addition, the role of other systems in constituting the 'problem' in a particular way will come under scrutiny. Concerns about problematic behaviour, for example, may come to be understood in the light of the limited networks of support available to children and their families. Interestingly, this approach can be seen as having an international application. In Uganda, it has been found that 'poverty affects coping behaviour because it reduces the external resources available for facilitating such behaviour' (Hartley *et al.*, 2005, p. 172).

The failure of external networks to provide adequate levels of support may itself contribute to certain behavioural problems, as primary carers become tired and stressed. Rejection and isolation may contribute to children's sense of powerlessness and exclusion, which may exacerbate behaviour classified as 'challenging':

> Many children were staying with their grandparents or other elderly relatives having been rejected by their parents and removed from their siblings. They did not attend school. Many of the children did not join in with other children and were sometimes kept in their rooms all day, away from any community activities. Some children with communication problems were observed screaming in sheer frustration at their inability to communicate. (Hartley *et al.*, 2005, p. 174)

Thus, the child's attempts to express her or his feelings and to challenge exclusionary practices may be open to interpretation as simply a manifestation of 'challenging behaviour'. Taking a 'systems' approach enables the practitioner to explore both the way in which the child is being disempowered, and the processes by which she or he becomes identified as the sole source of the problem.

Further to this, the process of locating the service user within a wider pattern of networks and relationships assists the social worker to consider the 'interactive' nature of these relationships. We thus gain a sense of the way in which social realities are negotiated and constructed between participants, rather than being fixed attributes or characteristics of the individuals who are 'objects of concern' (Smale *et al.*, 2000, p. 88). This is characterized in the form of 'feedback' mechanisms, or amplification processes, whereby the messages conveyed generate responses which, in turn, act as confirmation (or modification) of initial assumptions. Again, it is important also to reflect on the implications of this in terms of the relative capacity of those involved to define behaviour and its characteristics:

> Systems thinkers ... would see the attribution of individual blame within patterns of ... behaviour involving the reciprocal behaviour of several, if not many, people ... [and] as being dependent on the position of the person making the attribution. (Smale *et al.*, 2000, p. 97)

Thus, the very act of defining a situation, a person or a pattern of behaviour as problematic by someone in a position of authority or holding expertise may act as the starting point of a process whereby the response is interpreted effectively in terms of the initial definition.

The task of the practitioner is to incorporate awareness of these interactive processes into her or his assessment. In some ways, this represents an extension of the notion of the 'reflective practitioner' to encompass the systems and processes which impact on service users:

> we need to shift the focus somewhat and ask different and better questions about power relations. How do professionals convey authority in their interactions with clients? How do they exercise control? What strategies do clients adopt to resist this control? Who defines 'the facts' and how? These seem much more fruitful avenues for analysis because they do not make presumptions about power. (Taylor and White, 2000, p. 115)

We should, of course, broaden this discussion in acknowledgement of the likelihood that it is not just professionals and formal systems which have the ability to generate authoritative versions of 'the problem' and its causes. These prescriptive and often pejorative depictions can just as easily arise in family and community networks, and, in the same way as organizational accounts do, the initial portrayal of the subject of concern may carry considerable weight (Smale *et al.*, 2000, p. 97).

Reconceptualizing the service user's needs to take account of these systemic factors also leads to the consideration of a wider range of options for addressing concerns. In relation to the specific example of disabled children in Uganda, the importance is recognized of developing and supporting external resources to assist children and families, rather than concentrating only on individualized intervention programmes (Hartley *et al.*, 2005). This means that the focus of intervention may move away from the specific service user to one or more aspects of the wider networks which impact upon the individual.

At the same time as the value of systemic understandings is recognized, we must also take account of a number of further issues which arise. Firstly, it is important not to allow a systems approach to act as a vehicle for transforming a pathology of the individual into a means of blaming families, neighbourhoods or communities for the problems encountered by social work. The tendency to think in terms of 'cycles of disadvantage', 'deprived neighbourhoods' or to apply racial and cultural stereotypes may generate easy explanations without in any way providing us with a full or acceptable account of the cause of our concern. In social work practice, for example, the 'causes of crime' may appear to be clearly identified in terms of the upbringing and social circumstances of young offenders (Smith, 2003), but this kind of analysis also leaves a number of other questions unanswered, which are important in terms of generating effective critical practice. Notably, the way in which behaviours are defined as 'anti-social' or 'criminal' is left unexplored by this form of analysis. At the same time, however, the impact of particular forms of behaviour on other members of the community may also be omitted from our explanatory frame. In both respects, aspects of power need to be considered; firstly, in terms of the authority to define what and who will be criminalized, and, secondly, in terms of the social dynamics operating within particular neighbourhoods (which may be framed in terms of age, gender, ethnicity or other factors). A social work response which does not encompass these dimensions is open either to the accusation of merely 'excusing' unacceptable behaviour or of compounding embedded processes of discrimination and exclusion.

Finally, in this context, it is important to consider the implications for social work of organizational imperatives, which may appear to set limits to a systemic approach. We may encounter implicit or explicit exclusions within agency policies and procedures which inhibit our ability to look beyond individual circumstances and personalized 'needs'. Adams's reflections on the problems and possibilities offered by the notion of 'boundaries' are highly relevant here. Boundaries insert themselves (and are inserted) into social work practice in a number of ways: to create a sense of professional identity; to make workloads manageable; to define areas of responsibility; to establish lines of accountability; and to create uncontested areas of authority. They are thus important in the sense of giving social work practice a sense of its own legitimacy and integrity, but they also act to set limits to what practitioners are expected or entitled to do. This may include being discouraged from questioning the way in which organizations define problems:

> A senior manager produces an organisation chart to demonstrate that the problems lie 'out there', are not his responsibility and he cannot be held accountable for them ... The job descriptions of staff state that they carry out the procedures prescribed and do not go beyond these. They are taken as forbidding staff to cross boundaries, or only cross those authorised by management. Boundary crossing in other areas, such as networking, is perceived as a threat. (Adams, 2005, p. 113)

Practitioners may feel a substantial degree of pressure to restrict themselves to their own areas of recognized expertise. Not only are certain areas of practice apparently off-limits, but so are certain ways of analysing service users' problems.

For example, in relation to the issue of young offenders discussed above, social work matters (young people's well-being and personal development) are increasingly seen as irrelevant to the issue of accounting for and responding to their behaviour. Systems approaches may present challenges for practitioners, who will find it necessary to cross boundaries in order to take an integrated view of the relationship between the behaviour of young people who offend and their welfare needs. To engage with the 'problem' in its widest sense may necessitate taking a critical approach to the youth justice system. As Adams (2005) suggests, this may be an essential attribute of an effective practitioner in this setting, but it may also demand a certain readiness to take risks.

Reframing (again): whose problem is it anyway?

This discussion of boundaries, and the implied attribution of responsibility which goes with it, may prove a useful starting point for our consideration of appropriate strategies for redefining power relationships between service users, 'systems' and networks.

In practice the starting point for assessment and intervention for social workers is likely to be an identified concern about the needs and/or risks associated with a particular individual. This may come about through the routine process of referral to a statutory agency with primary responsibility for protecting vulnerable individuals or promoting their welfare. However, it is almost inevitable that this initial concern will also involve others, whether this be alleged perpetrators of abuse, carers under stress, concerned relatives or those at risk from unacceptable behaviour. This, in turn, brings into play the perceptions of others, and the network of relationships and influences which surround the individual who is the focus of professional interest. As we have already observed, these relationships are permeated by a diverse range of power dynamics. The starting point for the practitioner's intervention must, therefore, encompass not just the individual but the network of forces surrounding her or him. This, indeed, is one of the most important insights offered by systems theory. The fundamental observation that people and their social networks are interdependent (Pincus and Minahan, 1973, p. 3) requires social work to focus its interventions on these interactive systems and processes as much as on their consequences in terms of individuals' behaviour and needs. Any practice ideology which does not encompass an idea of the service user's 'connectedness' (Owusu-Bempah and Howitt, 2000; Owusu-Bempah, 2002; Korbin, 2003) is necessarily incomplete.

There is potential value in making use of various 'mapping' techniques which help to generate an understanding of the specific context (Rose and Aldgate, 2000; Bradley and Parker, 2003). 'Ecomaps', for example, are recommended as a way of generating an understanding of the relative impact of different external forces on families and individuals. This

> allows the service user and worker together to plot key figures and resources in the person's current network, the direction of flows of energy and resources and the quality of the connections, whether strong, tenuous or stressful. It gives a powerful visual summary of the client's life situation and can provoke reflection and discussion. (Gilligan, 1999, p. 82)

Not least, the value of this kind of mapping exercise is reflected in the process of actively engaging the service user, who is able to give her or his perspective on important influences and relationships in her or his life.

Further support for this is given in the context of work with children with disabilities who are abused. Given that disability often involves systemic discrimination and 'oppression', we should not then consider the abused child only in terms of his or her 'symptoms'

(Kennedy, 2002, p. 147). It is important to consider incidents of abuse within a broader pattern of oppression and marginalization which may incorporate the abuser as well as the abused.

The initial exercise of mapping interactions and dynamics, then, provides an opportunity to explore power relationships with and from the perspective of service users, which may reveal a much more varied and nuanced picture than a straightforward focus on the individual alone. Gilligan points out, too, that this approach helps us to distinguish between perspectives which may otherwise appear as undifferentiated:

> While children's needs and interests are often close to those of their parents, they must be seen as separate and distinct, especially by child care professionals working with children and young people at risk. (Gilligan, 1999, p. 71)

This, too, is potentially empowering in addressing the risk of ageism and helping to validate the child's distinctive perspective, and in bringing into focus relationships which might not otherwise have been given adequate weight (for example peer attachments or ties with absent relatives).

Further consequences of this approach to 'reframing' might also be to help us to recognize more fully the way that external factors impact on the lives of service users and their families, and thus to move away from an excessive concentration on the shortcomings of the care and support available. Indeed, this appears to be the aspiration behind recent developments in policy and guidance (Department of Health, 2000, p. 89), which have sought to provide models of assessment which give equal weight to 'family and environmental factors' in the task of assessing the welfare needs of children.

Empirical support for this ecological approach has been provided, where assessment and intervention have been informed by principles of networking and community empowerment intended to guard against the risk of parental stress and consequent harm to children. In one Canadian scheme:

> The [Parent Support Worker's] activity with mothers included helping them map their personal social networks ... The PSW then acted as a consultant to the mothers to help hem change these personal connections in ways that would activate support and reduce stress ... Overall, project results were encouraging ... the level of emotional support, information exchange and advice increased ... the personal social networks of the project parents began to cluster and give more sense of community. (Wachtel, 1994, p. 33)

This suggests two more important consequences of an approach based on building the capacity of groups, networks and systems. The object of social work interventions must change; and, as a consequence, the role of the social worker must also be reconceptualized. Firstly, practitioners must be prepared to work both with and beyond individuals. The aims of their interventions are to do with improving the capacity and resources of disadvantaged people, and this necessitates working with those relationships and systems which are capable of generating this kind of outcome.

In the same way as the Canadian model outlined above indicates, Adams (2003) argues that the social work practitioner must be prepared to work with people as members of groups and networks. Gilligan argues, for example, that schools have been an overlooked site and resource for social work with children. This has been evidenced by the apparent lack of interest in the educational experience of children for whom social work agencies have a responsibility (Gilligan, 1998, p. 14), despite the evidence that marginalization at school is a common experience for looked after children (Stein, 2002). Thus 'a key prerequisite for progress ... is a conviction within child and family social work ... that the school–social work relationship is a part of its "core business"' (Gilligan, 1998, p. 21).

This, in turn, leads us to reconsider the role of the social worker, who must be prepared to work '*between* people and resource systems' as well as '*within* systems' (Pincus and Minahan, 1973, p. 33). The social worker is to act as a 'facilitator' in order to build effective relationships between people and resource systems.

Systems theory itself does not address the issue of power directly, but its proponents show a clear understanding of the kind of strategies available to practitioners in seeking to bring influence to bear. Questions of credibility and authority come to the fore, as does the issue of the 'cost of exercising influence' (Pincus and Minahan, 1973, p. 268). The social worker is able, for example, to draw fairly freely on her or his own 'expertness' in order to determine outcomes in relation to an issue where this is seen as a legitimate exercise of professional authority (for example taking a view about the social functioning of an older person seeking additional support at home). However, the attempt to work between systems, and to represent service user interests in other spheres, may leave this claim to expertise open to challenge or rejection (for example where the social worker seeks to advance the professional opinion that a child's interests may not be served by being excluded from school). The consequences may be somewhat problematic:

> The exercise of influence can ... restrict future options of the worker because of the effects it may have on ongoing and future relationships ... Once the worker operates in the context of a conflictual relationship, it is difficult for him [sic] to assume roles such as a mediator and to use other means of influence, such as persuasion. (Pincus and Minahan, 1973, p. 269)

Nonetheless, it is a consequence of our earlier analysis that social workers must be prepared to work in support of service users' interests in areas where their 'rights' to intervene may be questioned. The importance of demonstrating solidarity and support for service users must be emphasized; at the same time this is not always a comfortable position for the practitioner to adopt.

Power thus becomes a crucial feature of the role of social work in its intervention in networks and systems. Social work practitioners will, in most cases, find themselves working alongside and on behalf of individuals and groups who are marginalized and disadvantaged. Attempting to change their relationships with other interests is therefore likely to involve a reordering of power in some way. This may involve a relatively straightforward 'brokerage' role, which focuses on enhancing mutual capacities and building 'social capital', along the lines suggested by the Canadian example above (Wachtel, 1994). It may involve networking to promote better information, access and participation rights, as in accessing resources to meet local needs; Adams (2003, p. 85) gives the example of his own involvement in community resource building. It may even involve the kind of 'reconciliation' between the demands of 'the state' and the interests of service users, as Davies (1994) suggests. But this role may also involve challenging the exclusionary and discriminatory aspects of existing institutions and community bodies, for instance in pursuing less punitive interventions with young people who offend (Smith, 1987). Questioning and challenge may well be a necessary feature of the social work task.

Generating power: changing relationships in networks and systems

As the preceding discussion has shown, social work is *and must be* about change, not just at the level of the atomized individual, but also in the systems and networks that frame the individual's experience and circumstances. At this point, we will turn to consider some of the opportunities and strategies available to social workers to undertake this wider project.

At its core, the challenge for practitioners here is to resist and develop alternatives to the processes of individualization which threaten to compromise much social work practice. This challenge arises because social work is fundamentally structured in such a way as to focus primarily on the needs of service users in isolation (a 'deficit' model). Working with groups and communities is not prioritized, or even seen as legitimate, in the context in which much mainstream practice is carried out. To reclaim this aspect of social work as an important and productive area of intervention is both necessary and a significant challenge. Despite recurrent endorsements of collective approaches to intervention in both policy (see, for example, Barclay, 1982) and practice (Dominelli, 2004), such forms of practice lie on the margins of social work (Payne, 2002). Some would argue that increasing emphasis on managerial and 'technical' priorities has in fact further diminished social workers' room for manoeuvre (Lymbery, 2001).

Despite these trends, much emphasis is placed on the importance of interventions at all levels in policy pronouncements on the expected skills and qualities of trained social workers (Quality Assurance Agency, 2000; Department of Health, 2002b; TOPSS, 2002). Qualified practitioners are expected to be equipped to 'interact with individuals, families, carers, groups and communities to achieve change and development and to improve life opportunities' (Department of Health, 2002b, p. 5). Additionally, social workers are encouraged to 'support the development of networks to meet assessed needs and planned outcomes' (*ibid.*).

This appears to provide encouragement to practitioners to take on a proactive approach to working with a range of interests in order to promote positive outcomes for service users. This is further underpinned by reference to the importance of advocacy on behalf of 'individuals, families, carers, groups and communities' (Department of Health, 2002b, p. 6). Social work practitioners therefore appear to have a mandate from authoritative sources to develop a wide range of interventions in order to promote the personal and social well-being of those who have welfare needs. The challenge is to give all forms of intervention equal and appropriate weight:

> We are ... encouraged to work from an ecological perspective, yet it is unclear how these requirements can be met within a climate that individualizes problems and solutions and where we have lost some of the skills and interventions required for collective action ... To intervene effectively in this area ... involves, importantly, an in-depth knowledge and understanding of the way that organizations ... operate. (Trevithick, 2005, p. 75)

Individualizing trends can be identified in such diverse areas as 'care management' for older people, and the Connexions service for young people, both of which are observed to be dominated by a 'case management' philosophy (Jeffs and Smith, 2001; Lymbery, 2004b). The task facing social work is to reclaim the right to engage constructively with the collective interests which are able to offer a sense of strength and cohesion to people, especially those who are marginalized or oppressed.

For practitioners, this probably means achieving three objectives: acquiring networking skills, developing relationships with local networks, groups and agencies, and, crucially, creating the space and time to prioritize work with collective service user interests. One approach recommended is 'to slice the community by topic, such as employment, education, volunteering, arts, faith and cultural communities, sport and exercise, and local neighbourhoods' (Bates and Butler, 2004, p. 122). Social work teams can thus realistically share the responsibility for making effective 'community connections' and, drawing on mutual resources, enhance opportunities for service users. It can be seen that this approach is also likely to increase the span of influence of the practitioners concerned, to the extent that they become seen as proactive contributors to a range of communal networks (the total 'power' capacity thus increases; see Chapter 2).

Building on their knowledge of shared community interests, social workers may be able to offer an effective contribution as 'facilitators' (Adams, 2003, p. 108), for example, in promoting the development and maintenance of 'self-help groups'. Whilst such groups may be organized around specific and typical social work concerns, such as mental health, the purpose of the intervention is to assist groups to establish their own means for mutual support and empowerment. The social worker can contribute positively in a number of ways (*ibid.*), including the provision of access to potential resources, promotion of the group's aims and objectives with other professionals, liaison and making connections, practical and professional advice, and the ability to act as a 'sounding board' for new ideas or for problem-solving.

In this context, the notion of the 'bridge builder' is quite helpful. The bridge builder's task is to identify areas of potential need, to locate possible partners and alliances, and to develop routes by which people may find the means to achieve their aims and desired outcomes:

 Bridge builders work as both 'travel agents' and 'travel companions' ... Travel agents know what is available in the community, provide comprehensive information about

> opportunities and occasionally create new locations, while travel companions accompany the person into community settings. (Bates and Butler, 2004, p. 125)

The role of bridge builder is necessarily complex because it involves developing different approaches and strategies depending on the context, and it often requires an ability to address the dynamics of oppression experienced by particular groups. According to Bates and Butler (2004, p. 127) it is not just a matter of developing appropriate skills, but also of being able to demonstrate a particular kind of commitment, including respect for different value systems, a readiness to work alongside groups and, sometimes, a willingness to challenge vested interests within and outside one's own agency. They also believe that social workers should be well-equipped to undertake this role because of their own value base and their anti-oppressive orientation to practice. Allied to this, the necessity of taking a holistic view of need, and being committed to a user-centred approach, should lead to a readiness to seek out solutions based on connections and common interests between service users.

Mullender (2002) argues that working with people in groups has real potential in terms of challenging oppression and promoting self-determination, citing the example of domestic violence, in particular. For her, it is the very act of making connections which brings into the open something which 'thrives ... behind closed doors' (p. 66). For both women and children who are abused in this way, the potential of groups is significant. They help those who are victimized to address the issues of responsibility and blame, in ways which are not available through individual work alone. Children, for example, become aware that life need not be characterized by perpetual fear and stress. Meeting and hearing from others is empowering in itself, and provides a very important opportunity to express feelings, to deal with guilt, to build self-esteem and to 'learn new ways of keeping safe' (Mullender, 2002, p. 68). Groups such as this can also empower those experiencing violence to feel that they have the capacity to resist and challenge what is happening. Like children, women who experience domestic violence can find strength in sharing their experiences and can develop the capacity to make choices and take control of their lives.

The opportunity to carry out this kind of work with groups and networks is often 'hard to find in most statutory social work ... settings' (Mullender, 2002, p. 67), but it is an integral part of the social work task (as we have already noted). She points out that the opportunity to develop this kind of supportive service through working collectively is to be found 'all over local authority settings' and in a variety of community services which are closely related to the social work arena. Increasingly this is the case, as initiatives such as Sure Start and Children's Centres become more widely established, and as social work practitioners are located with these new programmes.

practice illustration 9.1

Domestic violence and empowering networks

The practical goal achieved in securing a place in a refuge for a woman experiencing domestic violence and her children is important in itself, but it also creates an opportunity for her to gain access to supportive and empowering networks amongst her peers, volunteers and other workers.

Social workers need to consider their own potential role in linking with and developing enabling groups of this kind.

In order to practice effectively in this way, social workers need not only to gain space, time and permissions from their agencies, but also to have the appropriate 'networking skills' to be able to promote empowering groups and organizations (Trevithick, 2005, p. 226). These may be seen, however, as a development of the existing skills base, rather than the addition of a whole new body of competences. For example, the recruitment of people and establishment of appropriate groups will depend on an appreciation of diversity and difference. Social workers will thus be aware of the need to avoid making assumptions that experiencing domestic violence generates such a sense of commonality that women's religious and cultural differences can be overlooked. Other social work skills, such as mediating, advocacy and assessment are equally likely to be of value in identifying and supporting social networks as they are in working with individuals.

As Adams (2003) notes, social work involvement in network building and support has its complications. For instance, the use of professional resources to promote independence and self-sufficiency amongst groups and organizations leads to difficult decisions about the appropriate time to withdraw, as well as creating the risk that the group's agenda conflicts with those of social work practitioners or agencies. Of course, this serves to re-emphasize a central underlying theme of changing the balance in power relationships, which is that of giving up control, whether as professionals or as agencies, and that we must be ready to be challenged. Bearing in mind the strategies available to service users (Chapter 7), we should accept that 'real participation' (Adams, 2003, p. 184) involves conceding responsibility for fundamental decisions to the people who are at the centre of the initiative in question, that is, service users. We can, and should, therefore expect that sometimes our own role and activities will be questioned. A certain level of discomfort should perhaps be accepted as part of the job, providing an important safeguard against complacency or oppressive practice.

taking it further

■ Pincus and Minahan's *Social Work Practice: Model and Method* (F. E. Peacock, 1973) represented a major breakthrough in that it enabled social workers to begin to rebuild connections between individual troubles and social ills.
■ Audrey Mullender's chapter 'Persistent Oppressions: The Example of Domestic Violence' in Adams *et al.*'s *Critical Practice in Social Work* (Palgrave Macmillan, 2002) is extremely helpful in demonstrating the opportunities for effective networking and collective action within statutory sector social work.
■ Roger Adams's discussion of 'boundaries' and the limiting effect they have on practice is an important contribution to thinking about the influence of structural arrangements and the creation of self-imposed constraints. See 'Working Within and Across Boundaries: Tensions and Dilemmas' in Adams *et al.*'s *Social Work Futures* (Palgrave Macmillan, 2005).

http://www.womensaid.org.uk

This offers a wide range of advice and resources to survivors of abuse, including suggestions about how to develop mutually supportive networks

http://www.sosig.ac.uk

This is the site of the Social Science Information Gateway, which offers a wide range of general social science and specific social work reference material, including theoretical, research and practice sources. Look for entries relating to 'networking' and 'social action'.

10 Power: Meeting the Challenge

The political nature of social work

It has been observed on a number of occasions that social work practice is experienced as a kind of dichotomy. The tension between concern for individuals and their needs, on the one hand, and the desire to transform unequal and unfair social circumstances, on the other, is sometimes divisive. Social workers have, over the years, felt under some pressure to identify themselves with one camp or the other (Cooper, 2002, p. 8). This has been described as the basis of a kind of 'civil war within the profession'. Social work was for a long time perceived as either being about achieving structural change through expressing solidarity with oppressed groups and advocating for social justice, or about meeting individual needs through counselling and casework. The two perspectives were viewed from within as being incompatible, and, in different ways, as betraying the *real* needs of service users and the *real* meaning of social work practice. Whilst attempts were made to bridge the divide, these were limited and largely unsuccessful. Nevertheless, as Cooper observes, such dialogue gradually became more easily achievable, particularly as insights from feminism and anti-psychiatry demonstrated the connectedness between subjective worlds and external social realities. He argues that the domain of practice represented by social work requires an ability to work across and between apparently fixed barriers:

> for us as social workers ... there is really no choice but to go on having these kinds of cross-boundary dialogues. We necessarily, by virtue of being social care workers, occupy a psychosocial domain ... [O]ur activity is also framed by its location within the public sector. We cannot avoid the question of our relationship to the state. (Cooper, 2002, p. 9)

This implies that social workers must be prepared to take an integrated approach, recognizing the links between individual need and structural inequalities, and adapting the scope and substance of their professional activities accordingly. Importantly, here, the key practical task is the development of techniques for unifying different aspects of our interventions. Thus, effective practice requires social workers to move beyond either simplistic 'position-taking' (Simpkin, 1983) or pragmatic adaptation to statutory requirements (Davies, 1994).

Attempts to compartmentalize social work create significant impediments to practice. The suggestion, for example, that social work draws its legitimacy *only* from legislation and agency policy (Davies, 1994, p. 45) clearly fails to take account of the structural dynamics which problematize the practitioner's position as an authority figure. The difficulty with functionalist arguments is that they exclude from the very definition of social work aspects of intervention which are central to its aims of achieving social justice (and individual rights). Transformative practice appears to be excluded by definition. The suggestion that the worker should take the side of the client '*against the state*' (*ibid.*) and be prepared to challenge agency policy is deemed both impractical and 'of doubtful validity'. This critic of radical perspectives in social work concludes that 'the individualist approach of traditional social work is both necessary and sufficient to justify the existence of the profession' (Davies, 1994, p. 46). By contrast, the argument of the present text is that it is clearly *necessary* to focus on individual experiences and needs, but it is emphatically *not sufficient* to restrict ourselves to this limited and incomplete view of the practice agenda.

Interestingly, this argument has resurfaced in the language of debates framed in terms of 'modernity', 'late modernity' and 'postmodernity' (Ferguson, 2001; 2003; Garrett, 2003). On the one hand, it is suggested that changing patterns of social and cultural life requires a refocusing of the core activities of social work on 'self-actualization' (Ferguson, 2001, p. 53), rather than on achieving structural changes. According to this line of argument, 'emancipatory politics' should be subsumed under a more personalized concern with 'life politics'. Thus, the principles of empowerment and improving life chances can best be pursued through recognizing social work as

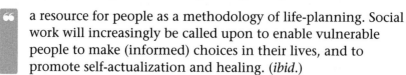

> a resource for people as a methodology of life-planning. Social work will increasingly be called upon to enable vulnerable people to make (informed) choices in their lives, and to promote self-actualization and healing. (*ibid.*)

Whilst it is difficult to take issue with this on its own terms, this position has been contested, in that it 'unduly emphasises human agency and personal choice' (Garrett, 2003, p. 394). A restricted focus on the individual reflects an 'elite' worldview according to this critic, who suggests that

> life politics – a politics of choice, lifestyle and self-actualization – will fail to equip social work to respond to structurally generated oppression which many users of social services have to confront. (*ibid.*)

Indeed, it is suggested that the increasingly international and global focus of ideas and practice in social work only serves to underpin the importance of a structural approach to practice (Dominelli, 2004; Lyons, 2006; see also Chapter 4). Social work in the context of 'forced migration' is incomplete if it does not address the broader political dimensions of its role and functions in pursuing forms of 'emancipatory practice' (Garrett, 2003, p. 394) and retaining its commitment to human rights (Humphries, 2004).

Knowing our place: recognizing the impact of social work

Following the framework of the previous chapters, I will now set out some of the implications for practice of the preceding argument. Social work must take an active approach to linking the individual and intensely personal needs, which are usually its starting point, to the parallel task of securing changes in both the immediate and wider environment. In order to achieve a holistic approach to practice, social workers must first bring an appreciation of their own structural location and the associated 'baggage' which exercises a significant influence on both the opportunities available to them and the constraints which they experience. The place which the social worker occupies and the perceptions associated with this are thus implicated in all aspects of practice. Social work *is not and cannot be* a neutral activity, so the choices made by the practitioner about how to approach a particular intervention are of significance for a number of distinct but connected reasons. In other words, the way in which we 'frame' our interventions is critical in determining the substance of what we actually do. Parton emphasizes this in his development of arguments for a 'social constructionist' approach to practice:

> it is important to recognize that the terms by which we understand our world and ourselves are neither required nor demanded by 'what there is'. Constructionism insists that we develop a critical stance towards our taken-for-granted ways of understanding the world, including ourselves. (Parton, 2003, p. 8)

We must therefore be cautious and sometimes sceptical about taking the world and the 'categories that we use to divide and interpret it' as given. All our interventions must be informed by a critical edge, which seeks to question even the most basic assumptions about what is 'routine' and what is 'normal' practice. As Parton, again, has observed, the inherent tendency for agencies and procedural requirements to impose routinized expectations on the social domain incorporates particular ways of ordering the world at the very core of practice. Structural inequalities are thereby reproduced in the mundane aspects of the social work task. The machinery by which referrals are taken, assessments are organized according to standard procedures and people are problematized is simultaneously defining the social work task for us, and conveying strong messages about the nature of the relationship between 'service users', agencies and practitioners. It is argued, however, that 'systems and organizational frameworks which operate *as if* issues are resolvable in any kind of scientific or calculative/probabilistic sense are in great danger of missing the point' (Parton, 2000, p. 460).

---

practice illustration 10.1

Taking a referral

The process of taking a referral at the very start of the social work process is beset with inbuilt attributes which structure our assumptions and practice orientations. A referral is likely to be:

- Individualized
- Problem-orientated
- From an authoritative source
- Outcome focused (with the implied message: 'solve this problem for us').

Enabling and empowerment are not likely to be highlighted as key objectives.

The task for the practitioner is to reframe these initial assumptions, asking:

- *What are the 'social' dimensions of this referral?*
- *How can we seek collective solutions?*
- *How is the problem seen from other perspectives?*
- *What changes do the least powerful people in this situation want to achieve?*

As Trevithick (2005, p. 35) observes, the search for certainty and determinacy is crucially tied up with the question of how far social work acts 'as an agent of control'. Rather than seeking predictability and standardization, social workers should seek to bring their practice more closely into line with the lived experiences of service users. Thus, Parton (2000, p. 460) asserts that 'notions of ambiguity, indeterminacy and uncertainty are at the core of social work and should be built upon and not defined out', leading to a greater scope for 'creativity' in thought and deed. Even if we can sustain the belief, as Davies (1994) appears to, that the relationship between knowledge, policies, procedures and practice is unilinear and straightforward, this implies that we must try to come to terms with the unpredictability of the contexts in which practitioners operate and the part which they play in achieving specific outcomes.

As we have already observed, this again illustrates the value of a 'reflective' (Ruch, 2005) or 'reflexive' (Taylor and White, 2000) orientation to practice. This is of particular importance in the present context because it helps to illustrate how structural aspects of the practitioner–service-user relationship are interpreted and sustained, and how power and authority are negotiated in the process of intervention. This approach is helpful for both practitioner and service users to the extent that it frees both from prior assumptions. Authority and legitimacy are not necessarily 'given' (indeed, they may actively be questioned; see Chapter 7), but they are realized (or not) in the course of a specific intervention (Taylor and White, 2000, p. 100). The attempt to establish an authentic 'professional' identity (see Chapter 6) and to achieve legitimacy through this process is thus bound up with the 'reframing' of structural relationships which suggest a hierarchy of knowledge, expertise and authority (see Chapter 5).

In terms of challenging the structural dynamics of power in social work, these observations have important implications. Firstly, the process of 'distancing' creates a gap between professionals and service users. As Taylor and White observe, this can be identified in the distinction between 'everyday' and 'institutional' modes of expression. In their research, they found that no practitioner introduced

> any personal elements into the conversation [with service users] or [referred] to their own experiences. Specifically, they do not divulge whether they are parents themselves, although this is ... highly significant ... for the service users. (Taylor and White, 2000, p. 103)

Equally, as is observed by one of these authors elsewhere, professional identities are established and sustained in the dialogues between those involved in practice (White and Featherstone, 2005, p. 210). Although the negotiation of professional legitimacy is accomplished in and through individual interactions with more or less sceptical service users, there is also a cumulative effect, whereby 'institutional identity and authority' are established (Taylor and White, 2000, p. 117). For social workers, it is also important to acknowledge that these perceptions may precede them. In other words, they are not simply achieved through atomized dialogues, but will be built upon prior experiences and expectations, on both sides. These authors conclude their discussion with some very pertinent questions addressed to practitioners:

> Even when you are giving information you may well be indicating what your service's expectations of clients are. We are not suggesting that you stop talking to clients/patients for fear of saying the wrong thing! ... But we are suggesting that you listen much more carefully to your own practice talk and that of others. How do you say things? Why do you say them in that way? How do you try to achieve compliance from service users? How does resistance manifest itself and how do you deal with it? What are the situations in which you feel 'powerless' with clients? Are there times when clients' voices are silenced or not listened to? (*ibid.*)

As these authors conclude, it is not just the quality of the practitioner's performance of her or his role which should be attended to ('reflection'), but also the nature and context of the service-user–practitioner relationship ('reflexivity'), which will have a critical bearing on the conduct of practice (Taylor and White, 2000, p. 198).

In seeking to develop our understanding of the complexity of the power relationships implicated in practice, we must, therefore, take account of both the structural dimensions of interpersonal interactions *and* the external impact of structural forces on specific interventions. Social workers therefore play a part, not just in reflecting or sustaining these relationships, but in creating and modifying them, in all aspects of their practice. The distinction discussed previously between individualized and structural practice is neither helpful, nor accurate, in its depiction of the choices available to social work practitioners.

As Mullaly (1997, p. 165) observes, this recognition that 'the personal is political' owes much to the feminist traditions which have exercised such an important influence on the development of theory and practice. As he also points out, this realization 'has two major implications for' the way in which we approach social work practice. The first of these is that all aspects of the practitioner's work have 'political' dimensions. There is no such thing as neutral or apolitical social work, although the reduction of structural and systemic problems to purely personal issues is an inherent risk in the way in which social work is often constituted. The resultant localization of our attribution of the causes of (and responsibility for) the service users' problems inhibits practitioners from seeking wider solutions which are not just about changing the individual's circumstances, relationships or behaviour. For Mullaly, the second consequence is that the search for 'political' change is an integral and necessary part of the social work task:

> This does not preclude intervention at the individual or family level, but instead of dealing with each of these levels by itself the connection between private troubles and the structural source of these troubles is made in every case. (*ibid.*)

The consequence of this, of course, is that social workers must be prepared to turn their attention towards the wider context when carrying out assessments and planning interventions. This is important again for a number of reasons. Firstly, this perspective enables the social worker to provide a holistic analysis to service users, locating their personal troubles within the wider pattern of social and structural influences which shape their lives.

practice illustration 10.2

Integrated assessment models

Some initiatives have been undertaken to promote integrated assessment, such as the *Framework for the Assessment of Children in Need and Their Families* (Department of Health, 2000). Although this framework does not provide a basis for making connections between the different dimensions which impact on children's lives, it does at least allow for the possibility that structural factors (such as low income and poor housing) need to be taken into account in assessing need.

For those undertaking assessments of children's needs using this tool, it is important to treat each element as being of equal significance, and to be ready to tackle any issues identified, including material disadvantage.

A more complete and realistic picture of needs and circumstances emerges. On the one hand, the processes by which external forces become internalized as 'guilt and blame' (Mullaly, 1997, p. 166) become clearer, and, on the other, the importance of addressing structural causes of individual ills becomes a more central imperative for constructive and empowering practice.

If we consider for a moment the issues arising from social work intervention with people with learning difficulties, these observations can be illustrated in concrete terms. This is an area of practice which has historically been centrally influenced by individualizing assumptions derived from the 'medical model', and where interventions are typically structured around assumptions of service users' inadequacies and incompetence. McIntosh (2002), for example, traces the history of the disabling impact of 'examination' and 'classification' in this context. These power relationships tend to preclude recognition of either the rights or the competences of people with learning difficulties, and, in this way, the scope of 'services' to be made available to them becomes restricted.

By contrast a 'social analysis' (Kagan and Burton, 2005) starts from a position which requires that the 'person-in-context' is 'the unit of analysis and change'. It is therefore essential that practice seeks to retain a sense of this dynamic link between service users, their perceptions and the factors which shape their circumstances, including the part which we as practitioners play, based on our particular structural location and the impact of our own actions.

Sites and sources of power: their meaning for practice

At this point, then, it is important to emphasize the underlying message that social work (and social workers) cannot be apolitical. It is not possible to opt to practise in a value-neutral power vacuum. Davies (1994), for example, correctly identifies a number of contexts (mental health admissions, provision of residential care and adoption proceedings) in which social workers necessarily exercise considerable professional and statutory authority. However, by rendering these processes unproblematic, he de-emphasizes the way in which these power relations are complex, conflictual and contradictory. Not only is it rarely the case that social workers can carry out their statutory functions in a purely routine fashion, but they must also remain critically aware of the impact of their (and others') structural relationships on service users, individually and collectively. An integral, and central, aspect of practice must therefore be to exercise an independent and critical perspective on the entire domain of practice, including those structural and systemic factors which influence peoples' lives. It is not simply a matter of adopting the kind of caricatured 'revolutionary' position which Davies (1994, p. 117) portrays, but of seeking to engage with those aspects of power which service users experience as oppressive and damaging (aspects of asylum legislation and policy, for example), in order to be able to carry out effective enabling practice.

Humphries (2004) illustrates this point well, observing that changing asylum and immigration policy has 'drawn' social work 'into a role of constriction and punishment in its work' in this area of practice (p. 93). As noted previously, the impact of global and transnational factors on asylum seekers and other immigrants is certain to have a direct bearing on the immediate issues of concern to them (see Kohli and Mather, 2003, for example). Experiences of oppression and loss of control will be central to their lives, and social work interventions will necessarily interact with these aspects of their present needs and circumstances. The social work response must therefore take account of this interaction; it must, therefore, also 'take a view' of the compounding effects of oppressive policies on a particularly vulnerable group of people. Humphries argues that this has often not proved to be the case in the past:

 social workers and social services ... have not resisted the gate-keeping and inhumane role thrust upon them. It is no wonder they are despised and feared by the people they purport to help. (Humphries, 2004, p. 104)

Humphries, and others (e.g. Christie), stress that the part social workers play in mediating and challenging oppression is crucial, and that 'anti-oppressive practice' itself needs to be understood in a broad sense. It is not simply about practicing in an anti-discriminatory manner with those we encounter as service users, but it is also important to take a 'strong' multiculturalist position (Christie, 2003, p. 230). By this, Christie means that it should be an integral part of the job of the social worker 'to be proactive in developing policies and practices that promote anti-racism'. It is therefore no less important a part of social work practice to be engaged in challenging unequal and damaging power relationships than to be developing appropriate culturally sensitive services for those who are subject to major traumas, such as the upheavals of war (Okitikpi and Aymer, 2003, p. 213).

Social work cannot achieve its aims in terms of improving individuals' lives unless it is geared to changing those aspects of power which have a direct impact on their sense of well-being. Failure to demonstrate solidarity in this way will not only diminish the likelihood of achieving effective interventions, but it will also reduce the potential for social workers to achieve relationships of openness and trust with service users. Social work:

> needs to begin to act collectively and in solidarity with those affected and impoverished by reactionary policies, rather than in fragmented, commercialized and exploited situations ... Surely it is time for social workers to find that combination of genuine caring for people in big trouble, with the informed anger and rage to galvanize them into action against manifest injustice. (Humphries, 2004, p. 105)

This highly pertinent example demonstrates a number of important requirements which apply to social work practice in general. Practice must be:

- Connected
- Reflective
- Critical
- Proactive
- Creative
- Change-orientated.

Interventions must be based on an understanding that personal troubles will *always* have a broader, structural dimension, which have to be 'factored in' to the processes of assessment and service planning. At the same time, as the above example demonstrates, the connection must be made between the tasks of changing individual circumstances and changing those external factors which limit individual freedoms and opportunities.

In addition, social workers must retain a sense of their own place in either sustaining or transforming power relationships. Anti-oppressive practice will require a commitment to constantly (re-)evaluating the impact of one's own role and actions. This, in turn, may necessitate a readiness to question and sometimes oppose the operational frameworks within which practitioners are located, and which exercise direct constraints on their actions. Following on from this, social workers must take a proactive view of the need for change in terms of the systems and structures which contextualize their work, and which are, as we have seen, capable of imposing or perpetuating inequalities and oppression (Humphries, 2004).

In order to prepare themselves for this kind of role, practitioners will need to explore the context within which oppressive power dynamics can be identified. Inevitably, too, this will mean seeking out alternative sources of solidarity and strength in order to pose an effective challenge. In the same way that many service users' experiences are fragmented and individualized, so practitioners also may feel that their work and working relationships are organized in such a way as to prevent them from establishing the kind of connections which might help them to advocate change. So, the forging of alliances may help to secure continuing legitimacy for forms of practice which might otherwise be questioned. As Valtonen (2001) puts it, 'professional networking' is an essential part of the social work agenda. Thus, resettlement work with socially excluded service users cannot overlook the impact of the state of the labour market in shaping opportunities (or lack of them) for those pursuing their entitlement as citizens to social integration. Seeking alliances in order to promote the 'right to work' of marginalized groups thus becomes integral to the role of the social work practitioner in such circumstances.

Recognition of the validity of this aspect of the social work task is important to the extent that it provides justification for 'indirect' forms of practice which focus on changing aspects of institutional bureaucracies or other social networks (Valtonen, 2001, p. 959). Social workers should not be made to feel that this aspect of their activities is not somehow *real* social work because it does not involve direct day-to-day contact with people who are defined as 'service users'.

Having established that 'making links' is a necessary part of the practitioner's role, it may help briefly to consider some of the opportunities available for building up effective alliances to support and legitimize this aspiration. Alternative power sources may be needed if social workers are to take action to challenge established interests and conventional assumptions about what is or is not an acceptable occupational activity.

By virtue of their own position, social workers are able to claim membership of professional networks, which offer potential sources of support and reinforcement. Thus, for example, the British Association of Social Workers is a source of both professional advice and campaigning activity. The association's code of ethics is explicit about the 'duty' of social workers to challenge injustice. They must

> Bring to the attention of those in power and the general public, and where appropriate challenge ways in which the policies or activities of government, organisations or society create or contribute to structural disadvantage, hardship and suffering, or militate against their relief. (BASW, 2002, p. 3)

This is helpful in two ways. Firstly, it provides strong professional backing for social workers to take an active part in tackling power imbalances which impact adversely on service users; and, secondly, it provides a vehicle through which these aims can be pursued. BASW has, itself, been a strong critic of unfair policies and practices in key areas such as youth justice and immigration (Konstandis, 2003; Mapstone, 2005). The association's role is of particular value because it effectively defines these campaigning activities as part of the *professional* function of social work. For those who have sought to reframe social work as a progressive and inclusive activity which has at its core a commitment to stand alongside service users (e.g. Fook, 2002; Parton, 2003), this represents an important endorsement. The emergence of the Social Work Manifesto, too (*The Guardian*, 16 March 2006), suggests that there continues to be a groundswell of support for a radical and committed form of practice.

As well as recognizing the importance of those networks which provide a form of endorsement for the identity of social work as an empowering activity, we should also acknowledge the significance of other potential alliances, notably those which coalesce around service user and other collective interests. The relationship between practitioners and organizations of and for service users offers significant opportunities in this respect. For social work practitioners, of course, this means recognizing and endorsing the validity of service users' experience, understandings and expertise (Beresford, 2001), and thus accepting that 'professionalism' stems not just from one's formal standing, but also from the ability to demonstrate empathy and solidarity with those on the receiving end of interventions. Unless social workers are willing to engage in such partnership-building activities, it is difficult to see how they can take a holistic approach to the challenge of reflecting on and, where necessary, reshaping power dynamics. The lack of social work involvement in this context is likely to be interpreted by service users as a sign of distance and a continuing commitment to a 'paternalistic provider-led approach to meeting people's needs' (Beresford, 2001, p. 350). As Beresford also points out, the development of effective networks needs to be undertaken at a number of distinct levels, including:

> - Education and training
> - Theory building, research and evaluation
> - Practice development
> - Standard setting and outcome measurement.
> (Beresford, 2001, p. 351)

The emergence and growing influence of organizations such as Shaping Our Lives gives substance to these aspirations, creating a strong service-user lobby capable of engaging with and progressively influencing practitioners and agencies.

In terms of developing an effective sense of trust and mutual commitment between social workers and 'service users' (Butler and Drakeford, 2005), such partnerships are a necessary prerequisite for the design and delivery of user-centred and user-friendly services.

'Reframing' social work: solidarity and commitment

To recap, the argument of this chapter has been that, firstly, social work is *necessarily* a political activity, and that, therefore, practitioners must seek an active engagement with their professional organizations and other networks in order to be able to take a holistic perspective on power, equality and justice into their work. Proceeding from this, we will now consider some of the ways in which this may lead to a reshaping of the way in which social work is understood and practiced.

As already observed, a number of authors (such as Fook, 2002) have argued that social work with individuals needs to be informed by the notion of 'reframing', such that established and often damaging relationships or patterns of behaviour may be questioned and subsequently transformed for the better. The aim here will be to illustrate a number of ways in which a similar strategy can be applied to the contextual factors which shape power relationships between social work practitioners and service users. As Johnson has suggested, it may often be as, or even more, valuable to apply social work principles and methods to indirect interventions as to direct practice. This provides a useful starting point to our 'reframing' exercise, in that we are encouraged to reverse the conventional wisdom that social work's 'focus is person-in-environment' and instead take as the starting point:

> ❝ 'Environment-person' ... Indeed, by attending to the environment first, the social worker might be serving people to a greater extent than if it were ignored, and offering a culturally sensitive practice to those clients who reject both individualism and the Western separation of self and community. (Johnson, 1999, p. 331)

Proper social work?

As a social worker who deals frequently with families who are rehoused in a particular geographical area of the local authority in which you work, you might find that problems of poor health and social isolation are concentrated amongst this group. The question then is how to go about identifying strategies to address a problem which cannot and should not be individualized, and yet still be able to justify this as *proper social work*.

This necessitates taking an approach to practice which highlights the consistency between the core purposes of social work and forms of collective and structural intervention which support empowerment and social justice. In order to achieve these aims, social work needs to be:

- Questioning
- Contextually aware
- Strategic
- Assertive
- Committed
- On the side of the oppressed
- Willing to take risks.

There is a danger that prescribing a course of action for others can readily be challenged on the basis that 'it's all right for you to talk', but, nonetheless, it must be stressed that social work practitioners are constantly engaged in making the choice between acknowledging and addressing the power relations which are inextricably bound up with their practice, or ignoring them and thus limiting their chances of pursuing fair and just outcomes for service users.

In opting for the former, there is a need to recognize the professional and personal implications. Underlying all aspects of practice will be found a 'questioning' stance, which resists the tendency to take for granted existing structural relations. The problems of service users will not be dealt with in isolation, but will in each case be examined for the ways in which they represent inequalities of power and resources.

Having identified the areas of concern, social work practitioners must also be in a position to be able to do something about the issues identified. Much of the frustration experienced by practitioners may well revolve around their perceived inability to find strategic solutions to the individualized problems they encounter. It is important at this point to stress the need for realism. The suggestion here is that significant change in power relations is only possible if social work pursues an 'assertive' approach, based on its core professional aims and values. This is not, however, intended to imply that change will either be dramatic or certain. In contrast to Davies's (1994) caricature, the achievement of revolutionary change is not the benchmark by which progressive social work practice should be judged. The steps to be taken may appear relatively modest; what is important is that they are geared towards the long term goal of achieving fairness and social justice.

Social workers can seek to reframe their role in influencing structural power relations by undertaking a number of steps, which are intended to create possibilities, rather than guarantee solutions. Firstly, practice must be undertaken on the basis that the individual *is* collective. That is to say, the links between individual circumstances and social forces need to be made explicit in all aspects of social work interventions. This is of particular importance in respect of those groups who are pathologized by virtue of attributed characteristics, and where a purely individualized form of intervention can serve to reinforce discriminatory assumptions and practices.

A cogent example of contemporary relevance is the issue of young people categorized as offenders, who may be disadvantaged in various ways. In this context, the identity of 'offender' takes precedence over other needs and effectively negates consideration of the young person's perspective. In this way, not only is the individual disempowered, but responses to the crimes of the young become partial, focusing only on their status as 'criminals' liable to punishment. For social work practitioners, the copious evidence of the contributions of poverty and disadvantage to the likelihood of young people becoming reported for crimes (Smith, 2003), and the associated evidence of the discriminatory nature of the justice system (Bowling and Phillips, 2002), should be crucial elements in shaping interventions. Whilst this clearly has implications for individual interventions, a comprehensive approach also requires social workers to play a part in redefining the way in which such problems come to be classified. A return to core social work values, for example, provides the basis, rooted in the practitioner's professional identity, for reformulating the problem. Principles of self-worth, inclusion and citizenship (Dominelli, 2004) can be applied collectively as well as individually. These cannot be applied partially or provisionally, and this leads social workers to the position of being mandated to represent the interests of those who are marginalized or oppressed, groups which are sometimes viewed with a considerable degree of opprobrium. In this respect, there is a degree of risk involved for practitioners whose perspective may not be shared generally. As Johnson (1999, p. 330) puts it, this 'position is tension filled' because social workers necessarily act in the problematic space between 'the client and society'. They gain their authority to act (in part) from society and its institutions, but they are also morally and professionally bound to question the damaging consequences of its policies and 'the ways less-privileged members are treated'. Nevertheless, as Dominelli suggests: 'Social workers ... have to act as society's conscience, challenge unjust arrangements and promote definitions of welfare articulated through discussions with client groups' (Dominelli, 2004, p. 232).

The importance of reflecting the profession's core values can be linked with the need to articulate service user perspectives, collectively as well as individually. For Dominelli, this is encapsulated best in the notion of 'citizenship', 'because it provides the basis from which' to make claims to fundamental entitlements which should be available to all. Social workers should

> be critical of society's failure to guarantee its actuality for all inhabitants on a daily basis. In other words, social workers can identify the gap between theoretical and actual citizenship. The commitment to social justice enables them to locate individuals within collective entitlements and obligations, and ground their interventions in this arena. (*ibid.*)

It is important, of course, that social work does not claim a monopoly on this perspective, although it has been suggested that it is the only 'helping profession' which is specifically mandated to operate with the relationship between the individual and the social environment at the heart of practice (Johnson, 1999, p. 330; see also Lymbery, 2006). This should therefore place the profession at the forefront of the task of exploring and articulating the position of service users, especially where they are denied a voice or their perspective is devalued.

To return to the example cited, of young people in trouble, the implications for practice are that social workers must take an active, questioning and assertive stance. This may mean engaging with colleagues, for example in multi-agency youth offending teams, to promote the necessity of taking account of the young person's own perspective, and the contextual factors associated with their behaviour. We need not be indicating approval of unacceptable behaviour, or deny the importance of taking personal responsibility (Dominelli, 2004, p. 231), when we draw attention to those circumstances which in themselves are exclusionary and, as is well known, also criminogenic (Smith, 2003). It is the task of social work to promote a holistic view such that these factors are considered in combination and as interactive. Incidentally, this approach also enables us to promote interventions which engage with the notion of service user responsibility and self-determination (GSCC, 2002); for example, young people, 'victims' and communities can be engaged constructively in generating effective responses to the problem of crime (Dominelli, 2004, p. 241).

We can conclude, then, that in this context 'reframing' means introducing a distinctively 'social work' perspective to discussion of the factors associated with exclusion and disempowerment. This means asserting the legitimacy of this perspective, and ensuring that it is accorded as much weight as might be given to other professional viewpoints. The starting point may simply be the social worker's knowledge and understanding of oppression, and her or his capacity to make this explicit in interactions with representatives of other agencies. For example, the institutional nature of racial discrimination within the justice system (Bowling and Phillips, 2002) is clearly a continuing factor of relevance in constructing anti-discriminatory services. The role of social work in reinforcing awareness of the nature of oppression in this way should not be underestimated.

Structural change is a legitimate objective for social work

In concluding, I want to focus on some of the change strategies which are available to practitioners and which focus squarely on achieving a more favourable distribution of power in the interests of service users. We have explored the idea that social work has a legitimate and central role in promoting awareness of structural inequalities and power imbalances, and it will now be useful to consider some illustrative examples of the potential for achieving autonomy and control as a collective project.

In undertaking this exercise, we should begin by acknowledging the *possibilities* for social work in achieving or contributing to change by focusing on areas of practice which do provide evidence of progressive developments. Whilst retaining a sense of modesty and realism, it is reasonable to suggest that the coherent and sustained commitment of the profession to the goals of 'empowerment' and 'user participation' has achieved changes beyond the individual level, for example in the way that domestic violence is addressed (Mullender, 2002) and the way the 'medical model' has been challenged in the field of disability. This is not to claim that social work has achieved such outcomes alone, or unproblematically (see Sapey, 2002, for example), but it is to suggest that it has an important contribution to make in collective movements to change attitudes and practices in relation to oppressed groups.

As the previous sections have demonstrated, social work has a *legitimate* role in seeking to challenge the structural forces which deny influence and control to service users. However, it is also important to consider the tools which may be available to enable social workers to gain maximum impact in this respect. It has, for example, been suggested repeatedly that confrontational or purely negative tactics are likely to result only in glorious failure: 'People cannot continue to carry out structural practice in the agency after they are fired. Martyrs are of limited practical use for ongoing radical work within agencies' (Mullaly, 1997, p. 186).

In any case, the starting point for social work practice must surely be that the collectively agreed values and professional standards which are sanctioned by representative bodies (BASW, 2002) and state agencies (GSCC, 2002) actually incorporate a belief in achieving autonomy and self-determination for service users. There is no need to stand outside or against these consensual statements of intent in order to aspire to progressive or emancipatory practice. It is rather a matter of tactics and strategy as to how to apply these core values to maximum effect in the cause of social justice.

The key question for social workers is how to incorporate into their activities effective methods of promoting structural changes in order to redress power imbalances which work against the interests of service users. The suggestions to be made here are by no means new, but the intention is rather to reiterate their value in underpinning the achievement of constructive change.

1 Engagement

Whilst much of social work may feel as if it is crisis-led or procedurally driven (Jones, 2001), the starting point for empowering practice must be active engagement with service user and other community interests. Social workers should be prepared to establish links with community groups in order to ensure that their own voices are seen as legitimate. It is important to achieve this as a matter of underlying principle rather than at the point of crisis where suspicion and hostility may well undermine attempts to forge alliances. One study, in particular, has demonstrated the value of this kind of proactive approach in working with Travellers (Cemlyn, 2000). Where social workers (and sometimes their managers) have adopted a collaborative approach, based on cultural awareness and a knowledge of human rights, the consequences can be shown to be beneficial, both enhancing participation and improving outcomes:

> There were several references to individual social workers who had gone out of their way to engage with Travellers and pursue their rights, perhaps drawing on a wider remit than their organizational role, for instance the UN Convention [on the Rights of the Child], while individual managers have used their knowledge of Traveller issues to promote organizational change. (Cemlyn, 2000, p. 337)

The positive value of working on a number of levels, incorporating relevant knowledge, cultural awareness and proactive engagement is clear.

2 Awareness-raising

As the above indicates, as well as good intentions, social workers need to remain aware of the effects of exclusion and disenfranchisement for service users and, in turn, to build on this knowledge to promote wider understanding and social inclusion. It is continually important to seek out the connections between individual examples of risk or need and the contexts which create the preconditions for personal problems to arise. This is of particular importance for those 'hidden' groups in the population whose difficulties are not necessarily acknowledged widely. For example, the role of social work in respect of young carers can be seen as particularly significant as part of a process of sensitizing our own and other professions and policy-makers to the needs and aspirations of a substantial group which has been overlooked in the past (Thomas *et al.*, 2003). For a variety of reasons, including their own concerns about the consequences of being open about their role, young carers have tended to be overlooked by the helping professions. However, social workers are likely to encounter young people caring for other family members because of their responsibilities for assessing the care needs of both adults and children. It is argued, therefore, that social workers should go beyond their casework role to play a part in promoting wider recognition and a more effective response:

> Of the professional groups involved, social workers are most likely to be working with the families of ill and disabled people, and social work agencies have a pivotal role in linking community care services to Children Act duties ... For all these reasons, it can be argued that social work should be taking a much stronger lead in the planning and provision of services for young carers and their families. (Thomas *et al.*, 2003, p. 43)

One starting point for this kind of strategy might being a proactive commitment by practitioners collectively to record and report evidence of unmet needs.

3 Collaboration

Our structural analysis shows that power relationships necessarily involve interactions between different interests, and in the social work context they are also critically concerned with disadvantage and inequalities, especially as these factors affect service users. Clearly, then, the key objective of seeking to influence power relationships in the direction of greater fairness and equity requires social workers to build partnerships with other interests, especially those who are in the least advantageous position. In direct practice terms, this means developing links and providing support to groups run by and for service users, for example. These links should not be made just with the aim of facilitating the achievement of agency goals, but should be seen as enabling the articulation of service user aims and objectives. Social workers may thus find themselves in the potentially conflictual position of taking the side of organizations which are challenging agency policy or behaviour (Hanley, 2003).

Nevertheless, the value of seeking effective partnerships is clear. Practitioners are able to promote service user interests on the basis of an informed understanding, which gives greater authenticity and substance to their arguments. At the same time, the professional standing of practitioners provides endorsement and validation to the objectives of service users. This kind of active engagement is mutually reinforcing and offers greater chances of promoting mutual interests (Adams, 2003, p. 173). Such collaborative relationships are likely to be problematic, given the dangers of 'co-option', 'tokenism' and unresolved suspicions (Adams, 2003, p. 175), but there is no doubt that social work has an important role to play in facilitating empowering collaborations.

practice illustration 10.3

Working together

In one area, practitioners were able to promote the participation of frail older people by working with them collectively in the form of a service user 'panel'. In this example, it was concluded that mutual benefits could be obtained by enabling 'the knowledge of users to contribute to service developments' (Barnes and Bennett, 1999, p. 110).

Empowering social work of this kind need not be overtly confrontational or dramatic, but it can be pursued through the identification of common interests (for example, carers' groups; Adams, 2003, p. 88) and the creation of opportunities for people to meet, share ideas and generate their own agendas for change.

4 *Taking action*

Sometimes, however, social work practitioners concerned with power and inequality will be faced with decisions about how to resist or challenge those forces which lead to disadvantage or oppression. There may well be a point where the conflict between moral and professional values, on the one hand, and organizational rules, managerial requirements or even legislative provisions, on the other, confronts practitioners with stark choices. Direct advocacy, campaigning or whistle-blowing may appear to be the only strategies available which are consistent with the core aims of social work. As Dominelli indicates, this involves a redefinition (or perhaps reclamation) of the meaning of social work itself, in view of concerns that 'social workers' capacity to advocate or act on behalf of dispossessed individuals and groups has been compromised by their dependency on government' (Dominelli, 2004, p. 251).

Van Wormer (2004) comments on the value of 'whistle-blowing' as a 'direct act of exposure against an individual or agency', which is likely to be 'an exceedingly risky (career wise) and unpopular act' drawing on her own personal experience of taking on this role. It is an individualized strategy which clearly carries significant personal implications, yet must be recognized as a form of 'structural' intervention which can be both compatible with social work values and goals and highly effective. Thus, for example, child care staff have been influential in bringing to light cases of institutional abuse (Waterhouse, 2000).

Involvement with other forms of campaigning activity should also be seen as a legitimate component of the social work role, where this is necessary 'to challenge individual and social relations that create and maintain oppression' (Reichert, 2003, p. 229). It is difficult to see, for example, how social work practice with asylum seekers cannot explicitly align itself with moves to challenge discriminatory legislation and the violation of human rights. Such a stance may appear 'naive' or 'confrontational', and practitioners would be well-advised to seek the support of their agencies, representative organizations, other professionals and the 'union', but

> the alternative is simply to collapse into informing the Home Office concerning immigration status, interrogating service users concerning their status before offering services, enforcing homelessness and withdrawing financial support. (Hayes, 2005, p. 193)

As Humphries (2004) puts it, if social workers do not explicitly align themselves with those who are victimized by 'reactionary' and oppressive policies and practices, then they will become part of the problem. In the UK context, it is somewhat encouraging that social work's professional body (BASW) has offered practitioners an active lead in this respect (Konstandis, 2003). At some point, however, we are all likely to confront the stark question: 'whose side are you on?' A decisive and progressive response is needed.

Social workers, power and justice

The gist of this concluding chapter has been that 'structural social work' (Mullaly, 1997) which seeks to generate greater equality in power relationships is and should be central to a holistic view of the social work task. Activities which are sometimes (e.g. Davies, 1994) defined as being outside the remit of practitioners need to be seen as integral to the core purposes of the profession, and, indeed, if these are not pursued then social work is unlikely to be able to remain true to its underlying values. This does not mean that social workers should expect to operate in a constant state of conflict with their agencies, the law or the state, not least because all of these are riddled with contradictions and conflicting purposes. It is also the case that relatively modest and small-scale actions can be recognized in terms of their contribution to structural change, such as the addition of an item to the team's weekly agenda on the housing needs of lone parent families, or an enquiry addressed to professional colleagues as to why schools have differential exclusion rates.

The attempt to reshape power relationships as they affect social work service users should be informed by a number of key questions (see Chapter 1), rather than a set of fixed preconceptions:

- Who is oppressed/disadvantaged in this practice setting?
- Who/what is the oppressor?
- What form does this power imbalance take (e.g. structural, cultural, personal)?
- What levers are available to us (practitioner/service user) to achieve change (e.g. use of professional authority, negotiation, legal challenge)?
- How can we generalize change to achieve collective as well as individual benefits?
- With whom can we work to achieve these ends?

Social workers must retain a sense of the profession's liberating potential, and, if they do so, practitioners will be able to identify plentiful opportunities to achieve empowering outcomes, great and small, for service users.

Social work operates in a critical space, mediating between influential social forces, authoritative institutions, oppressive behaviour and, in most cases, individuals and groups who are socially excluded, discriminated against and marginalized in various ways. Whilst this inevitably creates tensions and challenges for practitioners, it is essential that they do not simply become a vehicle for 'passing on' forms of oppression and control. In addressing the questions with which we began (Chapter 1), social workers should be clear about their responsibilities for identifying who is suffering as a result of unequal power relationships and unfair treatment; and they should be engaged in a constant search for the means by which these relationships can be transformed in the interests of those who are losing out. Above all else, social work is about using power to achieve social justice.

Bibliography

Adams, R. (2002) *Social Policy for Social Work*, Basingstoke, Palgrave Macmillan.

Adams, R. (2003) *Social Work and Empowerment*, 3rd edn, Basingstoke, Palgrave Macmillan.

Adams, R. (2005) 'Working Within and Across Boundaries: Tensions and Dilemmas', in Adams, R., Dominelli, L. and Payne, M. (eds) *Social Work Futures*, Basingstoke, Palgrave Macmillan, pp. 99–114.

Adams, R., Dominelli, L. and Payne, M. (eds) (2005) *Social Work Futures*, Basingstoke, Palgrave Macmillan.

Aiers, A. (1998) *When Things Go Wrong*, London, National Institute for Social Work.

Althusser, L. (1977) *Lenin and Philosophy and Other Essays*, London, Verso.

Amphlett, S. (2000) 'System Abuse: Social Violence and Families', in Payne, H. and Littlechild, B. (eds) *Ethical Practice and the Abuse of Power in Social Responsibility*, London, Jessica Kingsley, pp. 175–209.

Arendt, H. (1970) *On Violence*, San Diego, Harcourt Brace.

Arnstein, S. (1969) 'A Ladder of Citizen Participation', *Journal of the American Institute of Planners*, 35, 4, pp. 216–24.

Askheim, O. (2005) 'Personal Assistance – Direct Payments or Alternative Public Service. Does it Matter for the Promotion of User Control?', *Disability & Society*, 20, 3, pp. 247–60.

Audit Commission (2003) *Human Rights: Improving Public Service Delivery*, London, Audit Commission.

Ayre, P. (2001) 'Child Protection and the Media: Lessons from the Last Three Decades', *British Journal of Social Work*, 31, pp. 887–901.

Bachrach, P. and Baratz, M. (1969) 'Two Faces of Power', in Bell, R., Edwards, D. and Wagner, R. (eds) *Political Power: A Reader in Theory and Research*, New York, Free Press, pp. 94–9.

Bailey, R. and Brake, M. (eds) (1975) *Radical Social Work*, London, Edward Arnold.

Ball, C. and McDonald, A. (2002) *Law for Social Workers*, Aldershot, Ashgate.

Banks, S. (2001) *Ethics and Values in Social Work*, 2nd edn, Basingstoke, Palgrave Macmillan.

Banks, S. (2004) *Ethics, Accountability and the Social Professions*, Basingstoke, Palgrave Macmillan.

Banks, S. (2006) *Ethics and Values in Social Work*, 3rd edn, Basingstoke, Palgrave Macmillan.

Barclay, P. (1982) *Social Workers, Their Roles and Tasks* (Barclay Report), London, National Institute for Social Work.

Barnardo's (2002) *Family Group Conferences: Principles and Practice Guidance*, London, Barnardo's.

Barnes, C. (2005) 'Notes on Capacity Building for Local Service Provider Organizations Controlled and Run by Disabled People often Referred to as CILs', London, SCOPE.

Barnes, M. and Bennett, G. (1999) 'Frail Bodies, Courageous Voices: Older People Influencing Community Care', *Health and Social Care in the Community*, 6, 2, pp. 102–11.

Barrett, M. and McIntosh, M. (1991) *The Anti-Social Family*, 2nd edn, London, Verso.

Bates, P. and Butler, S. (2004) 'Community Connections and Creative Mental Health Practice', in Lymbery, M. and Butler, S. (eds) *Social Work Ideals and Practice Realities*, Basingstoke, Palgrave Macmillan, pp. 107–32.

Bauman, Z. (1992) *Intimations of Postmodernity*, London, Routledge.

Beck, U. (1992) *Risk Society*, London, Sage.

Becker, H. (1963) *The Outsiders*, New York, Free Press.

Bell, R., Edwards, D. and Harrison Wagner, R. (1969) *Political Power: A Reader in Theory and Research*, New York, The Free Press

Beresford, P. (2001) 'Social Work and Social Care: The Struggle for Knowledge', *Educational Action Research*, 9, 3, pp. 343–53.

Biesteck, F. (1961) *The Casework Relationship*, London, Allen & Unwin.

Birchall, E. and Hallett, C. (1995) *Working Together in Child Protection*, London, HMSO.

Blackmore, P. (1999) 'Mapping Professional Expertise: Old Tensions Revisited', *Teacher Development*, 3, 1, pp. 19–38.

Blair, T. (2000) 'Foreword' in Cabinet Office (ed.), *Prime Minister's Review: Adoption*, London, Cabinet Office, pp. 3–4.

Booth, T. and Booth, W. (2004) *Parents with Learning Difficulties, Child Protection and the Courts*, Sheffield, University of Sheffield.

Bowling, B. and Phillips, C. (2002) *Racism, Crime and Justice*, Harlow, Longman.

Bradley, G. and Parker, J. (2003) *Social Work Practice: Assessment, Planning, Intervention and Review*, Brighton, Learning Matters.

Bradshaw, Y., Kendall, I., Blackmore, M., Johnson, N. and Jenkinson, S. (1998) 'Complaining Our Way to Quality: Complaints, Contracts and the Voluntary Sector', *Social Policy & Administration*, 32, 3, pp. 209–25.

Braye, S. and Preston-Shoot, M. (1995) *Empowering Practice in Social Care*, Buckingham, Open University Press.

Braye, S. and Preston-Shoot, M. (2005) *Teaching, Learning and Assessment of Law in Social Work Education*, Bristol, Policy Press.

Brayne, H. and Carr, H. (2003) *Law for Social Workers*, 8th edn, Oxford, Oxford University Press.

Brayne, H. and Carr, H. (2005) *Law for Social Workers*, 9th edn, Oxford, Oxford University Press.

Bridge, G. (1999) 'Putting the Children Act Independent Person Procedure under the Spotlight', *Social Policy & Administration*, 33, 2, pp. 197–213.

Bridge, G. and Street, C. (2001) 'When Things Go Wrong: Being an Independent Person under the Children Act 1989 Complaints Procedure', *Social Policy & Administration*, 35, 6, pp. 716–31.

British Association of Social Workers (BASW) (2002) *The Code of Ethics for Social Work*, Birmingham, BASW.

Brown, L. (2003) 'Mainstream or Margin? The Current Use of Family Group Conferences in Child Welfare Practice in the UK', *Child and Family Social Work*, 8, pp. 331–40.

Burman, S. (2004) 'Revisiting the Agent of Social Control Role: Implications for Substance Abuse Treatment', *Journal of Social Work Practice*, 18, 2, pp. 197–210.

Butler, I. and Drakeford, M. (2005) *Scandal, Social Policy and Social Welfare*, Bristol, Policy Press.

Butler, I. and Pugh, R. (2004) 'The Politics of Social Work Research', in Lovelock, R., Lyons, K. and Powell, J. (eds) *Reflecting on Social Work – Discipline and Profession*, Aldershot, Ashgate, pp. 55–71.

Carpenter, J. and Sbaraini, S. (1997) 'Involving Users and Carers in the Care Programme Approach in Mental Health', *Findings*, 97, York, Joseph Rowntree Foundation.

Carr, S. (2004) *Has Service User Participation Made a Difference to Social Care Services?*, London, Social Care Institute for Excellence.

Castells, M. (2004) *The Power of Identity*, 2nd edn, Oxford, Blackwell.

Cemlyn, S. (2000) 'Assimilation, Control, Mediation or Advocacy? Social Work Dilemmas in Providing Anti-oppressive Services for Traveller Children and Families', *Child and Family Social Work*, 5, pp. 327–41.

Chana, P. (2005) 'Domestic Violence: Impact of Culture on Experiences of Asian (Indian Subcontinent) Women', MA thesis, University of Leicester.

Charles, M. (2004) 'Creativity and Constraint in Child Welfare', in Lymbery, M. and Butler, S. (eds) *Social Work Ideals and Practice Realities*, Basingstoke, Palgrave Macmillan, pp. 179–99.

Chief Secretary to the Treasury (2003) *Every Child Matters*, London, The Stationery Office.

Christie, A. (2003) 'Unsettling the "Social" in Social Work: Responses to Asylum Seeking Children in Ireland', *Child and Family Social Work*, 8, pp. 223–31.

Clarke, J., Gewirtz, S. and McLaughlin, E. (2000) *New Managerialism, New Welfare?*, London, Sage.

Cleaver, H. and Freeman, P. (1995) *Parental Perspectives in Cases of Suspected Child Abuse*, London, HMSO.

Clegg, S. (1989) *Frameworks of Power*, London, Sage.

Cooper, A. (2002) 'Keeping our Heads: Preserving Therapeutic Values in a Time of Change', *Journal of Social Work Practice*, 16, 1, pp. 7–13.

Cornwall Social Services (2003) 'Cornwall Social Services Department Individual Services (Children's care) Service Plan', http://www.cornwall.gov.uk/social/children/children06.htm, accessed 20 April 2005.

Corrigan, P. and Leonard, P. (1978) *Social Work Practice under Capitalism*, Basingstoke, Macmillan.

Crow, G. and Marsh, P. (1998) 'Family Group Conferences in Haringey', *Families & Welfare Findings Series*, 4, Sheffield, University of Sheffield.

Dahl, R. (1969) 'The Concept of Power', in Bell, R., Edwards, D. and Wagner, R. (eds) *Political Power: A Reader in Theory and Research*, New York, Free Press, pp. 79–93.

Dalrymple, J. and Burke, B. (1995) *Anti-Oppressive Practice: Social Care and the Law*, Buckingham, Open University Press.

Davies, M. (1981) *The Essential Social Worker*, Aldershot, Arena.

Davies, M. (1994) *The Essential Social Worker*, 3rd edn, Aldershot, Ashgate.

Davies, M. and Woolgrove, M. (1998) 'Mental Health Social Work and the Use of Supervision Registers for Patients at Risk', *Health and Social Care in the Community*, 6, 1, pp. 25–34.

Davis, A. (1996) 'Risk Work and Mental Health', in Kemshall, H. and Pritchard, J. (eds) *Good Practice in Risk Assessment and Risk Management: 1*, London, Jessica Kingsley, pp. 109–20.

Davis, A. and Garrett, P. (2004) 'Progressive Practice for Tough Times: Social Work, Poverty and Division in the Twenty-first Century', in Lymbery, M. and Butler, S. (eds) *Social Work Ideals and Practice Realities*, Basingstoke, Palgrave Macmillan, pp. 13–33.

Dawson, C. (2000) 'Implementing Direct Payments', *Findings*, N60, York, Joseph Rowntree Foundation.

Department for Education and Skills (DfES) (2004) *Every Child Matters: Next Steps*, London, The Stationery Office.

Department of Health (1990) *Community Care: Making it Happen*, London, HMSO.

Department of Health (1998a) *Modernizing Social Services*, London, The Stationery Office.

Department of Health (1998b) 'The Quality Protects Programme: Transforming Children's Services', LAC 98(28), London, Department of Health.

Department of Health (1999) *Working Together to Safeguard Children*, London, The Stationery Office.

Department of Health (2000) *Framework for the Assessment of Children in Need and Their Families*, London, The Stationery Office.

Department of Health (2001) *National Adoption Standards for England*, London, Department of Health.

Department of Health (2002a) *Focus on the Future*, London, Department of Health.

Department of Health (2002b) *Requirements for Social Work Training*, London, Department of Health.

Department of Health (2002c) *Fair Access to Care Services*, http://www.dh.gov.uk/assetRoot/04/01/96/41/04019641.pdf, accessed 1 June 2006.

Department of Health (2003) *Social Services Performance Assessment Framework Indicators 2002–2003*, London, Department of Health.

Department of Health (2005) *Independence, Well-Being and Choice*, London, The Stationery Office.

Department of Health (2006) *Our Health, our Care, our Say: A New Direction for Community Services*, London, The Stationery Office.

Dominelli, L. (1998) 'Anti-oppressive Practice in Context', in Adams, R., Dominelli, L. and Payne, M. (eds) *Social Work: Themes, Issues and Critical Debates*, Basingstoke, Macmillan, pp. 3–22.

Dominelli, L. (2002) *Anti-Oppressive Social Work Theory and Practice*, Basingstoke, Palgrave Macmillan.

Dominelli, L. (2004) *Social Work: Theory and Practice for a Changing Profession*, Cambridge, Polity Press.

Dominelli, L. and McLeod, E. (1989) *Feminist Social Work*, Basingstoke, Macmillan.

Donzelot, J. (1979) *The Policing of Families*, Baltimore, Johns Hopkins.

Farmer, E. and Owen, M. (1995) *Child Protection Practice: Private Risks and Public Remedies*, London, HMSO.

Featherstone, B. (2004) *Family Life and Family Support*, Basingstoke, Palgrave Macmillan.

Feilzer, M. and Hood, R. (2004) *Differences or Discrimination?*, London, Youth Justice Board.

Ferguson, H. (2001) 'Social Work, Individualization and Life Politics', *British Journal of Social Work*, 31, pp. 41–55.

Ferguson, H. (2003) 'In Defence (and Celebration) of Individualization and Life Politics for Social Work', *British Journal of Social Work*, 33, pp. 699–707.

Ferguson, H. (2004) *Protecting Children in Time: Child Abuse, Child Protection and the Consequences of Modernity*, Basingstoke, Palgrave Macmillan.

Fisher, M., Marsh, P. and Philips, D. with Sainsbury, E. (1986) *In and Out of Care*, London, Batsford.

Fitchett, A. (2005) personal communication.

Fitzpatrick, T. (2001) *Welfare Theory: An Introduction*, Basingstoke, Palgrave Macmillan.

Flexner, A. (2001) 'Is Social Work a Profession?', *Research on Social Work Practice*, 11, 2, pp. 152–65.

Folgheraiter, F. (2004) *Relational Social Work*, London, Jessica Kingsley.

Fook, J. (2002) *Social Work: Critical Theory and Practice*, London, Sage.

Foucault, M. (1979) *Discipline and Punish*, Harmondsworth, Penguin.

Foucault, M. (1980) *Power/Knowledge*, New York, Pantheon Books.

Foucault, M. (1981) *The Will to Knowledge*, Harmondsworth, Penguin.

Fox Harding, L. (1996) *Family, State and Social Policy*, Basingstoke, Macmillan.

French, J. and Raven, B. (1968) 'The Bases of Social Power', in Cartwright, D. and Zander, A. (eds) *Group Dynamics: Research and Theory*, New York, Harper and Row, pp. 259–69.

French, S. and Swain, M. (2002) 'The Perspective of the Disabled People's Movement', in Davies, M. (ed) *The Blackwell Companion to Social Work*, 2nd edn, Oxford, Blackwell, pp. 394–400.

Gambrill, E. (2001) 'Social Work: An Authority-Based Profession', *Research on Social Work Practice*, 11, 2, pp. 166–75.

Garland, D. (1990) *Punishment and Modern Society*, Oxford, Clarendon Press.

Garland, D. (2001) *The Culture of Control*, Oxford, Oxford University Press.

Garrett, P. (2003) 'The Trouble with Harry: Why the "New Agenda of Life Politics" Fails to Convince', *British Journal of Social Work*, 33, p. 381–97.

General Social Care Council (GSCC) (2002) *Codes of Practice*, London, GSCC.

Gerth, H. and Mills, C. Wright (1948) 'Introduction: The Man and his Work', in Gerth, H. and Mills, C. Wright (eds) *From Max Weber*, London, Routledge and Kegan Paul, pp. 3–74.

Gerth, H. and Mills, C. Wright (1954) *Character and Social Structure*, London, Routledge and Kegan Paul.

Giddens, A. (1984) *The Constitution of Society*, Cambridge, Polity Press.

Giddens, A. (1991) *Modernity and Self-Identity*, Cambridge, Polity Press.

Giddens, A. (1999) *Runaway World*, London, Profile Books.

Gilligan, R. (1998) 'The Importance of Schools and Teachers in Child Welfare', *Child and Family Social Work*, 3, pp. 13–25.

Gilligan, R. (1999) 'Working with Social Networks: Key Resources in Helping Children at Risk', in Hill, M. (ed.) *Effective Ways of Working with Children and Their Families*, London, Jessica Kingsley, pp. 70–91.

Glendinning, C. and Rummery, K. (2003) 'Collaboration between Primary Health and Social Care: From Policy to Practice in Developing Services for Older People', in Leathard, A. (ed.) *Interprofessional Collaboration*, Hove, Brunner-Routledge, pp. 186–99.

Goodwin, S. (1997) 'Independence, Risk and Compulsion: Conflicts in Mental Health Policy', *Social Policy & Administration*, 31, 3, pp. 260–73.

Graham, M. (2002) 'Creating Spaces: Exploring the Role of Cultural Knowledge as a Source of Empowerment in Models of Social Welfare in Black Communities', *British Journal of Social Work*, 32, pp. 35–49.

Graham, M. (2004) 'Empowerment Revisited – Social Work, Resistance and Agency in Black Communities', *European Journal of Social Work*, 7, 1, pp. 43–56.

Gramsci, A. (1971) *Selections from Prison Notebooks*, London, Lawrence & Wishart.

Gregory, M. and Holloway, M. (2005) 'Language and the Shaping of Social Work', *British Journal of Social Work*, 35, 1, pp. 37–53.

Griffiths, R. (1988) *Community Care: Agenda for Action*, London, HMSO.

Hagel, A. (2002) *The Mental Health of Young Offenders*, London, Mental Health Foundation.

Hall, C., Juhila, K., Parton, N. and Poso, T. (eds) (2003) *Constructing Clienthood in Social Work and Human Services*, London, Jessica Kingsley.

Hanley, B. (2005) *Research as Empowerment?*, York, Joseph Rowntree Foundation.

Hanley, F. (2003) 'The Social Work Dilemma', http://www.basw.co.uk/printpage.php?articleide=75, accessed 24 August 2005.

Harris, J. (1999) 'State Social Work and Social Citizenship in Britain: From Clientelism to Consumerism', *British Journal of Social Work*, 29, pp. 915–37.

Harris, J. (2003) *The Social Work Business*, London, Routledge.

Hartley, S., Ojwang, P., Baguwemu, A., Ddamulira, M. and Chavuta, A. (2005) 'How Do Carers of Disabled Children Cope? The Ugandan Perspective', *Child: Care, Health & Development*, 31, 2, pp. 167–80.

Hasler, F., Zarb, G., and Campbell, J. (2000) 'Implementation of the Community Care (Direct Payments) Act, *Findings*, 430, York, Joseph Rowntree Foundation.

Hayes, D. (2005) 'Social Work with Asylum Seekers and Others Subject to Immigration Control', in Adams, R., Dominelli, L. and Payne, M. (eds) *Social Work Futures*, Basingstoke, Palgrave Macmillan, pp. 182–94.

Hayes, D. and Humphries, B. (2004) *Social Work, Immigration and Asylum*, London, Jessica Kingsley.

Healy, K. (2000) *Social Work Practices: Contemporary Perspectives on Change*, London, Sage.

Healy, K. (2005) *Social Work Theories in Context: Frameworks for Practice*, Basingstoke, Palgrave Macmillan.

Healy, K. and Meagher, G. (2004) 'The Reprofessionalization of Social Work: Collaborative Approaches for Achieving Professional Recognition', *British Journal of Social Work*, 34, pp. 243–60.

Hill, C. and Watkins, J. (2003) 'Statutory Health Assessments for Looked-after Children: What Do they Achieve?', *Child: Care, Health & Development*, 29, pp. 3–13.

Hobbes, T. (1998 [1651]) *Leviathan*, Oxford, Oxford University Press.

Holland, S. (2004) *Child and Family Assessment in Social Work Practice*, London, Sage.

Home Office (1998) *Supporting Families*, London, Home Office.

Housley, W. (2003) *Interaction in Multidisciplinary Teams*, Aldershot, Ashgate.

Howe, D. (1995) *Attachment Theory for Social Work Practice*, Basingstoke, Macmillan.

Howe, D. (1997) 'Psychosocial and Relationship-based Theories for Child and Family Social Work; Political Philosophy, Psychology and Welfare Practice', *Child and Family Social Work*, 2, pp. 161–9.

Hudson, B. (2002) 'Interprofessionality in Health and Social Care: The Achilles Heel of Partnership?', *Journal of Interprofessional Care*, 16, 1, pp. 7–17.

Hugman, R. (1991) *Power in Caring Professions*, Basingstoke, Macmillan.

Humphries, B. (2004) 'An Unacceptable Role for Social Work: Implementing Immigration Policy', *British Journal of Social Work*, 34, pp. 93–107.

Ibn Khaldun (2005 [1377]) *The Muqaddimah*, Oxford, Princeton University Press.

Illich, I. (1977) *Disabling Professions*, London, Boyars.

Jack, G. (1997) 'An Ecological Approach to Social Work with Children and Families', *Child and Family Social Work*, 2, pp. 109–20.

Jackson, S. (1998) 'Family Group Conferences in Youth Justice: The Issues for Implementation in England and Wales', *Howard Journal*, 37, 1, pp. 34–51.

Jackson, S. (1999) 'Family Group Conferences in Youth Justice: The New Panacea?', in Goldson, B. (ed.) *Youth Justice: Contemporary Policy and Practice*, Aldershot, Avebury, pp. 127–47.

Jackson, S. and Morris, K. (1999) 'Family Group Conferences: User Empowerment or Family Self-Reliance? – Development from Lupton', *British Journal of Social Work*, 29, pp. 621–30.

Jeffs, T. and Smith, M. (2001) 'Social Exclusion, Joined-up Thinking and Individualization – New Labour's Connexions Strategy', http://www.infed.org/personaladvisers/connexions_strategy.htm, accessed 26 July 2005.

Johnson, T. (1972) *Professions and Power*, London, Macmillan.

Johnson, Y. (1999) 'Indirect Work: Social Work's Uncelebrated Strength', *Social Work*, 44, 4, pp. 323–34.

Jones, C. (1983) *State Social Work and the Working Class*, London, Macmillan.

Jones, C. (2001) 'Voices from the Front Line: State Social Workers and New Labour', *British Journal of Social Work*, 31, pp. 547–62.

Juhila, K. (2003) 'Creating a "Bad" Client: Disalignment of Institutional Identities in Social Work Interaction', in Hall, C., Juhila, K., Parton, N. and Poso, T. (eds) *Constructing Clienthood in Social Work and Human Services*, London, Jessica Kingsley, pp. 83–95.

Juhila, K., Poso, T., Hall, C. and Parton, N. (2003) 'Introduction: Beyond a Universal Client', in Hall, C., Juhila, K., Parton, N. and Poso, T. (eds) *Constructing Clienthood in Social Work and Human Services*, London, Jessica Kingsley, pp. 11–24.

Kagan, C. and Burton, M. (2005) 'Community Psychological Perspectives and Work with People with Learning Difficulties', http://homepages.poptel. org.uk/mark.burton/clinpsylngdffo4a.pdf, accessed 28 September 2005.

Kemshall, H. (2002) *Risk, Social Policy and Welfare*, Buckingham, Open University Press

Kennedy, M. (2002) 'Disability and Child Abuse', in Wilson, K. and James, A. (eds) *The Child Protection Handbook*, 2nd edn, Edinburgh, Baillière Tindall, pp. 147–71.

Kirkevold, O. and Engedal, K. (2004) 'Concealment of Drugs in Food and Beverages in Nursing Homes: Cross Sectional Study', http://bmj.bmjjournals. com/cgi/content/abridged/330/7481/20, accessed 02 June 2005.

Kitzinger, J. (2004) *Framing Abuse*, London, Pluto Press.

Kohli, R. and Mather, R. (2003) 'Promoting Psychosocial Well-being in Unaccompanied Asylum Seeking Young People in the United Kingdom', *Child and Family Social Work*, 8, pp. 201–12.

Konstandis, S. (2003) 'Asylum Bill', http://www.basw.co.uk/printpage. php?articleide=148, accessed 25 August 2005.

Korbin, J. (2003) 'Neighbourhood and Community Connectedness in Child Maltreatment Research', *Child Abuse & Neglect*, 27, pp. 137–40.

Koubel, G. (1998) 'Power Play: Systems, Principles and Perspectives that Affect Inter-professional Working in Hospital Discharge', *Kent Journal of Practice Research*, http://health.canterbury.ac.uk/health-and-social/resources/ KJPR/V1N4.HTM, accessed 17 May 2005.

Kuhn, T. (1970) *The Structure of Scientific Revolutions*, 2nd edn, London, University of Chicago Press.

Laming, H. (2003) *The Victoria Climbié Inquiry: Report*, London, The Stationery Office.

Langan, M. (2000) 'Social Services: Managing the Third Way', in Clarke, J., Gewirtz, S. and McLaughlin, E. (eds) *New Managerialism New Welfare?*, London, Sage, pp. 152–68.

Leiba, T. and Weinstein, J. (2003) 'Who are the Participants in the Collaborative Process and What Makes Collaboration Succeed or Fail?', in Weinstein, J., Whittington, C. and Leiba, T. (eds) *Collaboration in Social Work Practice*, London, Jessica Kingsley.

Leicester, Leicestershire and Rutland Area Child Protection Committee (2001) *Child Protection Procedures, Protocols and Practice Guidance*, Leicester, Leicester City, Leicestershire and Rutland ACPC.

Leonard, P. (1997) *Postmodern Welfare*, London, Sage.

Lipsky, M. (1980) *Street-Level Bureaucracy*, New York, Russell Sage Foundation.

Local Government Ombudsman (2005) 'Social Services Report Summaries: Findings of Maladministration and Injustice', http://www.lgo.org.uk/socserv.htm, accessed 9 June 2005.

Lorenz, W. (2004) 'Research as an Element in Social Work's Ongoing Search for Identity', in Lovelock, R., Lyons, K. and Powell, J. (eds) *Reflecting on Social Work – Discipline and Profession*, Aldershot, Ashgate, pp. 145–62.

Lukes, S. (1974) *Power: A Radical View*, Basingstoke, Palgrave Macmillan.

Lukes, S. (1986) 'Introduction', in Lukes, S. (ed.) *Power*, New York, New York University Press, pp. 1–18.

Lukes, S. (2005) *Power: A Radical View*, 2nd edn, Basingstoke, Palgrave Macmillan.

Lupton, C. (1998) 'User Empowerment or Family Self-reliance? The Family Group Conference Model', *British Journal of Social Work*, 28, pp. 107–28.

Lymbery, M. (2001) 'Social Work at the Crossroads', *British Journal of Social Work*, 31, pp. 369–84.

Lymbery, M. (2004a) 'Responding to Crisis: The Changing Nature of Welfare Organizations', in Lymbery, M. and Butler, S. (eds) *Social Work Ideals and Practice Realities*, Basingstoke, Palgrave Macmillan, pp. 34–56.

Lymbery, M. (2004b) 'Managerialism and Care Management Practice with Older People', in Lymbery, M. and Butler, S. (eds) *Social Work Ideals and Practice Realities*, Basingstoke, Palgrave Macmillan, pp. 157–78.

Lymbery, M. (2006) 'United we Stand? Partnership Working in Health and Social Care and the Role of Social Work in Services for Older People', *British Journal of Social Work*, 36, 7, pp. 1119–1134.

Lymbery, M. and Butler, S. (eds) (2004) *Social Work Ideals and Practice Realities*, Basingstoke: Palgrave Macmillan.

Lyons, K. (2006) 'Globalization and Social Work: International and Local Implications', *British Journal of Social Work*, 36, pp. 365–80.

Lyons, K. and Taylor, I. (2004) 'Gender and Knowledge in Social Work', in Lovelock, R., Lyons, K. and Powell, J. (eds) *Reflecting on Social Work – Discipline and Profession*, Aldershot, Ashgate, pp. 72–94.

Machiavelli, N. (2005 [1513]) *The Prince*, Oxford, Oxford University Press.

McIntosh, P. (2002) 'An Archi-texture of Learning Disability Services: The Use of Michel Foucault', *Disability & Society*, 17, 1, pp. 65–79.

MacKenzie, I. (1999) 'Power', in Ashe, F., Finlayson, A., Lloyd, M., MacKenzie, I., Martin, J. and O'Neill, S. (eds) *Contemporary Social and Political Theory: An Introduction*, Buckingham, Open University Press, pp. 69–87.

Mapstone, N. (2005) 'BASW Submission to Howard League Investigation', http://www.basw.co.uk/articles.php?articleid=358, accessed 28 September 2005.

Marriott, K. (2001) *Living in Limbo: Young Separated Refugees in the West Midlands*, London, Save the Children Fund.

Marsh, P. and Fisher, M. (2000) 'Partnership with Users in Social Services', *Families & Welfare Findings Series*, 1, York, Joseph Rowntree Foundation.

Mayer, J. and Timms, N. (1970) *The Client Speaks*, London, Routledge & Kegan Paul.

Means, R. and Smith, R. (1998) *Community Care: Policy and Practice*, 2nd edn, Basingstoke, Palgrave Macmillan.

Middleton, L. (1999) *Disabled Children: Challenging Social Exclusion*, Oxford, Blackwell.

Miliband, R. (1973) *The State in Capitalist Society*, London, Quartet.

Mills, C. Wright (1951) *White Collar*, London, Oxford University Press.

Mills, C. Wright (1956) *The Power Elite*, London, Oxford University Press.

Mills, C. Wright (1963) *Power, Politics and People*, London, Oxford University Press.

Mind (2005) 'User Empowerment 5', http://www.mind.org.uk/NR/exeres/FB857A82-F189-4143-9350-66F666E5F960.htm?NRMODE=..., accessed 27 May 2005.

Moore, R., Gray, E., Roberts, C., Merrington, S., Waters, I., Fernandez, R., Hayward, G. and Rogers, R. (2004) *ISSP: The Initial Report*, London, Youth Justice Board.

Morrell, K. (2004) *Analysing Professional Work in the Public Sector: The Case of NHS Nurses*, Loughborough, Loughborough University Business School.

Morris, J. (1997) 'Care or Empowerment? A Disability Rights Perspective', *Social Policy & Administration*, 31, 1, pp. 54–60.

Morris, K. and Shepherd, C. (2000) 'Quality Social Work with Children and Families', *Child and Family Social Work*, 5, pp. 169–76.

Mount, F. (1982) *The Subversive Family*, London, Jonathan Cape.

Mullaly, B (1997) *Structural Social Work*, 2nd edn, Ontario, Oxford University Press.

Mullender, A. (2002) 'Persistent Oppressions: The Example of Domestic Violence', in Adams, R., Dominelli, L. and Payne, M. (eds) *Critical Practice in Social Work*, Basingstoke, Palgrave Macmillan, pp. 63–71.

Murphy, M. (1995) *Working Together in Child Protection*, Aldershot, Arena.

National Audit Office (2004) *The Drug Treatment and Testing Order: Early Lessons*, London, The Stationery Office.

NCH (2003) *Challenging Perspectives*, London, NCH: The Children's Charity.

Newbigging, K. (2005) *Direct Payments and Mental Health: New Directions*, Brighton, Pavilion.

O'Hagan, K. (1996) *Competence in Social Work Practice*, London, Jessica Kingsley.

Okitikpi, T. and Aymer, C. (2003) 'Social Work with African Refugee Children and their Families', *Child and Family Social Work*, 8, pp. 213–22.

Oliver, M. (1990) *The Politics of Disablement*, Basingstoke, Macmillan.

O'Neill, J. (2004) *Civic Capitalism*, Toronto, University of Toronto Press.

Owusu-Bempah, K. (2002) 'Culture, Ethnicity and Identity', in Davies, M. (ed) *The Blackwell Companion to Social Work*, 2nd edn, Oxford, Blackwell, pp. 304–12.

Owusu-Bempah, K. and Howitt, D. (2000) 'Socio-genealogical Connectedness: On the Role of Gender and Same Gender Parenting in

Mitigating the Effects of Parental Divorce', *Child and Family Social Work*, 5, 2, pp. 107–16.

Parsloe, P. (ed) (1999) *Risk Assessment in Social Care and Social Work*, London, Jessica Kingsley.

Parsons, T. (1964) *Essays in Sociological Theory*, New York, Free Press.

Parsons, T. (1969) 'On the Concept of Political Power', in Bell, R., Edwards, D. and Wagner, R. (eds) *Political Power: A Reader in Theory and Research*, New York, Free Press, pp. 251–84.

Parton, N. (1991) *Governing the Family*, Basingstoke, Macmillan.

Parton, N. (2000) 'Some Thoughts on the Relationship between Theory and Practice in and for Social Work', *British Journal of Social Work*, 30, pp. 449–63.

Parton, N. (2003) 'Rethinking *Professional* Practice: The contribution of Social Constructionism and the Feminist "Ethics of Care"', *British Journal of Social Work*, 33, 1, pp. 1–16.

Payne, M. (2002) 'The Role and Achievements of a Professional Association in the Late Twentieth Century: The British Association of Social Workers 1970–2000', *British Journal of Social Work*, 32, pp. 969–95.

Payne, M. (2005) *Modern Social Work Theory*, 3rd edn, Basingstoke, Palgrave Macmillan.

Pease, B. (2002) 'Rethinking Empowerment: A Postmodern Reappraisal for Emancipatory Practice', *British Journal of Social Work*, 32, pp. 135–47.

Pence, E. and Paymar, M. (1993) 'Domestic Violence Information Manual: The Duluth Domestic Abuse Intervention Project', http://www.eurowrc.org/05.education/education_en/12.edu_en.htm, accessed 12 May 2006.

Peterson, C., Maier, S. and Seligman, M. (1993) *Learned Helplessness: A Theory for the Age of Personal Control*, Oxford, Oxford University Press.

Pincus, A. and Minahan, A. (1973) *Social Work Practice: Model and Method*, Itasca, F. E. Peacock.

Poulantzas, N. (1973) *Political Power and Social Classes*, London, New Left Books.

Poulantzas, N. (1975) *Classes in Contemporary Capitalism*, London, New Left Books.

Powell, F. (2001) *The Politics of Social Work*, London, Sage.

Powell, F. and Geoghegan, M. (2004) *The Politics of Community Development*, Dublin, A. & A. Farmar.

Powell, J., Lovelock, R. and Lyons, K. (2004) 'Introduction', in Lovelock, R., Lyons, K. and Powell, J. (eds) *Reflecting on Social Work: Discipline and Profession*, Aldershot, Ashgate, pp. 1–19.

Priestley, M. (1999) *Disability Politics and Community Care*, London, Jessica Kingsley.

Quality Assurance Agency (2000) 'Subject Benchmark Statement for Social Work', Gloucester, QAA.

Reichert, E. (2003) *Social Work and Human Rights*, New York, Columbia University Press.

Robinson, L. (1998) *'Race': Communication and the Caring Professions*, Buckingham, Open University Press.

Roche, J. (2001) 'Social Work Values and the Law', in Cull, L.-A. and Roche, J. (eds) *The Law and Social Work*, Basingstoke, Palgrave Macmillan, pp. 11–19.

Rodger, J. (1996) *Family Life and Social Control*, Basingstoke, Macmillan.

Rojek, C., Peacock, G. and Collins, S. (1988) *Social Work and Received Ideas*, London, Routledge.

Rose, W. and Aldgate, J. (2000) 'Knowledge Underpinning the Assessment Framework', in Department of Health, *Assessing Children in Need and their Families: Practice Guidance*, London, The Stationery Office.

Rotter, J. (1966) 'Generalized Expectancies for Internal versus External Control of Reinforcement', *Psychological Monographs*, 80, pp.1–28.

Ruch, G. (2005) 'Relationship-based Practice and Reflective Practice: Holistic Approaches to Contemporary Child Care Social Work', *Child and Family Social Work*, 10, pp. 111–23.

Sapey, B. (2002) 'Physical Disability', in Adams, R., Dominelli, L. and Payne, M. (eds) *Critical Practice in Social Work*, Basingstoke, Palgrave Macmillan, pp. 181–9.

Sharland, E., Seal, H., Croucher, M., Aldgate, J. and Jones, D. (1996) *Professional Intervention in Child Sexual Abuse*, London, HMSO.

Shaw, I. and Woodward, L. (2004) 'The Medicalization of Unhappiness? The Management of Mental Distress in Primary Care', in Shaw, I. and Kauppinen, K. (eds) *Constructions of Health and Illness: European Perspectives*, Aldershot, Ashgate, pp. 124–36.

Simmel, G. (1986) 'Domination and Freedom', in Lukes, S. (ed.) *Power*, New York, New York University Press, pp. 203–10.

Simons, K. (1995) 'Complaints Procedures in Social Services Departments', *Findings*, 67, York, Joseph Rowntree Foundation.

Simpkin, M. (1983) *Trapped within Welfare*, 2nd edn, London, Macmillan.

Sinclair, R. (1998) 'Involving Children in Planning their Care', *Child and Family Social Work*, 3, pp. 137–42.

Smale, G., Tuson, G. and Statham, D. (2000) *Social Work and Social Problems*, Basingstoke, Palgrave Macmillan.

Smith, R. (1987) 'The Practice of Diversion', *Youth and Policy*, 19, pp. 10–14.

Smith, R. (2003) *Youth Justice: Ideas, Policy, Practice*, Cullompton, Willan.

Smith, R. (2004) 'Globalization, Individualization and Childhood: The Challenge for Social Work', *New Global Development: Journal of International and Comparative Social Welfare*, Twentieth Anniversary Special, XX: 2, pp. 71–8.

Smith, R. (2005) *Values and Practice in Children's Services*, Basingstoke, Palgrave Macmillan.

Smith, R., Dahme, H.-J. and Wohlfahrt, N. (2002) 'The Marketization of Social Care in the UK and Germany', unpublished.

Stainton, T. and Boyce, S. (2004) '"I Have Got my Life Back": Users' Experience of Direct Payments', *Disability & Society*, 19, 5, pp. 443–54.

Stalker, K., Cadogan, L., Petrie, M., Jones, C. and Murray, J. (1999) 'If You Don't Ask You Don't Get', Edinburgh, Scottish Office Central Research Unit.

Stein, M. (2002) 'Leaving Care', in McNeish, D., Newman, T. and Roberts, H. (eds) *What Works for Children?*, Buckingham, Open University Press, pp. 59–82.

Straw, J. (1998) 'Foreword', in Home Office (ed.) *Supporting Families*, London, Home Office, p. 2.

Taylor, C. and White, S. (2000) *Practising Reflexivity in Health and Welfare*, Buckingham, Open University Press.

Thomas, N., Stainton, T., Jackson, S., Cheung, W., Doubtfire, S. and Webb, A. (2003) ' "Your Friends Don't Understand": Invisibility and Unmet Need in the Lives of "Young Carers" ', *Child and Family Social Work*, 8, pp. 35–46.

Thompson, N. (2001) *Anti-Discriminatory Practice*, Basingstoke, Palgrave Macmillan.

Thompson, N. (2002) 'Social Movements, Social Justice and Social Work', *British Journal of Social Work*, 32, pp. 711–22.

Thompson, N. (2003a) *Communication and Language: A Handbook of Theory and Practice*, Basingstoke, Palgrave Macmillan.

Thompson, N. (2003b) *Promoting Equality: Challenging Discrimination and Oppression*, 2nd edn, Basingstoke, Palgrave Macmillan.

Titterton, M. (1999) 'Training Professionals in Risk assessment and Risk Management: What Does the Research Tell Us?', in Parsloe, P. (ed.) *Risk Assessment in Social Care and Social Work*, London, Jessica Kinglsey, pp. 217–47.

TOPSS (Training Organisation for the Personal Social Services) (2002) *The National Occupational Standards for Social Work*, Leeds, TOPSS.

Trevithick, P. (2003) 'Effective Relationship-based Practice: A Theoretical Exploration', *Journal of Social Work Practice*, 17, 2, pp. 163–76.

Trevithick, P. (2005) *Social Work Skills: A Practice Handbook*, 2nd edn, Buckingham, Open University Press.

Tunstill, J. (2003) 'Adoption and Family Support: Two Means in Pursuit of the Same End', in Douglas, A. and Philpot, T. (eds) *Adoption: Changing Families, Changing Times*, London, Routledge, pp. 99–105.

Valtonen, K. (2001) 'Social Work with Immigrants and Refugees: Developing a Participation-based Framework for Anti-Oppressive Practice', *British Journal of Social Work*, 31, pp. 955–60.

van Wormer, K. (2004) *Confronting Oppression, Restoring Justice*, Alexandria, Council on Social Work Education.

Wachtel, A. (1994) 'Improving Child and Family Welfare', Ottawa, National Clearinghouse on Family Violence.

Waterhouse, R. (2000) *Lost in Care*, London, The Stationery Office.

Weber, M. (1948a) 'Politics as a Vocation', in Gerth, H. and Wright Mills, C. (eds) *From Max Weber*, London, Routledge and Kegan Paul, pp. 77–128.

Weber, M. (1948b) 'Bureaucracy', in Gerth, H. and Wright Mills, C. (eds) *From Max Weber*, London, Routledge and Kegan Paul, pp. 196–244.

Weber, M. (1957) *The Theory of Social and Economic Organisation*, Chicago, Free Press.

Weber, M. (1978) *Economy and Society*, Berkeley, University of California Press.

Weinstein, J., Whittington, C. and Leiba, T. (eds) (2003) *Collaboration in Social Work Practice*, London, Jessica Kingsley.

Westbury, E. and Tutty, L. (1999) 'The Efficacy of Group Treatment for Survivors of Childhood Abuse', *Child Abuse & Neglect*, 23, 1, pp. 31–44.

Westwood, S. (2002) *Power and the Social*, London, Routledge.

White, S. (2003) 'The Social Worker as Moral Judge: Blame, Responsibility and Case Formulation', in Hall, C., Juhila, K., Parton, N. and Poso, T. (eds)

Constructing Clienthood in Social Work and Human Services, London, Jessica Kingsley, pp. 177–92.

White, S. and Featherstone, B. (2005) 'Communicating Misunderstandings: Multi-agency Work as Social Practice', *Child and Family Social Work*, 10, pp. 207–16.

Whittington, C. (2003) 'A Model of Collaboration', in Weinstein, J., Whittington, C. and Leiba, T. (eds) *Collaboration in Social Work Practice*, London, Jessica Kingsley, pp. 39–61.

Wilding, P. (1982) *Professional Power and Social Welfare*, London, Routledge & Kegan Paul.

Wilensky, H. (1964) 'The Professionalization of Everyone?', *American Journal of Sociology*, 70, 2, pp. 137–58.

Williams, J. (2001) '1998 Human Rights Act: Social Work's New Benchmark', *British Journal of Social Work*, 31, pp. 831–44.

Wilson, A. and Beresford, P. (2000) '"Anti-Oppressive Practice": Emancipation or Appropriation?', *British Journal of Social Work*, 30, pp. 553–73.

Wistow, G., Knapp, M., Hardy, B., Forder, J., Kendall, J. and Manning, R. (1996) *Social Care Markets*, Buckingham, Open University Press.

Woodcock, J. (2002) 'Practical Approaches to Work with Refugee Children', in Dwivedi, K. (ed.) *Meeting the Needs of Ethnic Minority Children*, London, Jessica Kingsley, pp. 264–82.

Youth Justice Board (2000) *Intensive Supervision and Surveillance Programme: Service Specification*, London, Youth Justice Board.

Zufferey, C. and Kerr, L. (2004) 'Identity and Everyday Experiences of Homelessness: Some Implications for Social Work', *Australian Social Work*, 57, 4, pp. 343–53.

Author Index

Adams, R.   36, 38, 96, 99, 100, 101, 150, 151, 159, 165, 180, 183, 184, 186, 188, 189, 210
Aiers, A.   137
Aldgate, J.   181
Althusser, L.   29–30, 31, 74, 110, 127
Amphlett, S.   120
Arendt, H.   36
Arnstein, S.   141
Askheim, O.   168
Audit Commission   137–8
Aymer, C.   199
Ayre, P.   85, 86, 87, 88

Bachrach, P.   40
Bailey, R.   74
Ball, C.   6
Banks, S.   52, 114, 115, 117, 124
Baratz, M.   40
Barclay, P.   185
Barnardo's   139
Barnes, C.   142
Barnes, M.   210
Barrett, M.   67, 68
Bates, P.   186–7
Bauman, Z.   33, 34, 53–4
Beck, U.   90
Becker, H.   43
Bennett, G.   210
Beresford, P.   121, 125, 126, 202
Biesteck, F.   27
Blackmore, P.   106
Blair, T.   91
Booth, T.   131, 132
Booth, W.   131, 132
Bowling, B.   205, 206
Boyce, S.   168

Bradley, G.   181
Bradshaw, Y.   137
Brake, M.   74
Braye, S.   95, 157
Brayne, H.   94, 95, 102
Bridge, G.   137, 138
British Association of Social Workers (BASW)   201, 207, 211
Brown, L.   168
Burke, B.   59–60
Burman, S.   129
Burton, M.   198
Butler, I.   119, 202
Butler, S.   170, 186–7

Carpenter, J.   140, 141
Carr, H.   94, 95, 102
Carr, S.   137, 138, 145, 167
Castells, M.   47, 76, 77–8, 85
Cemlyn, S.   208
Chana, P.   153
Charles, M.   167
Chief Secretary to the Treasury   114
Christie, A.   199
Clarke, J.   90, 103, 112
Cleaver, H.   12, 119, 120, 121
Clegg, S.   27–8, 31–2, 33, 38, 39, 48, 52, 69, 74
Cooper, A.   191
Cornwall Social Services   92
Corrigan, P.   59, 74–5, 76, 110
Crow, G.   139, 140

Dahl, R.   19, 29
Dalrymple, J.   59–60
Davies, M.   74, 132, 171, 172, 184, 192, 195, 198–9, 204, 212
Davis, A.   6, 150

Dawson, C. 143
Department for Education and Skills (DfES) 118
Department of Health 3, 91, 92, 94, 98, 99, 100, 109, 114, 182, 185, 197
Dominelli, L. 7, 10, 14, 22, 27, 28, 31, 35, 43–4, 46, 52, 57, 59, 60, 62–3, 68, 70, 71–2, 78, 152, 171, 172, 185, 193, 205–6, 210–11
Donzelot, J. 30, 66, 75, 85
Drakeford, M. 202

Engedal, K. 132, 133

Farmer, E. 121
Featherstone, B. 67, 196
Ferguson, H. 135, 192
Fisher, M. 1, 12, 140, 141
Fitchett, A. 176
Fitzpatrick, T. 10, 13, 14, 23
Flexner, A. 109, 110
Folgheraiter, F. 55–6, 57, 156, 159–60
Fook, J. 34, 35, 37, 39, 55, 78, 154, 155, 161–3, 202, 203
Foucault, M. 22, 32–3, 39, 69, 110, 153, 177
Fox Harding, L. 68
Freeman, P. 12, 119, 120, 121
French, J. 20, 21
French, S. 45

Gambrill, E. 109, 110
Garland, D. 14, 33, 43, 70, 71
Garrett, P. 150, 192–3
General Social Care Council (GSCC) 2, 13, 101, 119, 142, 206, 207
Geoghegan, M. 69
Gerth, H. 19–20, 48, 50, 51
Giddens, A. 35–6, 54–5, 77, 78, 90
Gilligan, R. 181, 182, 183
Glendinning, C. 118
Goodwin, S. 129
Gramsci, A. 11, 41
Gregory, M. 164
Griffiths, R. 50

Hagel, A. 132
Hall, C. 121
Hanley, F. 210
Harris, J. 10, 51, 89, 90, 97, 99, 100, 102, 138, 140
Hartley, S. 177, 179
Hasler, F. 143
Hayes, D. 11, 211
Healy, K. 83, 84, 96, 103, 112–13, 114, 115, 122, 124
Hill, C. 132, 133
Hobbes, T. 18, 29
Holland, S. 155
Holloway, M. 164
Home Office 67
Housley, W. 10
Howe, D. 79, 156
Howitt, D. 181
Hudson, B. 116
Hugman, R. 110, 115
Humphries, B. 11, 111, 193, 199, 200, 211

Ibn Khaldun 18
Illich, I. 113

Jack, G. 175
Jackson, S. 139, 140, 168, 169
Jeffs, T. 186
Johnson, T. 104, 105, 106, 107, 109, 112, 115
Johnson, Y. 203, 205, 206
Jones, C. 1, 3, 17, 83, 89, 92, 97–8, 100, 103, 110, 125, 208
Juhila, K. 122, 134

Kagan, C. 198
Kemshall, H. 71
Kennedy, M. 182
Kerr, L. 164
Kirkevold, O. 132, 133
Kitzinger, J. 85, 86, 87, 88, 102
Kohli, R. 199
Konstandis, S. 201, 211
Korbin, J. 181
Koubel, G. 116–17
Kuhn, T.S. 11

Laming, H.   85, 117
Langan, M.   112
Leiba, T.   116, 124
Leicester, Leicestershire and Rutland
   Area Child Protection
   Committee   94
Leonard, P.   13, 14, 34, 35, 59,
   74–5, 76, 110
Lipsky, M.   100
Local Government Ombudsman
   137
Lorenz, W.   122, 123
Lukes, S.   19, 20, 21, 30, 40, 41,
   44–5, 45–6, 53, 57, 69, 73
Lupton, C.   139
Lymbery, M.   98, 99, 100, 101, 112,
   165, 167, 168, 170, 185, 186, 206
Lyons, K.   122, 193

Machiavelli, N.   18
MacKenzie, I.   21, 23, 29, 34, 46, 47
Mapstone, N.   201
Marriott, K.   64
Marsh, P.   139, 140, 141
Mather, R.   199
Mayer, J.   157
McDonald, A.   6
McIntosh, M.   67, 68
McIntosh, P.   198
McLeod, E.   10
Meagher, G.   112–13, 115, 124
Means, R.   100
Middleton, L.   45
Miliband, R.   31, 74
Mills, C. Wright   19–20, 31, 48, 50,
   51, 105–6
Minahan, A.   173–4, 181, 183–4,
   189
Mind   130
Moore, R.   128–9
Morrell, K.   106, 107, 108, 113
Morris, J.   163, 164
Morris, K.   139, 140, 168, 169
Mount, F.   68
Mullaly, B.   72, 80, 83, 84, 110–11,
   196–7, 207, 211
Mullender, A.   187, 189, 207
Murphy, M.   88

National Audit Office   131
Newbigging, K.   143, 144

O'Hagan, K.   104
Okitikpi, T.   199
Oliver, M.   141–2, 145
O'Neill, J.   24
Owen, M.   121
Owusu-Bempah, K.   181

Parker, J.   181
Parsloe, P.   87
Parsons, T.   9, 18, 20–1, 23–5, 27,
   28, 30, 35, 39, 40, 49, 105, 159
Parton, N.   86, 88, 193, 194, 195, 202
Paymar, M.   25
Payne, M.   173, 174–5, 185
Pease, B.   153
Pence, E.   25
Peterson, C.   130, 133, 145, 159
Phillips, C.   205, 206
Pincus, A.   173–4, 181, 183–4, 189
Poulantzas, N.   9, 21–2, 48, 75
Powell, F.   69, 72, 73, 74, 76, 77,
   80, 83
Powell, J.   119
Preston-Shoot, M.   95, 157
Priestley, M.   142, 143
Pugh, R.   119

Quality Assurance Agency   185

Raven, B.   20, 21
Reichert, E.   211
Robinson, L.   43
Roche, J.   93–4, 95, 96
Rodger, J.   68
Rojek, C.   41
Rose, W.   181
Rotter, J.   130, 154, 160
Ruch, G.   156, 157, 158–9, 195
Rummery, K.   118

Sbaraini, S.   140, 141
Sharland, E.   119, 121
Shaw, I.   108
Shepherd, C.   139
Simmel, G.   49–50

Simons, K.   137
Simpkin, M.   110, 192
Sinclair, R.   141
Smale, G.   69, 72, 73, 126, 130, 151,
   152, 166–7, 170, 172, 175–6,
   178, 179
Smith, M.   186
Smith, R.   6, 50, 60, 63, 64, 78, 91,
   92, 96, 100, 179, 184, 205, 206
Stainton, T.   168
Stalker, K.   121
Stein, M.   183
Straw, J.   90–1
Street, C.   137, 138
Swain, M.   45

Taylor, C.   178, 195, 196
Taylor, I.   122
Thomas, N.   209
Thompson, N.   43, 59, 60–1, 78, 80,
   84, 85, 149
Timms, N.   157
Titterton, M.   87
Trevithick, P.   156–7, 158, 160, 161,
   170, 185, 188, 195
Tunstill, J.   92

Valtonen, K.   201
Van Wormer, K.   211

Wachtel, A.   182, 184
Waterhouse, R.   211
Watkins, J.   132, 133
Weber, M.   24, 29, 31, 48, 49,
   92–3
Weinstein, J.   116, 124
Westwood, S.   18, 19, 22
White, S.   122, 178, 195–6
Whittington, C.   118, 124
Wilding, P.   105, 106, 107, 108,
   110
Wilensky, H.   107
Williams, J.   136
Wilson, A.   121
Wistow, G.   98, 99
Woodcock, J.   79
Woodward, L.   108
Woolgrove, M.   132

Youth Justice Board   128

Zufferey, C.   164

Subject Index

action, taking 210–11
action system 174
active resistance 135
adoption 90–2
advocacy 101, 185, 210–11
age/ageism 67, 71, 182
agency 31
  and structure 37–8
allocative resources 35–6
altruism 112
anti-social behaviour 61
Anti-Social Behaviour Orders
  (ASBOs) 61, 70
assertiveness 204
assessment
  changing power relationships
    165–7
  child and family assessments 30,
    155, 197
  integrated assessment models
    197
  social care market and 97–8
asylum seekers 78–9, 199, 211
audience response 85
audit, external 89–90
authoritative resources 35–6
authority 2, 24, 49–50, 51
  legal 92–6
  sources of for social workers 2
  typology of 29
autonomy 33
awareness-raising 208–9

Beckford, Jasmine 86
Best Value Inspectorate 89
Black people 22, 43, 55
blameworthiness 122
Boateng, Paul 89

boundaries 43, 111, 180
British Association of Social
  Workers (BASW) 88, 201–2,
  211
brokerage role 184
bureaucracy 29, 48–9

campaigning 201–2, 210–11
capacity, power as 20–1, 22
capacity building 159
care management 112, 186
care orders 110
care packages 98–9
care planning 140–1
carers 5, 64, 67, 95, 126, 162, 165,
  177, 181, 185, 209–10
case management 186
Centres for Integrated Living (CILs)
  142
challenge 162–3
  service user strategy 126, 136–8
change
  changing relationships: in
    networks and systems 184–9;
    user-led services 165–9
  language, choice and 160–5
change agent system 174
charismatic authority 29
'child in the world' model 63–5
child protection 5–6, 117–18, 129
  media and 85, 86–8
  parents with learning difficulties
    131
  social work professionalism and
    service users 119–21
children 114
  child and family assessments 30,
    155, 197

children (*cont.*)
  with disabilities   45, 176–8, 179;
    abuse   181–2
  looked-after children   132–3;
    ethnicity and identity   46
  networks for victims of domestic
    violence   187, 188
  young carers   209
Children Act 1989   30, 73, 94
Children Act 2004   94, 95–6
Children's Centres   188
choice   98–9, 138
  language, change and   160–5
Chronically Sick and Disabled
    Persons Act 1970   163
circuits of power   31–2
citizenship   163–4, 205–6
class   22, 107
Cleveland child sexual abuse case
    86, 88
client identity   134–5
client system   174
Climbié, Victoria   117–18
Codes of Practice   109
coercive power   19–21
collaboration
  interprofessional working
    114–18
  service user strategy   126, 138–41
  structural change   209–10
collective identity   44, 45
Commission for Care Standards
    89
commitment   203
commodified view of power   37
community
  site of power   62, 63, 64, 69–72
  see also systems
community care   97–100
competence   87–8
complaints procedures   136–7
compliance   19, 50
  service user strategy   126, 127–30
compulsory mental health
    admissions   110
Connexions service   186
constructionism   193
consumerism   138

context
  contexts of power in social work
    7–9
  importance of   58–9
control
  service user strategy   126, 141–4
  youth justice   127–9
courts   110
creditworthiness   122
Crime Reduction Partnerships   70
criminal justice   70
  see also young offenders
critical reconstructive process   162–3
culture
  domestic violence and   153
  PCS model   60–2
currency, power as   23–8

debilitative power   67
decision-making   167
deconstruction   162
defensiveness   87
Derbyshire Centre for Integrated
    Living   142
direct payments   142–4, 168
disability   163–4
  children with disabilities   45,
    176–8, 179;   abuse 181–2
  service users and control   141–4
Disability Discrimination Act 1995
    94, 136
discourse   34, 84, 92, 116, 162–3
distancing   195
distrust   89–90
doctors   116, 117–18
domestic violence   25, 153, 187,
    188
domination   35, 48
drug treatment   129, 131
Drug Treatment and Testing Orders
    131
drug users   131
Duluth Domestic Abuse Intervention
    Project   25
dyads   22

ecological theories   175
ecomaps   181–2

economic globalization 76–7
efficiency 89–90
eligibility criteria 97, 100
elites, power 31
emotional communication 54
empowerment 21, 36–8, 207
  empowering relationships *see* relationships
engagement 208
episodic power 33–4
ethics 95–6
ethnicity 46, 153
evidence-based practice 122
exchange model of assessment 166–7
expert power 20
expertise, professional 34, 107–8, 111, 113–14, 183

facilitation role 183–4, 186–8
facilitative resource, power as 23–8
family 30, 50
  changing nature of relationships 54
  site of power 62, 63, 64, 65–8
family group conferences (FGCs) 25–6, 139–40, 168
feedback mechanisms 178
feminism 46–7
financial assessment 99–100
fit, models of 175
formal resource systems 173
Framework for the Assessment of Children in Need and Their Families 197
functionalism 30, 107–8, 192

gatekeeping role 97
gender 67, 113
general practitioners (GPs) 116, 118
General Social Care Council (GSCC) 109
globalization 62, 63, 64, 76–9, 85
government 88–92
groups 183
  see also systems
guidance 94

hegemony 41, 52
homelessness 164
hospital discharge 116–17
human nature 44
Human Rights Act 1998 73, 94, 136, 137

identity 55
  client 134–5
  community and 69–70
  globalization and 77–8
  personal aspect of power 42–7
  professional 2, 103–8, 195–6
  situated subjectivity 55
  working with individuals 153–5
ideology 92
image 45
immigration policy 199
impartiality 111
indeterminacy 33–4, 53–4, 195
individuals 59
  relationships *see* relationships
  tension between individual and structural levels 59–60, 83–4, 149–50, 171–2, 191–3, 204–5
inequality, perpetuation of 6, 8, 21, 28, 35, 47, 68, 110, 111, 125, 210
informal resource systems 173
inspection 89
instrumental power 18
integrated assessment models 197
Intensive Supervision and Surveillance Programme (ISSP) 127–9
interagency stereotyping 88
interests 19, 21–2, 40–2, 68
  professions and 105–6, 107; self-interest 105, 106, 107, 111
internal self 154
international dimension 62, 63, 64, 76–9, 85
International Federation of Social Workers 88
interprofessional working 114–18

joint working 114–18
justice 211–12

language 8
  and discourse 160–5
lateness 3–5
law 92–6
league tables 89
learned helplessness 130
learning difficulties, people with 6, 131, 198
legal-rational authority 29
legitimacy 24, 27
  law and 92–6
legitimate power 19–21
legitimizing identity 47
life politics 192–3
Local Authority Social Services Act (LASSA) 1970 94
locus of control 130
looked-after children 46, 132–3

maintenance school of thought 171–2
managerialism 111–12
managerialization 90, 91
mapping techniques 181–2
market forces 96–101
media 84–8
medicalization 107–8
medication, covert administration of 132
mental health 6, 129, 130, 132, 143
  compulsory admissions 110
Mental Health Act 1983 94
moderate need 98
modes of power 10, 40–57
  interests and difference 40–2
  positional power 42, 47–52, 58
  relational power 42, 52–6, 58, 118
  role of identity 42–7
moral order 66
multiculturalism 199
multidimensional model of power 62–3
mutuality
  between practioner and service user 2, 157–8
  between professions 115

narrative reconstruction 161, 163
National Adoption Standards 92
natural powers 18
needs
  assessment see assessment
  categorization of 98
negative attribution 43
networks/networking 173–89, 200–2
  changing relationships in systems and 184–9
  exploring power relationships 176–80
  networking skills 186–8
  reframing 180–4
'new social movements' 141–4
NHS and Community Care Act 1990 94
non-cooperation 126, 131–3
non-decision-making 40
normalization 52
norms 45, 66
nursing homes, covert administration of medication in 132

older people 41, 97–8, 132, 210
oppression 7–8, 60, 71–2
organizational context 27–8
  see also professionalism
Orkney child sexual abuse case 86, 87
'othering' 43, 70–2

paedophiles 70–1
participation, user 138, 207
passive resistance 135
PCS model 60–2, 149
performance indicators 89
performativity 90
personal attributes 2, 60–2
personal development 156
personal power 42–7
planning of care 140–1
pluralism 73–4
political nature of social work 191–3, 196–7
positional power 42, 47–52, 58

possession, power as 18–19, 28–32
postmodernism 33–5, 53–4
potential, power as 23–8
power 1–9
    contexts of power in social work
        7–9
    defining 1, 19–23
    modes of *see* modes of power
    place in social work 3–7
    power of, over and to 68
    sites of *see* sites of power
    theories about *see* theories about
        power
    typologies of 20
power credit 27
power elite 31
powerlessness 17, 42, 70, 88, 105,
    177
primary care trusts 118
procedural model of assessment
    166
proceduralization 87, 112
process, power as 18–19, 32–5
product, power as 35–8
professionalism 11, 100–1, 103–24,
    195–6
    expertise 34, 107–8, 111, 113–14,
        183
    and managerialism 111–12
    power as process 34
    power of professions 104–8
    reprofessionalization 112–14
    and service users 118–23
    social work and other professions
        114–18
    transformative profession
        108–11
project identity 47
punishment 33

questioning model of assessment
    166
questioning stance 204

Race Relations Act 1976 94
racism 38, 149
radical social work 74–5
reconstruction 162–3

referent power 20
referrals, taking 194
reflective practice 158–9, 178,
    195–7
reformulation 159–60
reframing
    empowering relationships 160–5
    'proper social work' 203–7
    social work 203–11
    solidarity and commitment 203
    structural change 207–11
    systems, networks and 180–4
refugees 64–5, 78–9
relational power 42, 52–6, 58, 118
relational practice 55–6, 156–60
relationships 3–5, 8, 12, 22,
    149–70
    changing 165–9
    exploring 156–60
    reframing 160–5
    understanding 151–6
relative autonomy 75–6
renegotiation of prior
    understandings 159–60
reprofessionalization 112–14
resistance 162
    service user strategy 126, 133–6
resistance identity 47
resources
    allocative and authoritative 35–6
    resource systems 173
    social work and the market
        96–101
'responsibilizing' 70
reward power 20
rights 163–4
    challenge 136–8
    law and language of 95–6
risk 6, 12, 24, 59, 69, 87, 100, 116,
    118, 129, 131, 139, 150, 152,
    163, 165, 174, 180, 181–2, 188,
    197, 204–5, 209
routine interventions 3–5

safeguarding 93, 96, 105, 189
schools 183
self-actualization 192
self-help groups 186–7

self-interest 105, 106, 107, 111
self-management 141–4
self-regulation 153
service delivery, collaboration in
    planning 140–1
service ethic 105
service-user movements 138, 141–4
service users 3, 7–8, 202
  collaboration with and structural
    change 209–10
  social work professionalism and
    118–23
  strategies 11–12, 125–45;
    challenge 126, 136–8;
    collaboration 126, 138–41;
    compliance 126, 127–30;
    control 126, 141–4; non-
    cooperation 126, 131–3;
    resistance 126, 133–6
  user-led services 165–9
sex offenders 70–1
Shaping Our Lives 151, 202
shared meanings 43
sites of power 10–11, 58–80
  community as local authority
    62, 63, 64, 69–72
  family 62, 63, 64, 65–8
  global dimension 62, 63, 64,
    76–9
  importance of context 58–9
  meaning for social work practice
    198–202
  state institutions 62, 63, 64,
    73–6
  three frameworks 59–65
situated subjectivity 55
situational power 18, 67
social analysis 198
social capital 24
social constructionism 193
social exclusion 71–2
social order 20–1
social position 45–6
  positional power 42, 47–52, 58
social roles 51
Social Services Inspectorate 89
social work 13, 191–212
  bridge builders 186–7

contexts of power in 7–9
place of power in 3–7
political nature of 191–3, 196–7
power and justice 211–12
professionalism see
    professionalism
'proper social work' 203–7
recognizing the impact of 193–8
reframing 203–11
sites and sources of power and
    their meaning for practice
    198–202
statutory role of the social worker
    94
structural change as legitimate
    objective for 207–11
Social Work Manifesto 202
societal resource systems 173
solidarity 199–200, 203
sovereignty 48
state 29–31, 48–9, 50, 52
  institutions as site of power 62,
    63, 64, 73–6
state apparatuses 29–30
status 50–1, 107
storage 35–6
'street-level bureaucracy' 100
structural change 191–2, 203–7
  legitimate objective for social work
    207–11
structural influences on practice
    11, 83–102
  government 88–92
  law and legitimacy 92–6
  market 96–101
  media 84–8
structural social work, principles of
    72
structure
  and agency 37–8
  PCS model 60–2
  state power and 29–32
  tension between individual and
    structural levels 59–60, 83–4,
    149–50, 171–2, 191–3, 204–5
substantial need 98
support systems 173
Sure Start 188

surveillance   33
  youth justice   127–9
system abuse   120–1
systems   12–13, 171–90
  changing relationships in
    networks and   184–9
  exploring power relationships
    176–80
  practice and the impact of   103–4
  reframing   180–4
  social work between lifeworld and
    system   123
  systems thinking and
    understanding power   172–6

taking action   210–11
target system   174
targets   90–1
theories about power   10, 17–39
  defining power   19–23
  historical ideas   18–19
  power as possession   18–19, 28–32
  power as potential   23–8
  power as process   18–19, 32–5
  power as product   35–8
traditional authority   29
traits, professionalism and   106–7,
  109
transformative profession   108–11
Travellers   208
trust   54
typologies of power   20

UN Convention on the Rights of the
  Child 1991   136

uncertainty   33–4, 53–4, 195
underclass   72
unsubstantiated child abuse
  allegations   120–1
user-led services   165–9
  see also service users

values   114
  core social work values   95–6,
    101, 205
vulnerability   117, 138
vulnerable people   5, 6, 73, 125,
  153, 181, 192, 199

weakness (position of)   3, 12, 27,
  118, 163, 166
welfare state   75
  impact of globalization   77
whistle-blowing   211
Wiltshire and Swindon User
  Network   138
women
  domestic violence   25, 153, 187,
    188
  widows and identity   46

young carers   209
young offenders   179, 180, 205,
  206
  ISSP   127–9
young people   128, 168, 172, 180,
  184, 186, 205–206, 209

zero-sum problem   24–5